Full-Stack React Projects

Modern web development using React 16, Node, Express, and MongoDB

Shama Hoque

BIRMINGHAM - MUMBAI

Full-Stack React Projects

Commissioning Editor: Amarabha Banerjee
Acquisition Editor: Akshay Ghadi
Content Development Editor: Francis Carneiro
Technical Editor: Diksha Wakode
Copy Editor: Safis Editing
Project Coordinator: Devanshi Doshi
Proofreader: Safis Editing
Indexer: Aishwarya Gangawane
Graphics: Jason Monteiro
Production Coordinator: Shraddha Falebhai

Production reference: 1230518

Published by Packt Publishing Ltd.
Livery Place
35 Livery Street
Birmingham
B3 2PB, UK.

ISBN 978-1-78883-553-4

www.packtpub.com

`mapt.io`

Mapt is an online digital library that gives you full access to over 5,000 books and videos, as well as industry leading tools to help you plan your personal development and advance your career. For more information, please visit our website.

Why subscribe?

- Spend less time learning and more time coding with practical eBooks and Videos from over 4,000 industry professionals

- Improve your learning with Skill Plans built especially for you

- Get a free eBook or video every month

- Mapt is fully searchable

- Copy and paste, print, and bookmark content

PacktPub.com

Did you know that Packt offers eBook versions of every book published, with PDF and ePub files available? You can upgrade to the eBook version at `www.PacktPub.com` and as a print book customer, you are entitled to a discount on the eBook copy. Get in touch with us at `service@packtpub.com` for more details.

At `www.PacktPub.com`, you can also read a collection of free technical articles, sign up for a range of free newsletters, and receive exclusive discounts and offers on Packt books and eBooks.

Contributors

About the author

Shama Hoque has 8 years of experience as a software developer and mentor, with a master's in software engineering from Carnegie Mellon University.

From Java programming to full-stack development with JavaScript, the applications she has worked on include national Olympiad registration websites, universally accessible widgets, video conferencing apps, and medical 3D reconstruction software.

Currently, she makes web-based prototypes for R&D start-ups in California, while training aspiring software engineers and teaching web development to CS undergrads in Bangladesh.

This book would not have been possible without the continuous support of my family and friends. First and foremost, I want to thank my brother, Shamiul, for providing valuable technical insight and guidance. I am also grateful to my parents and my friend, Shahrukh, for doing their part in boosting my morale and encouraging me when I needed it the most.

About the reviewer

Sai Kishore Komanduri does software architecture and engineering at MGRM NET, where he leads a team of engineers building e-governance enterprise applications.

Prior to this, he was a software engineer and developer evangelist at Hashnode, a premier social network for software developers, where he worked across the whole breadth of Hashnode's MERN tech stack.

I would like to offer my profound thanks to Dr. Murthy, Chairman of MGRM, for his invaluable, and all-round mentorship.

Packt is searching for authors like you

If you're interested in becoming an author for Packt, please visit `authors.packtpub.com` and apply today. We have worked with thousands of developers and tech professionals, just like you, to help them share their insight with the global tech community. You can make a general application, apply for a specific hot topic that we are recruiting an author for, or submit your own idea.

Table of Contents

Preface

This book explores the potential of developing full-stack JavaScript web applications by combining the power of React with industry tested server-side technologies, such as Node, Express, and MongoDB. The JavaScript landscape has been growing rapidly for some time now. With an abundance of options and resources available on this subject matter, it is easy to get lost when you need to choose from these frequently changing parts, learn about them, and make them work together to build your own web applications. In an attempt to address this pain point, the book adopts a practical approach to help you set up and build a diverse range of working applications using this popular JavaScript stack.

Who this book is for

This book is aimed at JavaScript developers who may have some experience with React, but no previous experience with full-stack development involving Node, Express, and MongoDB, and who want practical guidelines to start building different types of web applications with this stack.

What this book covers

Chapter 1, *Unleashing React Applications with MERN*, introduces the MERN stack technologies and the applications developed in this book. We will discuss the context and relevance of developing web applications with React, Node, Express, and MongoDB.

Chapter 2, *Preparing the Development Environment*, helps set up the MERN stack technologies for development. We will explore essential development tools, install Node, MongoDB, Express, React, and other required libraries, and then run code to check the setup.

Chapter 3, *Building a Backend with MongoDB, Express, and Node*, implements the backend of a skeleton MERN application. We will build a standalone server-side application with MongoDB, Express, and Node, which stores user details and has APIs for user authentication and CRUD operations.

Chapter 4, *Adding a React Frontend to Complete MERN*, completes the MERN skeleton application by integrating a React frontend. We will implement a working frontend with React views for interacting with the user CRUD and auth APIs on the server.

Chapter 5, *Starting with a Simple Social Media Application*, builds a social media application by extending the skeleton application. We will explore the capabilities of the MERN stack by implementing social media features, such as post sharing, liking, and commenting; following friends; and an aggregated newsfeed.

Chapter 6, *Exercising New MERN Skills with an Online Marketplace*, implements basic features in an online marketplace application. We will implement buying- and selling-related features with support for seller accounts, product listings, and product search by category.

Chapter 7, *Extending the Marketplace for Orders and Payments*, builds the marketplace application further with a shopping cart, order management, and payments processing. We will add a shopping cart feature and allow users to place orders with the items in their carts. We will also integrate Stripe to collect and process payments.

Chapter 8, *Building a Media Streaming Application*, implements media uploading and streaming using MongoDB GridFS. We will start building a basic media streaming application, allowing registered users to upload video files that will be stored on MongoDB and streamed back so that viewers can play each video in a simple React media player.

Chapter 9, *Customizing the Media Player and Improving SEO*, upgrades the media viewing capabilities with a custom media player and autoplay media list. We will implement customized controls on the default React media player, add a playlist that can be autoplayed, and improve SEO for the media details by adding selective server-side rendering with data for just the media detail view.

Chapter 10, *Developing a Web-Based VR Game*, uses React 360 to develop a 3D virtual reality infused game for the web. We will explore the 3D and VR capabilities of React 360 and build a simple web-based VR game.

Chapter 11, *Making the VR Game Dynamic using MERN*, builds a dynamic VR game application by extending the MERN skeleton application and integrating React 360. We will implement a game data model that allows users to create their own VR games and incorporate the dynamic game data with the game developed using React 360.

Chapter 12, *Following Best Practices and Developing MERN Further*, reflects on the lessons learned in previous chapters and suggests improvements for further MERN-based application development. We will expand on some of the best practices already applied, such as modularity in the app structure, other practices that should be applied, such as writing test code, and possible improvements, such as optimizing bundle size.

To get the most out of this book

The content in this book is organized with the assumption that you have familiarity with basic web-based technologies, a working knowledge of programming constructs in JavaScript, and a general idea of how React applications work. As you go through the book, you will uncover how these concepts come together when building full-fledged web applications with React, Node, Express, and MongoDB.

In order to maximize your learning experience while reading through the chapters, it is recommended that you run the associated version of the application code in parallel, using the relevant instructions provided in each chapter.

Download the example code files

You can download the example code files for this book from your account at www.packtpub.com. If you purchased this book elsewhere, you can visit www.packtpub.com/support and register to have the files emailed directly to you.

You can download the code files by following these steps:

1. Log in or register at www.packtpub.com.
2. Select the **SUPPORT** tab.
3. Click on **Code Downloads & Errata**.
4. Enter the name of the book in the **Search** box and follow the onscreen instructions.

Once the file is downloaded, please make sure that you unzip or extract the folder using the latest version of:

- WinRAR/7-Zip for Windows
- Zipeg/iZip/UnRarX for Mac
- 7-Zip/PeaZip for Linux

The code bundle for the book is also hosted on GitHub at https://github.com/PacktPublishing/Full-Stack-React-Projects. If there's an update to the code, it will be updated on the existing GitHub repository.

We also have other code bundles from our rich catalog of books and videos available at https://github.com/PacktPublishing/. Check them out!

Conventions used

There are a number of text conventions used throughout this book.

CodeInText: Indicates code words in text, database table names, folder names, filenames, file extensions, pathnames, dummy URLs, user input, and Twitter handles. Here is an example: "Mount the downloaded WebStorm-10*.dmg disk image file as another disk in your system."

A block of code is set as follows:

```
import path from 'path'
const CURRENT_WORKING_DIR = process.cwd()
app.use('/dist', express.static(path.join(CURRENT_WORKING_DIR, 'dist')))
```

When we wish to draw your attention to a particular part of a code block, the relevant lines or items are set in bold:

```
{
    "presets": [
      "env",
      "stage-2",
      "react"
    ],
    "plugins": [
      "react-hot-loader/babel"
    ]
}
```

Any command-line input or output is written as follows:

```
npm install babel-preset-react --save-dev
```

Bold: Indicates a new term, an important word, or words that you see on screen. For example, words in menus or dialog boxes appear in the text like this. Here is an example: "Select **System info** from the **Administration** panel."

 Warnings or important notes appear like this.

Tips and tricks appear like this.

Get in touch

Feedback from our readers is always welcome.

General feedback: Email `feedback@packtpub.com` and mention the book title in the subject of your message. If you have questions about any aspect of this book, please email us at `questions@packtpub.com`.

Errata: Although we have taken every care to ensure the accuracy of our content, mistakes do happen. If you have found a mistake in this book, we would be grateful if you would report this to us. Please visit `www.packtpub.com/submit-errata`, selecting your book, clicking on the Errata Submission Form link, and entering the details.

Piracy: If you come across any illegal copies of our works in any form on the internet, we would be grateful if you would provide us with the location address or website name. Please contact us at `copyright@packtpub.com` with a link to the material.

If you are interested in becoming an author: If there is a topic that you have expertise in and you are interested in either writing or contributing to a book, please visit `authors.packtpub.com`.

Reviews

Please leave a review. Once you have read and used this book, why not leave a review on the site that you purchased it from? Potential readers can then see and use your unbiased opinion to make purchase decisions, we at Packt can understand what you think about our products, and our authors can see your feedback on their book. Thank you!

For more information about Packt, please visit `packtpub.com`.

1
Unleashing React Applications with MERN

React may have opened up new frontiers for frontend web development and changed the way we program JavaScript user interfaces, but we still need a solid backend to build a complete web application. Although there are myriad options when selecting backend technologies, the benefits and appeal of using a full JavaScript stack are undeniable, especially when there are robust and widely-adopted backend technologies such as Node, Express, and MongoDB. Combining the potential of React with these industry-tested, server-side technologies creates a diverse array of possibilities when developing real-world web applications.

This book guides you through setting up for MERN-based web development, to building real-world web applications of varying complexities.

Before diving into the development of these web applications, we are going to answer the following questions in this chapter to set the context for using MERN:

- What is the MERN stack?
- Why is MERN relevant today?
- When is MERN a good fit for developing web apps?
- How is this book organized to help master MERN?

MERN stack

MongoDB, Express, React, and Node are used in tandem to build web applications and make up the MERN stack. In this lineup, Node and Express bind the web backend together, MongoDB serves as the NoSQL database, and React makes the frontend that the user sees and interacts with.

All four of these technologies are free, open-source, cross-platform, and JavaScript-based, with extensive community and industry support. Each technology has a unique set of attributes, which when integrated together make a simple but effective full JavaScript stack for web development.

Node

Node was developed as a JavaScript runtime environment built on Chrome's V8 JavaScript engine. Node made it possible to start using JavaScript on the server-side to build a variety of tools and applications beyond previous use cases that were limited to within a browser.

Node has an event-driven architecture capable of asynchronous, non-blocking I/O. Its unique non-blocking I/O model eliminates the waiting approach to serving requests. This allows building scalable and lightweight real-time web applications that can efficiently handle many requests.

Node's default package management system, the Node package manager or npm, comes bundled with the Node installation. Npm gives access to hundreds of thousands of reusable Node packages built by developers all over the world and boasts that it is currently the largest ecosystem of open source libraries in the world.

Learn more about Node at `https://nodejs.org/en/` and browse through available npm modules at `https://www.npmjs.com/`.

Express

Express is a basic framework for building web applications and APIs with a Node server. It provides a simple layer of fundamental web application features that complements Node.

In any web application developed with Node, Express can be used as a routing and middleware web framework that has minimal functionality of its own—an Express application is essentially a series of middleware function calls.

Middleware functions are functions that have access to the HTTP request and response objects, and also the next middleware function in the web application's request-response cycle.

It is possible to insert almost any compatible middleware of your choice into the request handling chain, in almost any order, making Express very flexible to work with.

Find out what is possible with Express.js at `expressjs.com`.

MongoDB

MongoDB is a top choice when deciding on a NoSQL database for any application. It is a document-oriented database that stores data in flexible, JSON-like documents. This means fields can vary from document to document and data models can evolve over time in response to changing application requirements.

Applications that place a high priority on availability and scalability benefit from MongoDB's distributed architecture features. It comes with built-in support for high availability, horizontal scaling using sharding, and multi-data center scalability across geographic distributions.

MongoDB has an expressive query language, enabling ad hoc queries, indexing for fast lookups, and real-time aggregation that provides powerful ways to access and analyze data while maintaining performance even when data size grows exponentially.

Explore MongoDB features and services at `https://www.mongodb.com/`.

React

React is a declarative and component-based JavaScript library for building user interfaces. Its declarative and modular nature makes it easy for developers to create and maintain reusable, interactive, and complex user interfaces.

Large applications that display a lot of changing data can be fast and responsive if built with React, as it takes care of efficiently updating and rendering just the right UI components when specific data changes. React does this efficient rendering with its notable implementation of a virtual DOM, setting React apart from other web UI libraries that handle page updates with expensive manipulations directly in the browser's DOM.

Developing user interfaces using React also forces frontend programmers to write well-reasoned and modular code that is reusable, easier to debug, test, and extend.

 Check out resources on React at `https://reactjs.org/`.

Since all four technologies are JavaScript-based, these are inherently optimized for integration. However, how these are actually put together in practice to form the MERN stack can vary based on application requirements and developer preferences, making MERN customizable and extensible to specific needs.

Relevance of MERN

JavaScript has come a long way since its inception and it is ever-growing. The MERN stack technologies have challenged the status quo and broken new ground for what is possible with JavaScript. But when it comes to developing real-world applications that need to be sustainable, is it a worthy choice? Some of the reasons that make a strong case for choosing MERN for your next web application are briefly outlined in the following.

Consistency across the technology stack

As JavaScript is used throughout, developers don't need to learn and change gears frequently to work with very different technologies. This also enables better communication and understanding across teams working on different parts of the web application.

Less time to learn, develop, deploy, and extend

Consistency across the stack also makes it easy to learn and work with MERN, reducing the overhead of adopting a new stack and the time to develop a working product. Once the working base of a MERN application is set up and a workflow established, it takes less effort to replicate, further develop, and extend any application.

Widely adopted in the industry

Organizations of all sizes have been adopting the technologies in this stack based on their needs because they can build applications faster, handle highly diverse requirements, and manage applications more efficiently at scale.

Community support and growth

Developer communities surrounding the very popular MERN stack technologies are quite diverse and growing on a regular basis. With lots of people continuously using, fixing, updating, and willing to help grow these technologies, the support system will remain strong for the foreseeable future. These technologies will continue to be maintained, and resources are very likely to be available in terms of documentation, add-on libraries, and technical support.

The ease and benefits of using these technologies are already widely recognized. Because of the high-profile companies that continue adoption and adaptation, and the growing number of people contributing to the code bases, providing support, and creating resources, technologies in the MERN stack will continue to be relevant for a long time to come.

Range of MERN applications

Given the unique features attributed to each technology, along with the ease of extending functionalities of this stack by integrating other technologies, the range of applications that can be built with this stack is actually quite diverse.

These days, web applications are, by default, expected to be rich client apps that are immersive, interactive, and don't fall short on performance and availability. The grouping of MERN strengths makes it perfect for developing web applications that meet these very aspects and demands.

Moreover, novel and upcoming attributes of some of these technologies, such as low-level operation manipulation with Node, large file streaming capabilities with MongoDB GridFS, and virtual reality features on the web using React 360, make it possible to build even more complex and unique applications with MERN.

It may seem reasonable to pick specific features in the MERN technologies, and argue why these don't work for certain applications. But given the versatile nature of how a MERN stack can come together and be extended; these concerns can be addressed in MERN on a case-by-case basis. In this book, we will demonstrate how to make such considerations when faced with specific requirements and demands in the application being built.

MERN applications developed in this book

To demonstrate the breadth of possibilities with MERN and how you can easily start building a web application with varying features, this book will showcase everyday use web applications alongside complex and rare web experiences:

The preceding screenshot gives a glimpse of the four different MERN applications developed in the rest of this book

Social media platform

For the first MERN application, we will build a basic social media application inspired by Twitter and Facebook. This social media platform will implement simple features such as post sharing, liking and commenting, following friends, and an aggregated news feed.

Online marketplace

E-commerce web applications of all sorts are abundant on the internet, and these will not go out of style anytime soon. Using MERN, we will build an online marketplace application covering core aspects, such as support for seller accounts, product listings, a shopping cart for customers, and payment processing.

Media streaming application

To test out some advanced MERN capabilities, a more immersive application, such as a media streaming application, is the next pick. Inspired by features from Netflix and YouTube, this application will implement content uploading and viewing capabilities with a media content upload feature for content providers, and real-time content streaming for viewers.

VR game for the web

The release of React 360 makes it possible to apply web VR capabilities to React user interfaces. We will explore how to create rare web experiences with React 360 in MERN by putting together a basic virtual reality game application for the web. Users will be able to make and play VR games, where each game will have animated VR objects that the player can collect to complete the game.

Book structure

This book aims to help JavaScript developers who have zero-to-some experience with the MERN stack, to set up and start developing web applications of varying complexity. It includes guidelines for building out and running the different applications supplemented with code snippets and explanations of key concepts.

The book is organized into five parts, progressing from basic to advanced topics, taking you on a journey of building MERN from the ground up, then using it to develop different applications with simple to complex features, while demonstrating how to extend the capabilities of the MERN stack based on application requirements.

Getting started with MERN

Chapter 1, *Unleashing React Applications with MERN* and Chapter 2, *Preparing the Development Environment* set the context for developing web applications in a MERN stack and guide you through setting up your development environment.

Building MERN from the ground up – a skeleton application

Chapter 3, *Building a Backend with MongoDB, Express, and Node* and Chapter 4, *Adding a React Frontend to Complete MERN* show how to bring the MERN stack technologies together to form a skeleton web application with minimal and basic features. This skeletal MERN application acts as a base for the four main applications developed in the rest of the book.

Developing basic web applications with MERN

In this part, you will become familiar with the core attributes of a MERN stack web application by building out two real-world applications—a simple social media platform in Chapter 5, *Starting with a Simple Social Media Application,* and an online marketplace in Chapter 6, *Exercising New MERN Skills with an Online Marketplace* and Chapter 7, *Extending the Marketplace for Orders and Payments.*

Advancing to complex MERN applications

Chapter 8, *Building a Media Streaming Application,* Chapter 9, *Customizing Media Player and Improve SEO,* Chapter 10, *Developing a Web-Based VR Game,* and Chapter 11, *Making the VR Game Dynamic using MERN* show how this stack can be used to develop applications with more complex and immersive features, such as media streaming and virtual reality using React 360.

Going forward with MERN

Finally Chapter 12, *Following Best Practices and Developing MERN Further* wraps up the preceding chapters and applications developed by expanding on best practices to follow to make successful MERN applications, suggesting improvements and further developments.

You may choose to use the book out of the prescribed order based on your experience level and preference. A developer who is very new to MERN can follow the path set out in the book. For a more seasoned JS developer, the chapters in the *Building MERN from the ground up - a skeleton application* section would be a good place to start setting up the base application, then pick any of the four applications to build and extend.

Getting the most out of this book

The content in this book is practical-oriented and covers the implementation steps, code, and concepts relevant to building out each MERN application. It is recommended that, rather than attempting to just read through the chapters, you should run the relevant code in parallel, and browse through the application features while following the explanations in the book.

Chapters that discuss code implementations will point to GitHub repositories containing the complete code with instructions on how to run the code. You can pull the code, install, and run it before reading through the chapter:

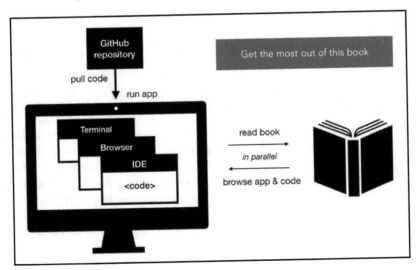

You may consider the recommended following steps outlined to follow the implementations in this book:

- Before diving into the implementation details discussed in the chapter, pull code from the relevant GitHub repository
- Follow instructions with the code to install and run the application
- Browse the features of the running application, while reading the feature descriptions in the relevant chapter
- With the code running in development mode and also open in the editor, refer to the steps and explanations in the book to get a deeper understanding of the implementations

This book aims to provide a quick onboarding with working code for each application. You can experiment with, improve, and extend this code as desired. For an active learning experience, you are encouraged to refactor and modify the code while following the book. In some examples, the book chooses verbose code over succinct and cleaner code because it is easier to reason about for newcomers. In some other implementations, the book sticks with more widely used and traditional conventions over modern and upcoming JavaScript conventions. This is done to minimize disparity when you refer to online resources and documentation while researching the discussed technologies and concepts on your own. These instances where the code in the book can be updated, serve as good opportunities to explore and grow skills beyond what is covered in the book.

Summary

In this chapter, we discovered the context for developing web applications in the MERN stack, and how this book will help you develop with this stack.

MERN stack projects integrate MongoDB, Express, React, and Node to build web applications. Each of the technologies in this stack has made relevant strides in the world of web development. These are widely adopted and continue to improve with the support of growing communities. It is possible to develop MERN applications with diverse requirements, ranging from everyday use applications to more complex web experiences. The practical-oriented approach in this book can be used to grow MERN skills from basic to advanced, or for diving right into building the more complex applications.

In the next chapter, we will start gearing up for MERN application development by setting up the development environment.

2

Preparing the Development Environment

Before building applications with the MERN stack, we first need to prepare the development environment with each technology, and also with tools to aid development and debugging. This chapter guides you through understanding workspace options, essential development tools, how to set up the MERN technologies in your workspace, and the steps to check this setup with actual code.

We are going to cover the following topics:

- Workspace options
- Code editors
- Chrome Developer Tools
- Git setup
- MongoDB setup
- Node setup
- npm modules to complete the MERN stack
- Code to check MERN setup

Selecting development tools

There are plenty of options available when it comes to selecting basic development tools such as text editors or IDEs, version control software, and even the development workspace itself. In this section, we go over options and recommendations relevant to web development with MERN so you can make informed decisions when selecting these tools based on individual preferences.

Workspace options

Developing on a local machine is the most common practice among programmers, but with the advent of good cloud development services, such as Cloud9 (https://aws.amazon.com/cloud9/?origin=c9io), it's now possible to use either or both. You can set up your local workspace with MERN technologies, and this will be assumed to be the case in the rest of the book, but you can also choose to run and develop the code in the cloud services that come equipped for Node development.

Local and cloud development

You can choose to use both types of workspaces to enjoy the benefits of working locally without worrying about bandwidth/internet issues and to work remotely when you don't physically have your favorite local machine. To do this, you can use Git to version control your code, store your latest code on remote Git hosting services such as GitHub or BitBucket, and then share the same code across all your workspaces.

IDE or text editors

Most cloud development environments will come integrated with source code editors. But for your local workspace, you can pick any based on your preference as a programmer, then customize it for MERN development. For example, the following popular options can each be customized as required:

- **Atom** (https://atom.io/): A free, open-source text editor for GitHub that has many MERN stack relevant packages available from other developers
- **SublimeText** (https://www.sublimetext.com/): A proprietary, cross-platform text editor that also has many MERN stack relevant packages available, along with support for JavaScript development
- **Visual Studio Code** (https://code.visualstudio.com/): A feature-rich source code editor by Microsoft with extensive support for modern web application development workflow, including support for MERN stack technologies
- **WebStorm** (https://www.jetbrains.com/webstorm/): A full-fledged JavaScript IDE by JetBrains, with support for MERN stack-based development

Chrome Developer Tools

Loading, viewing and debugging the frontend is a very crucial part of the web development process. The Chrome Developer Tools, which are a part of the Chrome Browser, have many great features that allow debugging, testing, and experimenting with the frontend code, and the look, feel, responsiveness, and performance of the UI. Additionally, the React Developer Tools extension is available as a Chrome plugin, and it adds React debugging tools to the Chrome Developer Tools.

Git

Any development workflow is incomplete without a version control system that enables tracking code changes, code sharing, and collaboration. Over the years, Git has become the de facto version control system for many developers and is the most widely used distributed source code management tool. For code development in this book, Git will help primarily to track progress as we go through the steps to build out each application.

Installation

To start using Git, first install it on your local machine or cloud development environment based on your system specifications. Relevant instructions to download and install the latest Git, along with documentation on using Git commands can be found at: `https://git-scm.com/downloads`.

Remote Git hosting services

Cloud-based Git repository hosting services such as GitHub and BitBucket help share your latest code across workspaces and deployment environments, and also to back up your code. These services pack in a lot of useful features to help with code management and the development workflow. To get started, you can create an account and set up remote repositories for your code bases.

All these essential tools will enrich your web development workflow and increase productivity once you complete the necessary setup in your workspace and start building MERN applications.

Setting up MERN stack technologies

MERN stack technologies are being developed and upgraded as this book is being written, so for the work demonstrated throughout this book, we use the latest stable versions at the time of writing. Installation guidelines for most of these technologies are dependent on the system environment of your workspaces, so this section points to all relevant installation resources, and also acts as a guide for setting up a fully functioning MERN stack.

MongoDB

MongoDB must be set up and running in the development environment before any database features are added to MERN applications. At the time of writing, the current stable version of MongoDB is 3.6.3, and this version of the MongoDB Community Edition is used for developing the applications in this book. The rest of this section provides resources on how to install and run MongoDB.

Installation

You need to install and start MongoDB on your workspace to be able to use it for development. The installation and startup process for MongoDB depends on workspace specifications:

- Cloud development services will have their own instructions for installing and setting up MongoDB. For example, the how-to steps for Cloud9 can be found at: `https://community.c9.io/t/setting-up-mongodb/1717`.
- The guides for installation on your local machine are detailed at: `https://docs.mongodb.com/manual/installation/`.

Running the mongo shell

The *mongo* shell is an interactive tool for MongoDB and a good place to get familiar with MongoDB operations. Once MongoDB is installed and running, you can run the *mongo* shell on the command line. In the *mongo* shell, you can try commands to query and update data as well as perform administrative operations.

Node

Backend server implementation for the MERN applications relies on Node, and also npm. At the time of writing, 8.11.1 is the latest stable Node version available, and it comes bundled with npm version 5.6.0. However, the latest version available for npm is 5.8.0, so after installing Node, npm will need to be upgraded as discussed in the following section.

Installation

Node can be installed via direct download, installers, or the Node version manager:

- You can install Node by directly downloading the source code or a pre-built installer specific to your workspace platform. Downloads are available at `nodejs.org/en/download`.
- Cloud development services may come with Node preinstalled, such as in Cloud9, or will have specific instructions for adding and updating Node.

To test if the installation was successful, you can open the command line and run `node -v` to see if it correctly returns the version number.

Upgrading npm versions

In order to install npm version 5.8.0, run the following install command from the command line, and check the version with `npm -v`:

```
npm install -g npm@5.8.0
npm -v
```

Node version management with nvm

If you need to maintain multiple versions of Node and npm for different projects, nvm is a useful command-line tool to install and manage different versions on the same workspace. You have to install nvm separately. Instructions for setup can be found at: `github.com/creationix/nvm`.

npm modules for MERN

The remaining MERN stack technologies are all available as npm modules and can be added to each project using `npm install`. These include key modules, such as React and Express, which are required to run each MERN application, and also modules that will be necessary during development. In this section, we list and discuss the modules, then see how to use the modules in a working project in the following section.

Key modules

To integrate the MERN stack technologies and run your applications, we will need the following npm modules:

- **React**: To start using React, we will need two modules:
  - `react`
  - `react-dom`
- **Express**: To use Express in your code, you will need the `express` module
- **MongoDB**: To use MongoDB with Node applications, you also need to add the driver, which is available as an npm module named `mongodb`

devDependency modules

To maintain consistency throughout the development of the MERN applications, we will use JavaScript ES6 across the stack. As a consequence, and also to aid the development process, we will use the following additional npm modules to compile and bundle the code and to automatically reload the server and browser app as the code is updated during development:

- Babel modules are needed for converting ES6 and JSX to suitable JavaScript for all browsers. The modules needed to get Babel working are:
  - `babel-core`
  - `babel-loader` for transpiling JavaScript files with Webpack

- `babel-preset-env`, `babel-preset-react`, and `babel-preset-stage-2` to provide support for React, the latest JS features, and some stage-x features such as declaring class fields that are not currently covered under `babel-preset-env`

- Webpack modules will help bundle the compiled JavaScript, both for the client-side and server-side code. Modules needed to get Webpack working are:
  - `webpack`
  - `webpack-cli` to run Webpack commands
  - `webpack-node-externals` to ignore external Node module files when bundling in Webpack
  - `webpack-dev-middleware` to serve the files emitted from Webpack over a connected server during development of the code
  - `webpack-hot-middleware` to add hot module reloading into an existing server by connecting a browser client to a Webpack server and receiving updates as code changes during development

- `nodemon` to watch server-side changes during development, so the server can be reloaded to put changes into effect.

- `react-hot-loader` for faster development on the client side. Every time a file changes in the React frontend, `react-hot-loader` enables the browser app to update without re-bundling the whole frontend code.

 Although `react-hot-loader` is meant for aiding development flow, it is safe to install this module as a regular dependency rather than a devDependency. It automatically ensures hot reloading is disabled in production and the footprint is minimal.

Checking your development setup

In this section, we will go through the development workflow and write code step-by-step to ensure the environment is correctly set up to start developing and running MERN applications.

We will generate these project files in the following folder structure to run a simple setup project:

```
| mern-simplesetup/
  | -- client/
    | --- HelloWorld.js
    | --- main.js
  | -- server/
    | --- devBundle.js
    | --- server.js
  | -- .babelrc
  | -- nodemon.json
  | -- package.json
  | -- template.js
  | -- webpack.config.client.js
  | -- webpack.config.client.production.js
  | -- webpack.config.server.js
```

> The code discussed in this section is available on GitHub in the repository at: `github.com/shamahoque/mern-simplesetup`. You can clone this code and run it as you go through the code explanations in the rest of this chapter.

Initializing package.json and installing npm modules

We will begin by using npm to install all the required modules. It is a best practice to add a `package.json` file in every project folder to maintain, document, and share the npm modules being used in the MERN application. The `package.json` file will contain meta information about the application, as well as list the module dependencies.

Perform the steps outlined in the following to generate a `package.json` file, modify it, and use it to install the npm modules:

- `npm init`: From the command line, enter your project folder and run `npm init`. You will be asked a series of questions and then a `package.json` file will be auto-generated with your answers.

- dependencies: Open the `package.json` in your editor and modify the JSON object to add the key modules and `react-hot-loader` as regular dependencies.

The file path mentioned before a code block indicates the location of the code in the project directory. This convention has been maintained throughout the book to provide better context and guidance as you follow along with the code.

`mern-simplesetup/package.json`:

```
"dependencies": {
    "express": "^4.16.3",
    "mongodb": "^3.0.7",
    "react": "^16.3.2",
    "react-dom": "^16.3.2",
    "react-hot-loader": "^4.1.2"
}
```

- devDependencies: Modify `package.json` further to add the following npm modules required during development as devDependencies.

`mern-simplesetup/package.json`:

```
"devDependencies": {
    "babel-core": "^6.26.2",
    "babel-loader": "^7.1.4",
    "babel-preset-env": "^1.6.1",
    "babel-preset-react": "^6.24.1",
    "babel-preset-stage-2": "^6.24.1",
    "nodemon": "^1.17.3",
    "webpack": "^4.6.0",
    "webpack-cli": "^2.0.15",
    "webpack-dev-middleware": "^3.1.2",
    "webpack-hot-middleware": "^2.22.1",
    "webpack-node-externals": "^1.7.2"
}
```

- npm install: Save `package.json` and from the command line, run `npm install` to fetch and add all these modules to your project.

Configuring Babel, Webpack, and Nodemon

Before we start coding up the web application, we need to configure Babel, Webpack, and Nodemon to compile, bundle, and auto reload the changes in the code during development.

Babel

Create a `.babelrc` file in your project folder and add the following JSON with `presets` and `plugins` specified.

`mern-simplesetup/.babelrc`:

```
{
    "presets": [
      "env",
      "stage-2"
      "react"
    ],
    "plugins": [
      "react-hot-loader/babel"
    ]
}
```

The `react-hot-loader/babel` plugin is required by the `react-hot-loader` module to compile `React` components.

Webpack

We will have to configure Webpack for bundling both the client and server code and the client code separately for production code. Create `webpack.config.client.js`, `webpack.config.server.js`, and `webpack.config.client.production.js` files in your project folder. All three files will have the following code structure:

```
const path = require('path')
const webpack = require('webpack')
const CURRENT_WORKING_DIR = process.cwd()

const config = { ... }

module.exports = config
```

The `config` JSON object will differ with values specific to the client or server-side code, and development versus production code.

Client-side Webpack configuration for development

Update the `config` object with the following in your `webpack.config.client.js` file, to configure Webpack for bundling and hot loading React code during development.

`mern-simplesetup/webpack.config.client.js`:

```
const config = {
    name: "browser",
    mode: "development",
    devtool: 'eval-source-map',
    entry: [
        'react-hot-loader/patch',
        'webpack-hot-middleware/client?reload=true',
        path.join(CURRENT_WORKING_DIR, 'client/main.js')
    ],
    output: {
        path: path.join(CURRENT_WORKING_DIR , '/dist'),
        filename: 'bundle.js',
        publicPath: '/dist/'
    },
    module: {
        rules: [
            {
                test: /\.jsx?$/,
                exclude: /node_modules/,
                use: [
                    'babel-loader'
                ]
            }
        ]
    }, plugins: [
            new webpack.HotModuleReplacementPlugin(),
            new webpack.NoEmitOnErrorsPlugin()
        ]
}
```

- mode sets `process.env.NODE_ENV` to the given value and tells Webpack to use its built-in optimizations accordingly. If not explicitly set, it defaults to the value `'production'`. It can also be set via the command line by passing the value as a CLI argument.

- `devtool` specifies how source maps are generated, if at all. Generally, a source map provides a way of mapping code within a compressed file back to its original position in a source file to aid debugging.
- `entry` specifies the entry file where Webpack starts bundling, in this case with the `main.js` file in the `client` folder.
- `output` specifies the output path for the bundled code, in this case, set to `dist/bundle.js`.
- `publicPath` allows specifying the base path for all assets in the application.
- `module` sets the regex rule for the file extension to be used for transpilation, and the folders to be excluded. The transpilation tool to be used here is `babel-loader`.
- `HotModuleReplacementPlugin` enables hot module replacement for `react-hot-loader`.
- `NoEmitOnErrorsPlugin` allows skipping emitting when there are compile errors.

Server-side Webpack configuration

Modify the code to require `nodeExternals`, and update the `config` object with the following in your `webpack.config.server.js` file to configure Webpack for bundling server-side code.

`mern-simplesetup/webpack.config.server.js`:

```
const config = {
    name: "server",
    entry: [ path.join(CURRENT_WORKING_DIR , './server/server.js') ],
    target: "node",
    output: {
        path: path.join(CURRENT_WORKING_DIR , '/dist/'),
        filename: "server.generated.js",
        publicPath: '/dist/',
        libraryTarget: "commonjs2"
    },
    externals: [nodeExternals()],
    module: {
        rules: [
            {
                test: /\.js$/,
                exclude: /node_modules/,
                use: [ 'babel-loader' ]
            }
```

```
        ]
    }
}
```

The `mode` option is not set here explicitly but will be passed as required when running the Webpack commands with respect to running for development or building for production.

Webpack starts bundling from the server folder with `server.js`, then outputs the bundled code in `server.generated.js` in the `dist` folder.

Client-side Webpack configuration for production

For preparing the client-side code for production, update the `config` object with the following code in your `webpack.config.client.production.js` file.

`mern-simplesetup/webpack.config.client.production.js`:

```
const config = {
    mode: "production",
    entry: [
        path.join(CURRENT_WORKING_DIR, 'client/main.js')
    ],
    output: {
        path: path.join(CURRENT_WORKING_DIR , '/dist'),
        filename: 'bundle.js',
        publicPath: "/dist/"
    },
    module: {
        rules: [
            {
                test: /\.jsx?$/,
                exclude: /node_modules/,
                use: [
                    'babel-loader'
                ]
            }
        ]
    }
}
```

This will configure Webpack for bundling the React code to be used in production mode, where the hot reloading plugin or debug configuration will no longer be required.

Nodemon

Create a `nodemon.js` file in your project folder, and add the following configuration.

`mern-simplesetup/nodemon.js`:

```
{
    "verbose": false,
    "watch": [ "./server" ],
    "exec": "webpack --mode=development --config
    webpack.config.server.js
            && node ./dist/server.generated.js"
}
```

This configuration will set up `nodemon` to watch for changes in the server files during development, then execute compile and build commands as necessary.

Frontend views with React

In order to start developing a frontend, first create a root template file called `template.js` in the project folder, which will render the HTML with `React` components.

`mern-simplesetup/template.js`:

```
export default () => {
    return `<!doctype html>
      <html lang="en">
        <head>
          <meta charset="utf-8">
          <title>MERN Kickstart</title>
        </head>
        <body>
          <div id="root"></div>
          <script type="text/javascript" src="/dist/bundle.js">
        </script>
        </body>
      </html>`
}
```

When the server receives a request to the root URL, this HTML template will be rendered in the browser, and the `div` element with ID `"root"` will contain our `React` component.

Next, create a `client` folder where we will add two React files, `main.js` and `HelloWorld.js`.

The `main.js` file simply renders the top-level entry `React` component in the `div` element in the HTML document.

`mern-simplesetup/client/main.js`:

```
import React from 'react'
import { render } from 'react-dom'
import HelloWorld from './HelloWorld'

render(<HelloWorld/>, document.getElementById('root'))
```

In this case, the entry `React` component is the `HelloWorld` component imported from `HelloWorld.js`.

`HelloWorld.js` contains a basic `HelloWorld` component, which is hot-exported to enable hot reloading with `react-hot-loader` during development.

`mern-simplesetup/client/HelloWorld.js`:

```
import React, { Component } from 'react'
import { hot } from 'react-hot-loader'

class HelloWorld extends Component {
    render() {
      return (
          <div>
              <h1>Hello World!</h1>
          </div>
      )
    }
}

export default hot(module)(HelloWorld)
```

To see the `React` component rendered in the browser when the server receives a request to the root URL, we need to use the Webpack and Babel setup to compile and bundle this code, and add server-side code that responds to the root route request with the bundled code.

Server with Express and Node

In the project folder, create a folder called `server`, and add a file called `server.js` that will set up the server. Then, add another file called `devBundle.js`, which will help compile the React code using Webpack configurations while in development mode.

Express app

In `server.js`, we will first add code to import the `express` module in order to initialize an Express app.

`mern-simplesetup/server/server.js`:

```
import express from 'express'

const app = express()
```

Then we will use this Express app to build out the rest of the Node server application.

Bundle React app during development

In order to keep the development flow simple, we will initialize Webpack to compile the client-side code when the server is run. In `devBundle.js`, we will set up a compile method that takes the Express app and configures it to use the Webpack middleware to compile, bundle, and serve code, as well as enable hot reloading in development mode.

`mern-simplesetup/server/devBundle.js`:

```
import webpack from 'webpack'
import webpackMiddleware from 'webpack-dev-middleware'
import webpackHotMiddleware from 'webpack-hot-middleware'
import webpackConfig from './../webpack.config.client.js'

const compile = (app) => {
  if(process.env.NODE_ENV == "development"){
    const compiler = webpack(webpackConfig)
    const middleware = webpackMiddleware(compiler, {
      publicPath: webpackConfig.output.publicPath
    })
    app.use(middleware)
    app.use(webpackHotMiddleware(compiler))
  }
}

export default {
  compile
}
```

We will call this compile method in `server.js` by adding the following lines while in development mode.

`mern-simplesetup/server/server.js`:

```
import devBundle from './devBundle'
const app = express()
devBundle.compile(app)
```

These two highlighted lines are only meant for development mode and should be commented out when building the application code for production. In development mode, when these lines are executed, Webpack will compile and bundle the React code to place it in `dist/bundle.js`.

Serving static files from the dist folder

Webpack will compile client-side code in both development and production mode, then place the bundled files in the `dist` folder. To make these static files available on requests from the client side, we will add the following code in `server.js` to serve static files from `dist/folder`.

`mern-simplesetup/server/server.js`:

```
import path from 'path'
const CURRENT_WORKING_DIR = process.cwd()
app.use('/dist', express.static(path.join(CURRENT_WORKING_DIR, 'dist')))
```

Rendering templates at the root

When the server receives a request at the root URL /, we will render `template.js` in the browser. In `server.js`, add the following route handling code to the Express app to receive GET requests at /.

`mern-simplesetup/server/server.js`:

```
import template from './../template'
app.get('/', (req, res) => {
    res.status(200).send(template())
})
```

Finally, add server code to listen on the specified port for incoming requests.

`mern-simplesetup/server/server.js`:

```
let port = process.env.PORT || 3000
app.listen(port, function onStart(err) {
  if (err) {
    console.log(err)
  }
  console.info('Server started on port %s.', port)
})
```

Connecting the server to MongoDB

To connect your Node server to MongoDB, add the following code to `server.js`, and make sure you have MongoDB running in your workspace.

`mern-simplesetup/server/server.js`:

```
import { MongoClient } from 'mongodb'
const url = process.env.MONGODB_URI ||
'mongodb://localhost:27017/mernSimpleSetup'
MongoClient.connect(url, (err, db)=>{
  console.log("Connected successfully to mongodb server")
  db.close()
})
```

In this code example, `MongoClient` is the driver that connects to the running `MongoDB` instance using its `url` and allows us to implement the database related code in the backend.

npm run scripts

Update the `package.json` file to add the following npm run scripts for development and production.

`mern-simplesetup/package.json`:

```
"scripts": {
    "development": "nodemon",
    "build": "webpack --config webpack.config.client.production.js
```

```
               && webpack --mode=production --config
       webpack.config.server.js",
       "start": "NODE_ENV=production node ./dist/server.generated.js"
}
```

- `npm run development`: This command will get Nodemon, Webpack, and the server started for development
- `npm run build`: This will generate the client and server code bundles for production mode (before running this script, make sure to remove the `devBundle.compile` code from `server.js`)
- `npm run start`: This command will run the bundled code in production

Developing and debugging in real time

To run the code developed so far, and to ensure everything is working, you can go through the following steps:

1. **Run the application from the command line**: `npm run development`.
2. **Load in browser**: Open the root URL in the browser, which is `http://localhost:3000` if you are using your local machine setup. You should see a page with the title MERN Kickstart that just shows **Hello World!**.
3. **Develop code and debug live**: Change the `HelloWorld.js` component text `'Hello World!'` to just `'hello'`. Save the changes to see the instantaneous update in the browser, and also check the command line output to see that `bundle.js` is not re-created. Similarly, you can also see instant updates when you change the server-side code, increasing productivity during development.

If you have made it this far, congratulations, you are all set to start developing exciting MERN applications.

Summary

In this chapter, we discussed development tool options and how to install MERN technologies, and then we wrote code to check whether the development environment is set up correctly.

We began by looking at the recommended workspace, IDE, version control software, and browser options suitable for web development. You can select from these options based on your preferences as a developer.

Next, we set up the MERN stack technologies by first installing MongoDB, Node, and npm, and then adding the remaining required libraries using npm.

Before moving on to writing code to check this setup, we configured Webpack and Babel to compile and bundle code during development, and to build production ready code. We learned that it is necessary to compile the ES6 and JSX code that is used for developing a MERN application before opening the application on browsers.

Additionally, we made the development flow efficient by including React Hot Loader for frontend development, configuring Nodemon for backend development, and compiling both the client and server code in one command when the server is run during development.

In the next chapter, we use this setup to start building a skeleton MERN application that will function as a base for full-featured applications.

3

Building a Backend with MongoDB, Express, and Node

During the development of most web applications, there are common tasks, basic features, and implementation code repeated across the process. The same is true for the MERN applications developed in this book. Taking these similarities into consideration, we will first lay the foundations for a skeleton MERN application that can be easily modified and extended to implement a variety of MERN applications.

In this chapter, we will cover the following topics and start with the backend implementation of the MERN skeleton, using Node, Express, and MongoDB:

- User CRUD and auth in a MERN application
- Handling HTTP requests with an Express server
- Using a Mongoose schema for a user model
- APIs for user CRUD and auth
- Auth with JWT for protected routes
- Running backend code and checking APIs

Skeleton application overview

The skeleton application will encapsulate rudimentary features and a workflow repeated for most MERN applications. We will build the skeleton essentially as a basic but fully functioning MERN web application with user create, update, delete (**CRUD**), and **auth**entication-**auth**orization (**auth**) capabilities, which will also lay out how to develop, organize, and run code for general web applications built using this stack. The aim is to keep the skeleton as simple as possible so it is easy to extend, and can be used as a base application for developing different MERN applications.

Feature breakdown

In the skeleton application, we will add the following use cases with user CRUD and auth functionality implementations:

- **Sign up**: Users can register by creating a new account using an email address
- **User list**: Any visitor can see the list of all registered users
- **Authentication**: Registered users can sign in and sign out
- **Protected user profile**: Only registered users can view individual user details after signing in
- **Authorized user edit and delete**: Only a registered and authenticated user can edit or remove their own user account details

Focus of this chapter – the backend

In this chapter, we will focus on building a working backend for the skeleton application with Node, Express, and MongoDB. The completed backend will be a standalone server-side application that can handle HTTP requests to create a user, list all users, and view, update, or delete a user in the database while taking user authentication and authorization into consideration.

User model

The user model will define user details to be stored in the MongoDB database, and also handle user-related business logic such as password encryption and user data validation. The user model for this skeletal version will be basic with support for the following attributes:

Field name	Type	Description
name	String	Required field to store user's name
email	String	Required unique field to store user's email and identify each account (only one account allowed per unique email)
password	String	Required field for authentication, the database will store the encrypted password and not the actual string for security purposes
created	Date	Automatically generated timestamp when a new user account is created
updated	Date	Automatically generated timestamp when existing user details are updated

API endpoints for user CRUD

To enable and handle user CRUD operations on the user database, the backend will implement and expose API endpoints that the frontend can utilize in the views, as follows:

Operation	API route	HTTP method
Create a user	/api/users	POST
List all users	/api/users	GET
Fetch a user	/api/users/:userId	GET
Update a user	/api/users/:userId	PUT
Delete a user	/api/users/:userId	DELETE
User sign-in	/auth/signin	POST
User sign-out (optional)	/auth/signout	GET

Some of these user CRUD operations will have protected access, which will require the requesting client to be either authenticated, authorized, or both. The last two routes are for authentication and will allow the user to sign in and sign out.

Auth with JSON Web Tokens

To restrict and protect access to the user API endpoints according to the skeleton features, the backend will need to incorporate authentication and authorization mechanisms. There are a number of options when it comes to implementing user auth for web applications. The most common and time tested option is the use of sessions to store user state on both the client and server side. But a newer approach is the use of **JSON Web Token (JWT)** as a stateless authentication mechanism that does not require storing user state on the server side.

Both approaches have strengths for relevant real-world use cases. However, for the purpose of keeping the code simple in this book, and because it pairs well with the MERN stack and our example applications, we will use JWT for auth implementation. Additionally, the book will also suggest security enhancement options in future chapters.

How JWT works

When a user successfully signs in using their credentials, the server side generates a JWT signed with a secret key and a unique user detail. Then, this token is returned to the requesting client to be saved locally either in `localStorage`, `sessionStorage`, or a cookie in the browser, essentially handing over the responsibility of maintaining user state to the client side:

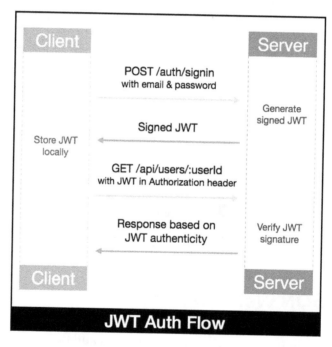

For HTTP requests made following a successful sign-in, specially requests for API endpoints that are protected and have restricted access, the client side has to attach this token to the request. More specifically, the `JSON Web Token` must be included in the request `Authorization` header as a `Bearer`:

```
Authorization: Bearer <JSON Web Token>
```

When the server receives a request for a protected API endpoint, it checks the `Authorization` header of the request for a valid JWT, then verifies the signature to identify the sender and ensures the request data was not corrupted. If the token is valid, the requesting client is given access to the associated operation or resource, otherwise an authorization error is returned.

In the skeleton application, when a user signs in with email and password, the backend will generate a signed JWT with the user's ID and with a secret key available only on the server. This token will then be required for verification when a user tries to view any user profiles, update their account details, or delete their user account.

Implementing the user model to store and validate user data, then integrating it with APIs to perform CRUD operations based on auth with JWT, will produce a functioning standalone backend. In the rest of the chapter, we will look at how to achieve this in the MERN stack and setup.

Implementing the skeleton backend

To start developing the backend part of the MERN skeleton, we will first set up the project folder, install and configure the necessary npm modules, and then prepare the run scripts to aid development and run the code. Then, we will go through the code step by step to implement the user model, API endpoints, and JWT-based auth to meet the specifications we defined earlier for the user-oriented features.

The code discussed in this chapter, and for the complete skeleton application is available on GitHub in the repository at `github.com/shamahoque/mern-skeleton`. The code for just the backend is available at the same repository in the branch named `mern-skeleton-backend`. You can clone this code and run the application as you go through the code explanations in the rest of this chapter.

Folder and file structure

The following folder structure only shows the files that are relevant for the MERN skeleton backend. With these files, we will produce a functioning, standalone server-side application:

```
| mern_skeleton/
   | -- config/
      | --- config.js
```

```
| -- server/
  | --- controllers/
    | ---- auth.controller.js
    | ---- user.controller.js
  | --- helpers/
    | ---- dbErrorHandler.js
  | --- models/
    | ---- user.model.js
  | --- routes/
    | ---- auth.routes.js
    | ---- user.routes.js
  | --- express.js
  | --- server.js
| -- .babelrc
| -- nodemon.json
| -- package.json
| -- template.js
| -- webpack.config.server.js
```

This structure will be further expanded in the next chapter, where we complete the skeleton application by adding a React frontend.

Setting up the project

If the development environment is already set up, we can initialize the MERN project to start developing the backend. First, we will initialize package.json in the project folder, configure and install development dependencies, set configuration variables to be used in the code, and update package.json with run scripts to help develop and run the code.

Initializing package.json

We will need a package.json file to store meta information about the project, list the module dependencies with version numbers, and to define run scripts. To initialize a package.json file in the project folder, go to the project folder from the command line and run npm init, then follow the instructions to add the necessary details. With package.json created, we can proceed with setup and development, and update the file as more modules are required throughout code implementation.

Development dependencies

In order to begin with development and to run the backend server code, we will configure and install Babel, Webpack, and Nodemon as discussed in Chapter 2, *Preparing the Development Environment*, with some minor adjustments for just the backend.

Babel

Since we will be using ES6 to write the backend code, we will configure and install Babel modules to convert ES6.

First, we configure Babel in the .babelrc file with presets for the latest JS features and some stage-x features not currently covered under babel-preset-env.

mern-skeleton/.babelrc:

```
{
    "presets": [
      "env",
      "stage-2"
    ]
}
```

Next, we install the Babel modules as devDependencies from the command line:

```
npm install --save-dev babel-core babel-loader babel-preset-env babel-preset-stage-2
```

Once the module installations are done, you will notice that the devDependencies list has been updated in the package.json file.

Webpack

We will need Webpack to compile and bundle the server-side code using Babel, and for configuration we can use the same webpack.config.server.js discussed in Chapter 2, *Preparing the Development Environment*.

From the command line, run the following command to install webpack, webpack-cli, and the webpack-node-externals module:

```
npm install --save-dev webpack webpack-cli webpack-node-externals
```

This will install the Webpack modules and update the package.json file.

Nodemon

To automatically restart the Node server as we update the code during development, we will use Nodemon to monitor the server code for changes. We can use the same installation and configuration guidelines discussed in Chapter 2, *Preparing the Development Environment*.

Config variables

In the config/config.js file, we will define some server-side configuration related variables that will be used in the code, but should not be hardcoded as a best practice, as well as for security purposes.

mern-skeleton/config/config.js:

```
const config = {
  env: process.env.NODE_ENV || 'development',
  port: process.env.PORT || 3000,
  jwtSecret: process.env.JWT_SECRET || "YOUR_secret_key",
  mongoUri: process.env.MONGODB_URI ||
    process.env.MONGO_HOST ||
    'mongodb://' + (process.env.IP || 'localhost') + ':' +
    (process.env.MONGO_PORT || '27017') +
    '/mernproject'
}

export default config
```

The config variables defined are:

- env: To differentiate between development and production mode
- port: To define the listening port for the server
- jwtSecret: The secret key to be used to sign JWT
- mongoUri: The location of the MongoDB database for the project

Running scripts

To run the server as we develop the code for only the backend, we can start with the npm run development script in the package.json file. For the complete skeleton application, we will use the same run scripts defined in Chapter 2, *Preparing the Development Environment*.

`mern-skeleton/package.json:`

```
"scripts": {
    "development": "nodemon"
}
```

`npm run development`: Running this in the command line from your project folder will basically start Nodemon according to the configuration in `nodemon.js`. The configuration instructs Nodemon to monitor the server files for updates, and on update to build the files again, then restart the server so the changes are immediately available.

Preparing the server

In this section, we will integrate Express, Node, and MongoDB to run a completely configured server before we start implementing the user specific features.

Configuring Express

To use Express, we will first install Express, then add and configure it in the `server/express.js` file.

From the command line, run the following command to install the `express` module with the `--save` flag, so the `package.json` file is automatically updated:

```
npm install express --save
```

Once Express is installed, we can import it into the `express.js` file, configure as required, and make it available to the rest of the app.

`mern-skeleton/server/express.js:`

```
import express from 'express'
const app = express()
  /*... configure express ... */
export default app
```

To handle HTTP requests and serve responses properly, we will use the following modules to configure Express:

- body-parser: Body parsing middleware to handle the complexities of parsing streamable request objects, so we can simplify browser-server communication by exchanging JSON in the request body:
    - Install the body-parser module: npm install body-parser --save
    - Configure Express: bodyParser.json() and bodyParser.urlencoded({ extended: true })
- cookie-parser: Cookie parsing middleware to parse and set cookies in request objects:
  Install the cookie-parser module: npm install cookie-parser --save
- compression: Compression middleware that will attempt to compress response bodies for all requests that traverse through the middleware:
  Install the compression module: npm install compression --save
- helmet: A collection of middleware functions to help secure Express apps by setting various HTTP headers:
  Install the helmet module: npm install helmet --save
- cors: Middleware to enable **CORS (Cross-origin resource sharing)**:
  Install the cors module: npm install cors --save

After the preceding modules are installed, we can update express.js to import these modules and configure the Express app before exporting it for use in the rest of the server code.

The updated mern-skeleton/server/express.js code should be as follows:

```
import express from 'express'
import bodyParser from 'body-parser'
import cookieParser from 'cookie-parser'
import compress from 'compression'
import cors from 'cors'
import helmet from 'helmet'

const app = express()

app.use(bodyParser.json())
app.use(bodyParser.urlencoded({ extended: true }))
```

```
app.use(cookieParser())
app.use(compress())
app.use(helmet())
app.use(cors())

export default app
```

Starting the server

With the Express app configured to accept HTTP requests, we can go ahead and use it to implement the server to listen for incoming requests.

In the `mern-skeleton/server/server.js` file, add the following code to implement the server:

```
import config from './../config/config'
import app from './express'

app.listen(config.port, (err) => {
  if (err) {
    console.log(err)
  }
  console.info('Server started on port %s.', config.port)
})
```

We first import the config variables to set the port number that the server will listen on, and then the configured Express app to start the server.

To get this code running and continue development, you can now run `npm run development` from the command line. If the code has no errors, the server should start running with Nodemon monitoring for code changes.

Setting up Mongoose and connecting to MongoDB

We will be using the `Mongoose` module to implement the user model in this skeleton, and also all future data models for our MERN applications. Here, we will start by configuring Mongoose, and utilizing it to define a connection with the MongoDB database.

First, to install the `mongoose` module, run the following command:

```
npm install mongoose --save
```

Then, update the `server.js` file to import the `mongoose` module, configure it to use native ES6 promises, and finally use it to handle the connection to the MongoDB database for the project.

`mern-skeleton/server/server.js`:

```
import mongoose from 'mongoose'

mongoose.Promise = global.Promise
mongoose.connect(config.mongoUri)

mongoose.connection.on('error', () => {
  throw new Error(`unable to connect to database: ${mongoUri}`)
})
```

If you have the code running in development, saving this update should restart the server that is now integrated with Mongoose and MongoDB.

 Mongoose is a MongoDB object modeling tool that provides a schema-based solution to model application data. It includes built-in type casting, validation, query building, and business logic hooks. Using Mongoose with this backend stack provides a higher layer over MongoDB with more functionality including mapping object models to database documents. Thus, making it simpler and more productive to develop with a Node and MongoDB backend. To learn more about Mongoose, visit `mongoosejs.com`.

Serving an HTML template at a root URL

With a Node, Express, and MongoDB enabled server now running, we can extend it to serve an HTML template in response to an incoming request at the root URL /.

In the `template.js` file, add a JS function that returns a simple HTML document that will render `Hello World` on the browser screen.

`mern-skeleton/template.js`:

```
export default () => {
    return `<!doctype html>
      <html lang="en">
        <head>
          <meta charset="utf-8">
          <title>MERN Skeleton</title>
        </head>
```

```
            <body>
                <div id="root">Hello World</div>
            </body>
        </html>`
    }
```

To serve this template at the root URL, update the `express.js` file to import this template, and send it in the response to a GET request for the `'/'` route.

`mern-skeleton/server/express.js`:

```
import Template from './../template'
...
app.get('/', (req, res) => {
  res.status(200).send(Template())
})
...
```

With this update, opening the root URL in a browser should show **Hello World** rendered on the page.

If you are running the code on your local machine, the root URL will be `http://localhost:3000/`.

User model

We will implement the user model in the `server/models/user.model.js` file, using Mongoose to define the schema with the necessary user data fields, to add built-in validation for the fields and to incorporate business logic such as password encryption, authentication, and custom validation.

We will begin by importing the `mongoose` module and use it to generate a `UserSchema`.

`mern-skeleton/server/models/user.model.js`:

```
import mongoose from 'mongoose'

const UserSchema = new mongoose.Schema({ ... })
```

The `mongoose.Schema()` function takes a schema definition object as a parameter to generate a new Mongoose schema object that can be used in the rest of the backend code.

User schema definition

The user schema definition object needed to generate the new Mongoose schema will declare all the user data fields and associated properties.

Name

The `name` field is a required field of type `String`.

mern-skeleton/server/models/user.model.js:

```
name: {
  type: String,
  trim: true,
  required: 'Name is required'
},
```

Email

The `email` field is a required field of type `String`, which must match a valid email format and must also be `unique` in the user collection.

mern-skeleton/server/models/user.model.js:

```
email: {
  type: String,
  trim: true,
  unique: 'Email already exists',
  match: [/.+\@.+\..+/, 'Please fill a valid email address'],
  required: 'Email is required'
},
```

Created and updated timestamps

The fields `created` and `updated` are `Date` values that will be programmatically generated to record timestamps for a user being created and updated.

mern-skeleton/server/models/user.model.js:

```
created: {
  type: Date,
  default: Date.now
},
updated: Date,
```

Hashed password and salt

The `hashed_password` and `salt` fields represent the encrypted user password that we will use for authentication.

`mern-skeleton/server/models/user.model.js`:

```
hashed_password: {
    type: String,
    required: "Password is required"
},
salt: String
```

The actual password string is not stored directly in the database for security purposes and is handled separately.

Password for auth

The password field is very crucial for providing secure user authentication in any application, and it needs to be encrypted, validated, and authenticated securely as a part of the user model.

As a virtual field

The `password` string provided by the user is not stored directly in the user document. Instead, it is handled as a `virtual` field.

`mern-skeleton/server/models/user.model.js`:

```
UserSchema
  .virtual('password')
  .set(function(password) {
    this._password = password
    this.salt = this.makeSalt()
    this.hashed_password = this.encryptPassword(password)
  })
  .get(function() {
    return this._password
  })
```

When the `password` value is received on user creation or update, it is encrypted into a new hashed value and set to the `hashed_password` field, along with the `salt` value in the `salt` field.

Encryption and authentication

The encryption logic and salt generation logic, which are used to generate the `hashed_password` and `salt` values representing the `password` value, are defined as `UserSchema` methods.

`mern-skeleton/server/models/user.model.js`:

```
UserSchema.methods = {
  authenticate: function(plainText) {
    return this.encryptPassword(plainText) === this.hashed_password
  },
  encryptPassword: function(password) {
    if (!password) return ''
    try {
      return crypto
        .createHmac('sha1', this.salt)
        .update(password)
        .digest('hex')
    } catch (err) {
      return ''
    }
  },
  makeSalt: function() {
    return Math.round((new Date().valueOf() * Math.random())) + ''
  }
}
```

Additionally, the `authenticate` method is also defined as a `UserSchema` method, which is used when a user supplied password must be authenticated for sign-in.

The `crypto` module in Node is used to encrypt the user-provided password string into a `hashed_password` with a randomly generated `salt` value. The `hashed_password` and the salt is stored in the user document when the user details are saved to the database on a create or update. Both the `hashed_password` and `salt` values are required in order to match and authenticate a password string provided during user sign-in, using the `authenticate` method defined previously.

Password field validation

To add validation constraints on the actual password string selected by the end user, we will need to add custom validation logic and associate it with the `hashed_password` field in the schema.

`mern-skeleton/server/models/user.model.js`:

```
UserSchema.path('hashed_password').validate(function(v) {
    if (this._password && this._password.length < 6) {
        this.invalidate('password', 'Password must be at least 6 characters.')
    }
    if (this.isNew && !this._password) {
        this.invalidate('password', 'Password is required')
    }
}, null)
```

To ensure that a password value is indeed provided, and has a length of at least six characters when a new user is created or existing password is updated, custom validation is added to check the password value before Mongoose attempts to store the `hashed_password` value. If validation fails, the logic will return the relevant error message.

Once the `UserSchema` is defined, and all the password related business logic is added as discussed previously, we can finally export the schema at the bottom of the `user.model.js` file, in order to use it in other parts of the backend code.

`mern-skeleton/server/models/user.model.js`:

```
export default mongoose.model('User', UserSchema)
```

Mongoose error handling

The validation constraints added to the user schema fields will throw error messages, if violated when user data is saved to the database. To handle these validation errors and other errors that the database may throw when we make queries to it, we will define a helper method to return a relevant error message that can be propagated in the request-response cycle as appropriate.

We will add the `getErrorMessage` helper method in the `server/helpers/dbErrorHandler.js` file. This method will parse and return the error message associated with the specific validation error or other error that occurred while querying MongoDB using Mongoose.

`mern-skeleton/server/helpers/dbErrorHandler.js`:

```
const getErrorMessage = (err) => {
    let message = ''
    if (err.code) {
        switch (err.code) {
```

```
                case 11000:
                case 11001:
                    message = getUniqueErrorMessage(err)
                    break
                default:
                    message = 'Something went wrong'
        }
    } else {
        for (let errName in err.errors) {
            if (err.errors[errName].message)
            message = err.errors[errName].message
        }
    }
    return message
}
```

```
export default {getErrorMessage}
```

Errors that are not thrown because of a Mongoose validator violation will contain an error code and in some cases need to be handled differently. For example, errors caused due to a violation of the unique constraint will return a different error object than Mongoose validation errors. The unique option is not a validator but a convenient helper for building MongoDB unique indexes, and thus we will add another getUniqueErrorMessage method to parse the unique constraint related error object and construct an appropriate error message.

mern-skeleton/server/helpers/dbErrorHandler.js:

```
const getUniqueErrorMessage = (err) => {
  let output
  try {
      let fieldName =
      err.message.substring(err.message.lastIndexOf('.$') + 2,
      err.message.lastIndexOf('_1'))
      output = fieldName.charAt(0).toUpperCase() + fieldName.slice(1) +
      ' already exists'
  } catch (ex) {
      output = 'Unique field already exists'
  }
  return output
}
```

By using the getErrorMessage function exported from this helper file, we will add meaningful error messages when handling errors thrown by Mongoose operations performed for user CRUD.

User CRUD API

The user API endpoints exposed by the Express app will allow the frontend to do CRUD operations on the documents generated according to the user model. To implement these working endpoints, we will write Express routes and corresponding controller callback functions that should be executed when HTTP requests come in for these declared routes. In this section, we will look at how these endpoints will work without any auth restrictions.

The user API routes will be declared using Express router in `server/routes/user.routes.js`, and then mounted on the Express app we configured in `server/express.js`.

`mern-skeleton/server/express.js`:

```
import userRoutes from './routes/user.routes'
...
app.use('/', userRoutes)
...
```

User routes

The user routes defined in the `user.routes.js` file will use `express.Router()` to declare the route paths with relevant HTTP methods, and assign the corresponding controller function that should be called when these requests are received by the server.

We will keep the user routes simple, by using the following:

- `/api/users` for:
  - Listing users with GET
  - Creating a new user with POST
- `/api/users/:userId` for:
  - Fetching a user with GET
  - Updating a user with PUT
  - Deleting a user with DELETE

The resulting `user.routes.js` code will look as follows (without the auth considerations that need to be added for protected routes).

`mern-skeleton/server/routes/user.routes.js:`

```
import express from 'express'
import userCtrl from '../controllers/user.controller'

const router = express.Router()

router.route('/api/users')
  .get(userCtrl.list)
  .post(userCtrl.create)

router.route('/api/users/:userId')
  .get(userCtrl.read)
  .put(userCtrl.update)
  .delete(userCtrl.remove)

router.param('userId', userCtrl.userByID)

export default router
```

User controller

The `server/controllers/user.controller.js` file will contain the controller methods used in the preceding user route declarations as callbacks when a route request is received by the server.

The `user.controller.js` file will have the following structure:

```
import User from '../models/user.model'
import _ from 'lodash'
import errorHandler from './error.controller'

const create = (req, res, next) => { ... }
const list = (req, res) => { ... }
const userByID = (req, res, next, id) => { ... }
const read = (req, res) => { ... }
const update = (req, res, next) => { ... }
const remove = (req, res, next) => { ... }

export default { create, userByID, read, list, remove, update }
```

The controller will make use of the `errorHandler` helper to respond to the route requests with meaningful messages when a Mongoose error occurs. It will also use a module called `lodash` when updating an existing user with changed values.

TIP `lodash` is a JavaScript library which provides utility functions for common programming tasks including manipulation of arrays and objects. To install `lodash`, run `npm install lodash --save` from command line.

Each of the controller functions defined previously are related to a route request, and will be elaborated on in relation to each API use case.

Creating a new user

The API endpoint to create a new user is declared in the following route.

`mern-skeleton/server/routes/user.routes.js`:

```
router.route('/api/users').post(userCtrl.create)
```

When the Express app gets a POST request at `'/api/users'`, it calls the `create` function defined in the controller.

`mern-skeleton/server/controllers/user.controller.js`:

```
const create = (req, res, next) => {
  const user = new User(req.body)
  user.save((err, result) => {
    if (err) {
      return res.status(400).json({
        error: errorHandler.getErrorMessage(err)
      })
    }
    res.status(200).json({
      message: "Successfully signed up!"
    })
  })
}
```

This function creates a new user with the user JSON object received in the POST request from the frontend within `req.body`. The `user.save` attempts to save the new user into the database after Mongoose does a validation check on the data, consequently an error or success response is returned to the requesting client.

Listing all users

The API endpoint to fetch all the users is declared in the following route.

mern-skeleton/server/routes/user.routes.js:

```
router.route('/api/users').get(userCtrl.list)
```

When the Express app gets a GET request at '/api/users', it executes the `list` controller function.

mern-skeleton/server/controllers/user.controller.js:

```
const list = (req, res) => {
  User.find((err, users) => {
    if (err) {
      return res.status(400).json({
        error: errorHandler.getErrorMessage(err)
      })
    }
    res.json(users)
  }).select('name email updated created')
}
```

The `list` controller function finds all the users from the database, populates only the name, email, created and updated fields in the resulting user list, and then returns this list of users as JSON objects in an array to the requesting client.

Loading a user by ID to read, update, or delete

All three API endpoints for read, update, and delete require a user to be retrieved from the database based on the user ID of the user being accessed. We will program the Express router to do this action first before responding to the specific request to read, update, or delete.

Loading

Whenever the Express app receives a request to a route that matches a path containing the `:userId` param in it, the app will first execute the `userByID` controller function before propagating to the `next` function specific to the request that came in.

mern-skeleton/server/routes/user.routes.js:

```
router.param('userId', userCtrl.userByID)
```

The `userByID` controller function uses the value in the `:userId` param to query the database by `_id`, and load the matching user's details.

`mern-skeleton/server/controllers/user.controller.js`:

```
const userByID = (req, res, next, id) => {
  User.findById(id).exec((err, user) => {
    if (err || !user)
      return res.status('400').json({
        error: "User not found"
      })
    req.profile = user
    next()
  })
}
```

If a matching user is found in the database, the user object is appended to the request object in the `profile` key. Then, the `next()` middleware is used to propagate control to the next relevant controller function. For example, if the original request was to read a user profile, the `next()` call in `userById` would go to the `read` controller function.

Reading

The API endpoint to read a single user's data is declared in the following route.

`mern-skeleton/server/routes/user.routes.js`:

```
router.route('/api/users/:userId').get(userCtrl.read)
```

When the Express app gets a GET request at `'/api/users/:userId'`, it executes the `userByID` controller function to load the user by the `userId` value in the param, and then the `read` controller function.

`mern-skeleton/server/controllers/user.controller.js`:

```
const read = (req, res) => {
  req.profile.hashed_password = undefined
  req.profile.salt = undefined
  return res.json(req.profile)
}
```

The `read` function retrieves the user details from `req.profile` and removes sensitive information, such as the `hashed_password` and `salt` values, before sending the user object in the response to the requesting client.

Updating

The API endpoint to update a single user is declared in the following route.

`mern-skeleton/server/routes/user.routes.js`:

```
router.route('/api/users/:userId').put(userCtrl.update)
```

When the Express app gets a PUT request at `'/api/users/:userId'`, similar to the `read`, it first loads the user with the `:userId` param value, and then the `update` controller function is executed.

`mern-skeleton/server/controllers/user.controller.js`:

```
const update = (req, res, next) => {
  let user = req.profile
  user = _.extend(user, req.body)
  user.updated = Date.now()
  user.save((err) => {
    if (err) {
      return res.status(400).json({
        error: errorHandler.getErrorMessage(err)
      })
    }
    user.hashed_password = undefined
    user.salt = undefined
    res.json(user)
  })
}
```

The `update` function retrieves the user details from `req.profile`, then uses the `lodash` module to extend and merge the changes that came in the request body to update the user data. Before saving this updated user to the database, the `updated` field is populated with the current date to reflect the last updated at timestamp. On successful save of this update, the updated user object is cleaned by removing the sensitive data, such as `hashed_password` and `salt`, before sending the user object in the response to the requesting client.

Deleting

The API endpoint to delete a user is declared in the following route.

`mern-skeleton/server/routes/user.routes.js`:

```
router.route('/api/users/:userId').delete(userCtrl.remove)
```

When the Express app gets a DELETE request at `'/api/users/:userId'`, similar to the read and update, it first loads the user by ID, and then the `remove` controller function is executed.

`mern-skeleton/server/controllers/user.controller.js`:

```
const remove = (req, res, next) => {
  let user = req.profile
  user.remove((err, deletedUser) => {
    if (err) {
      return res.status(400).json({
        error: errorHandler.getErrorMessage(err)
      })
    }
    deletedUser.hashed_password = undefined
    deletedUser.salt = undefined
    res.json(deletedUser)
  })
}
```

The `remove` function retrieves the user from `req.profile` and uses the `remove()` query to delete the user from the database. On successful deletion, the requesting client is returned the deleted user object in the response.

With the implementation of the API endpoints so far, any client can perform CRUD operations on the user model, but we want to restrict access to some of these operations with authentication and authorization.

User auth and protected routes

To restrict access to user operations such as user profile view, user update, and user delete, we will implement sign-in authentication with JWT, then protect and authorize the read, update, and delete routes.

The auth-related API endpoints for sign-in and sign-out will be declared in `server/routes/auth.routes.js` and then mounted on the Express app in `server/express.js`.

```
mern-skeleton/server/express.js:

   import authRoutes from './routes/auth.routes'
     ...
     app.use('/', authRoutes)
     ...
```

Auth routes

The two auth APIs are defined in the `auth.routes.js` file using `express.Router()` to declare the route paths with relevant HTTP methods, and assigned corresponding auth controller functions that should be called when requests are received for these routes.

The auth routes are as follows:

- `'/auth/signin'`: POST request to authenticate the user with email and password
- `'/auth/signout'`: GET request to clear the cookie containing a JWT that was set on the response object after sign-in

The resulting `mern-skeleton/server/routes/auth.routes.js` file will be as follows:

```
import express from 'express'
import authCtrl from '../controllers/auth.controller'

const router = express.Router()

router.route('/auth/signin')
  .post(authCtrl.signin)
router.route('/auth/signout')
  .get(authCtrl.signout)

export default router
```

Auth controller

The auth controller functions in `server/controllers/auth.controller.js` will not only handle requests to the sign-in and sign-out routes, but also provide JWT and `express-jwt` functionality to enable authentication and authorization for protected user API endpoints.

The `auth.controller.js` file will have the following structure:

```
import User from '../models/user.model'
import jwt from 'jsonwebtoken'
import expressJwt from 'express-jwt'
import config from './../../config/config'

const signin = (req, res) => { ... }
const signout = (req, res) => { ... }
const requireSignin = ...
const hasAuthorization = (req, res) => { ... }

export default { signin, signout, requireSignin, hasAuthorization }
```

The four controller functions are elaborated on in the following to show how the backend implements user auth using JSON Web Tokens.

Sign-in

The API endpoint to sign in a user is declared in the following route.

`mern-skeleton/server/routes/auth.routes.js`:

```
router.route('/auth/signin').post(authCtrl.signin)
```

When the Express app gets a POST request at `'/auth/signin'`, it executes the `signin` controller function.

`mern-skeleton/server/controllers/auth.controller.js`:

```
const signin = (req, res) => {
  User.findOne({
    "email": req.body.email
  }, (err, user) => {
    if (err || !user)
      return res.status('401').json({
        error: "User not found"
      })

    if (!user.authenticate(req.body.password)) {
      return res.status('401').send({
        error: "Email and password don't match."
      })
    }

    const token = jwt.sign({
```

```
    _id: user._id
  }, config.jwtSecret)

  res.cookie("t", token, {
    expire: new Date() + 9999
  })

  return res.json({
    token,
    user: {_id: user._id, name: user.name, email: user.email}
  })
})
}
```

The POST request object receives the email and password in req.body. This email is used to retrieve a matching user from the database. Then, the password authentication method defined in the UserSchema is used to verify the password received in the req.body from the client.

If the password is successfully verified, the JWT module is used to generate a JWT signed using a secret key and the user's _id value.

 Install the jsonwebtoken module to make it available to this controller in the import by running npm install jsonwebtoken --save from the command line.

Then, the signed JWT is returned to the authenticated client along with user details. Optionally, we can also set the token to a cookie in the response object so it is available to the client side if cookies is the chosen form of JWT storage. On the client side, this token must be attached as an Authorization header when requesting protected routes from the server.

Sign-out

The API endpoint to sign out a user is declared in the following route.

mern-skeleton/server/routes/auth.routes.js:

```
router.route('/auth/signout').get(authCtrl.signout)
```

When the Express app gets a GET request at '/auth/signout', it executes the signout controller function.

mern-skeleton/server/controllers/auth.controller.js:

```
const signout = (req, res) => {
  res.clearCookie("t")
  return res.status('200').json({
    message: "signed out"
  })
}
```

The signout function clears the response cookie containing the signed JWT. This is an optional endpoint and not really necessary for auth purposes if cookies are not used at all in the frontend. With JWT, user state storage is the client's responsibility, and there are multiple options for client-side storage besides cookies. On sign-out, the client needs to delete the token on the client side to establish that the user is no longer authenticated.

Protecting routes with express-jwt

To protect access to the read, update, and delete routes, the server will need to check that the requesting client is actually an authenticated and authorized user.

To check if the requesting user is signed in and has a valid JWT when a protected route is accessed, we will use the express-jwt module.

The express-jwt module is middleware that validates JSON Web Tokens. Run npm install express-jwt --save from the command line to install express-jwt.

Requiring sign-in

The requireSignin method in auth.controller.js uses express-jwt to verify that the incoming request has a valid JWT in the Authorization header. If the token is valid, it appends the verified user's ID in an 'auth' key to the request object, otherwise it throws an authentication error.

`mern-skeleton/server/controllers/auth.controller.js:`

```
const requireSignin = expressJwt({
  secret: config.jwtSecret,
  userProperty: 'auth'
})
```

We can add `requireSignin` to any route that should be protected against unauthenticated access.

Authorizing signed in users

For some of the protected routes such as update and delete, on top of checking for authentication we also want to make sure the requesting user is only updating or deleting their own user information. To achieve this, the `hasAuthorization` function defined in `auth.controller.js` checks if the authenticated user is the same as the user being updated or deleted before the corresponding CRUD controller function is allowed to proceed.

`mern-skeleton/server/controllers/auth.controller.js:`

```
const hasAuthorization = (req, res, next) => {
  const authorized = req.profile && req.auth && req.profile._id ==
  req.auth._id
  if (!(authorized)) {
    return res.status('403').json({
      error: "User is not authorized"
    })
  }
  next()
}
```

The `req.auth` object is populated by `express-jwt` in `requireSignin` after authentication verification, and the `req.profile` is populated by the `userByID` function in the `user.controller.js`. We will add the `hasAuthorization` function to routes that require both authentication and authorization.

Protecting user routes

We will add `requireSignin` and `hasAuthorization` to the user route declarations that need to be protected with authentication and also authorization.

Update the read, update, and delete routes in `user.routes.js` as follows.

`mern-skeleton/server/routes/user.routes.js`:

```
import authCtrl from '../controllers/auth.controller'
...
router.route('/api/users/:userId')
    .get(authCtrl.requireSignin, userCtrl.read)
    .put(authCtrl.requireSignin, authCtrl.hasAuthorization,
    userCtrl.update)
    .delete(authCtrl.requireSignin, authCtrl.hasAuthorization,
    userCtrl.remove)
...
```

The route to read a user's information only needs authentication verification, whereas the update and delete routes should check for both authentication and authorization before these CRUD operations are executed.

Auth error handling for express-jwt

To handle the auth-related errors thrown by `express-jwt` when it tries to validate JWT tokens in incoming requests, we need to add the following error-catching code to the Express app configuration in `mern-skeleton/server/express.js`, near the end of the code, after the routes are mounted and before the app is exported:

```
app.use((err, req, res, next) => {
  if (err.name === 'UnauthorizedError') {
    res.status(401).json({"error" : err.name + ": " + err.message})
  }
})
```

`express-jwt` throws an error named `UnauthorizedError` when the token cannot be validated for some reason. We catch this error here to return a `401` status back to the requesting client.

With user auth implemented for protecting routes, we have covered all the desired features of a working backend for the skeleton MERN application. In the next section, we will look at how we can check if this standalone backend is functioning as desired without implementing a frontend.

Checking the standalone backend

There are a number of options when it comes to selecting tools to check backend APIs, ranging from the command-line tool curl (`https://github.com/curl/curl`) to Advanced REST Client (`https://chrome.google.com/webstore/detail/advanced-rest-client/hgmloofddffdnphfgcellkdfbfbjeloo`)—a Chrome extension app with an interactive user interface.

To check the APIs implemented in this chapter, first have the server running from the command line, and use either of these tools to request the routes. If you are running the code on your local machine, the root URL is `http://localhost:3000/`.

Using ARC, we will showcase the expected behavior for five use cases of checking the implemented API endpoints.

Creating a new user

First, we will create a new user with the `/api/users` POST request, and pass name, email, and password values in the request body. When the user is successfully created in the database without any validation errors, we will see a **200 OK** success message as shown in the following screenshot:

Fetching the user list

We can see if the new user is in the database by fetching a list of all users with a GET request to `/api/users`. The response should contain an array of all the user objects stored in the database:

Trying to fetch a single user

Next, we will try to access a protected API without signing in first. A GET request to read any one of the users will return a **401 Unauthorized**, such as in the following example, a GET request to `/api/users/5a1c7ead1a692aa19c3e7b33` returns a **401**:

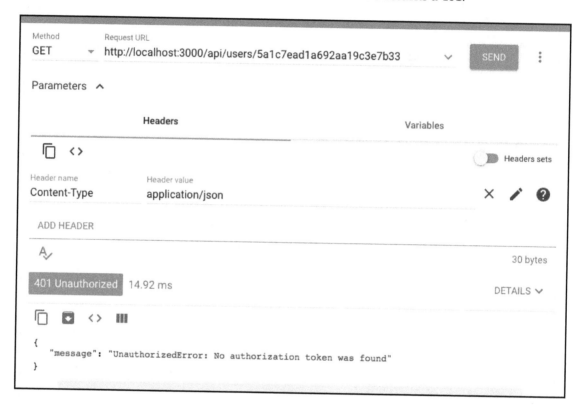

Signing in

To be able to access the protected route, we will sign in using the credentials of the user created in the first example. To sign in, a POST request is sent at /auth/signin with the email and password in the request body. On successful sign-in, the server returns a signed JWT and user details. We will need this token to access the protected route for fetching a single user:

Fetching a single user successfully

Using the token received after sign-in, we can now access the protected route that failed before. The token is set in the `Authorization` header in the Bearer scheme when making the GET request to `/api/users/5a1c7ead1a692aa19c3e7b33`, and this time the user object is returned successfully:

Summary

In this chapter, we developed a fully functioning standalone server-side application using Node, Express, and MongoDB, covering the first part of the MERN skeleton application. In the backend, we implemented the following features:

- A user model for storing user data, implemented with Mongoose
- User API endpoints to perform CRUD operations, implemented with Express
- User auth for protected routes, implemented with JWT and `express-jwt`

We also set up the development flow by configuring Webpack to compile ES6 code, and Nodemon to restart the server when the code changes. Finally, we checked the implementation of the APIs using the Advanced Rest API Client extension app for Chrome.

We are now ready to extend this backend application code in the following chapter, to add the React frontend and complete the MERN skeleton application.

4

Adding a React Frontend to Complete MERN

A web application is incomplete without a frontend. It is the part that users interact with and it is crucial to any web experience. In this chapter, we will use React to add an interactive user interface to the basic user and auth features implemented for the backend of the MERN skeleton application that we started building in the previous chapter.

We will cover the following topics to add a working frontend and complete the MERN skeleton application:

- Frontend features of the skeleton
- Setting up development with React, React Router, and Material-UI
- Backend user API integration
- Auth integration
- Home, Users, Sign-Up, Sign-In, User Profile, Edit, and Delete views
- Navigation menu
- Basic server-side rendering

Skeleton frontend

In order to fully implement the skeleton application features discussed in the *Feature breakdown* section of Chapter 3, *Building a Backend with MongoDB, Express, and Node*, we will add the following user interface components to our base application:

- **Home page**: A view that renders at the root URL to welcome users to the web application
- **User list page**: A view that fetches and shows a list of all the users in the database, and also links to individual user profiles

- **Sign-up page**: A view with a form for user sign-up, allowing new users to create a user account and redirecting them to a sign in page when successfully created
- **Sign-in page**: A view with a sign-in form that allows existing users to sign in so they have access to protected views and actions
- **Profile page**: A component that fetches and displays an individual user's information, is only accessible by signed-in users, and also contains edit and delete options, which are visible only if the signed-in user is looking at their own profile
- **Edit profile page**: A form that fetches the user's information in the form, allows them to edit the information, and is accessible only if the logged-in user is trying to edit their own profile
- **Delete user component**: An option that allows the signed-in user to delete only their own profile after confirming their intent
- **Menu navigation bar**: A component that lists all the available and relevant views to the user, and also helps to indicate the user's current location in the application

The following React component tree diagram shows all the React components we will develop to build out the views for this base application:

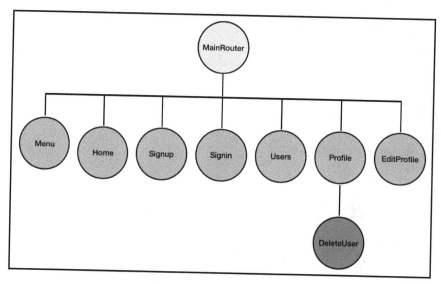

MainRouter will be the root React component that contains all the other custom React views in the application. **Home, Signup, Signin, Users, Profile**, and **EditProfile** will render at individual routes declared with React Router, whereas the **Menu** component will render across all these views, and **DeleteUser** will be a part of the **Profile** view.

The code discussed in this chapter, and for the complete skeleton, is available on GitHub in the repository at `github.com/shamahoque/mern-skeleton`. You can clone this code and run the application as you go through the code explanations in the rest of this chapter.

Folder and file structure

The following folder structure shows the new folders and files to be added to the skeleton to complete it with a React frontend:

```
| mern_skeleton/
   | -- client/
      | --- assets/
         | ---- images/
      | --- auth/
         | ---- api-auth.js
         | ---- auth-helper.js
         | ---- PrivateRoute.js
         | ---- Signin.js
      | --- core/
         | ---- Home.js
         | ---- Menu.js
      | --- user/
         | ---- api-user.js
         | ---- DeleteUser.js
         | ---- EditProfile.js
         | ---- Profile.js
         | ---- Signup.js
         | ---- Users.js
      | --- App.js
      | --- main.js
      | --- MainRouter.js
   | -- server/
      | --- devBundle.js
   | -- webpack.config.client.js
   | -- webpack.config.client.production.js
```

The client folder will contain the React components, helpers, and frontend assets, such as images and CSS. Besides this folder and the Webpack config for compiling and bundling the client code, we will also modify some of the other existing files to integrate the complete skeleton.

Setting up for React development

Before we can start developing with React in our existing skeleton code base, we first need to add configuration to compile and bundle the frontend code, add the React-related dependencies necessary to build the interactive interface, and tie it all together in the MERN development flow.

Configuring Babel and Webpack

To compile and bundle the client code to run it during development and also bundle it for production, we will update the configuration for Babel and Webpack.

Babel

For compiling React, first install the Babel React preset module as a development dependency:

```
npm install babel-preset-react --save-dev
```

Then, update .babelrc to include the module and also configure the react-hot-loader Babel plugin as required for the react-hot-loader module.

mern-skeleton/.babelrc:

```
{
    "presets": [
      "env",
      "stage-2",
      "react"
    ],
    "plugins": [
      "react-hot-loader/babel"
    ]
}
```

Webpack

To bundle client-side code after compiling it with Babel, and also to enable react-hot-loader for faster development, install the following modules:

```
npm install --save-dev webpack-dev-middleware webpack-hot-middleware file-
loader
npm install --save react-hot-loader
```

Then, to configure Webpack for the frontend development and to build the production bundle, we will add a `webpack.config.client.js` file and a `webpack.config.client.production.js` file with the same configuration code described in `Chapter 2`, *Preparing the Development Environment*.

Loading Webpack middleware for development

During development, when we run the server, the Express app should load the Webpack middleware relevant to the frontend with respect to the configuration set for the client-side code, so that the frontend and backend development workflow is integrated. To enable this, we will use the `devBundle.js` file discussed in `Chapter 2`, *Preparing the Development Environment*, to set up a `compile` method that takes the Express app and configures it to use the Webpack middleware. The `devBundle.js` in the `server` folder will be as follows.

`mern-skeleton/server/devBundle.js`:

```
import config from './../config/config'
import webpack from 'webpack'
import webpackMiddleware from 'webpack-dev-middleware'
import webpackHotMiddleware from 'webpack-hot-middleware'
import webpackConfig from './../webpack.config.client.js'

const compile = (app) => {
  if(config.env === "development"){
    const compiler = webpack(webpackConfig)
    const middleware = webpackMiddleware(compiler, {
      publicPath: webpackConfig.output.publicPath
    })
    app.use(middleware)
    app.use(webpackHotMiddleware(compiler))
  }
}

export default {
  compile
}
```

Then, import and call this `compile` method in `express.js` by adding the following highlighted lines only while developing.

`mern-skeleton/server/express.js`:

```
import devBundle from './devBundle'
const app = express()
devBundle.compile(app)
```

These two highlighted lines are only meant for development mode and should be commented out when building the code for production. This code will import the middleware and the Webpack configuration before initiating Webpack to compile and bundle the client-side code when the Express app runs in development mode. The bundled code will be placed in the `dist` folder.

Serving static files with Express

To ensure that the Express server properly handles the requests to static files such as CSS files, images, or the bundled client-side JS, we will configure it to serve static files from the `dist` folder by adding the following configuration in `express.js`.

`mern-skeleton/server/express.js`:

```
import path from 'path'
const CURRENT_WORKING_DIR = process.cwd()
app.use('/dist', express.static(path.join(CURRENT_WORKING_DIR, 'dist')))
```

Updating the template to load a bundled script

In order to add the bundled frontend code in the HTML view, we will update the `template.js` file to add the script file from the `dist` folder to the end of the `<body>` tag.

`mern-skeleton/template.js`:

```
...
<body>
    <div id="root"></div>
    <script type="text/javascript" src="/dist/bundle.js"></script>
</body>
```

Adding React dependencies

The frontend views will primarily be implemented using React. In addition, to enable client-side routing we will use React Router, and to enhance the user experience with a sleek look and feel we will use Material-UI.

React

Throughout this book, we will use React 16 to code up the frontend. To start writing the `React` component code, we will need to install the following modules as regular dependencies:

```
npm install --save react react-dom
```

React Router

React Router provides a collection of navigational components that enable routing on the frontend for React applications. To utilize declarative routing and have bookmarkable URL routes, we will add the following React Router modules:

```
npm install --save react-router react-router-dom
```

Material-UI

In order to keep the UI in our MERN applications sleek without delving too much into UI design and implementation, we will utilize the `Material-UI` library. It provides ready-to-use and customizable `React` components that implement Google's material design. To start using Material-UI components to make the frontend, we need to install the following modules:

```
npm install --save material-ui@1.0.0-beta.43 material-ui-icons
```

At the time of writing, the latest pre-release version of Material-UI is `1.0.0-beta.43` and it is recommended to install this exact version in order to ensure the code for the example projects do not break.

To add the `Roboto` fonts as recommended by Material-UI, and use the `Material-UI` icons, we will add the relevant style links into the `template.js` file, in the HTML document's `<head>` section:

```
<link rel="stylesheet"
href="https://fonts.googleapis.com/css?family=Roboto:100,300,400">
<link href="https://fonts.googleapis.com/icon?family=Material+Icons"
rel="stylesheet">
```

With development configuration all set up, and the necessary React modules added to the code base, we can now start implementing the custom React components.

Implementing React views

A functional frontend should integrate React components with the backend API and allow users to navigate seamlessly within the application based on authorization. To demonstrate how to implement a functional frontend view for this MERN skeleton, we will start by detailing how to render the home page component at the root route, then cover the backend API and user auth integration, before highlighting the unique aspects of implementing the remaining view components.

Rendering a home page

The process of implementing and rendering a working `Home` component at the root route will also expose the basic structure of the frontend code in the skeleton. We will start with the top-level entry component that houses the whole React app and renders the main router component that links all the React components in the application.

Entry point at main.js

The `client/main.js` file in the client folder will be the entry point to render the complete React app. In this code, we import the root or top-level React component that will contain the complete frontend and render it to the `div` element with the ID `'root'` specified in the HTML document in `template.js`.

`mern-skeleton/client/main.js`:

```
import React from 'react'
import { render } from 'react-dom'
import App from './App'

render(<App/>, document.getElementById('root'))
```

Root React component

The top-level React component that will contain all the components for the application's frontend is defined in the `client/App.js` file. In this file, we configure the React app to render the view components with a customized Material-UI theme, enable frontend routing, and ensure that React Hot Loader can instantly load changes as we develop the components.

Customizing the Material-UI theme

The Material-UI theme can be easily customized using the `MuiThemeProvider` component, and by configuring custom values to theme variables in `createMuiTheme()`.

`mern-skeleton/client/App.js`:

```
import {MuiThemeProvider, createMuiTheme} from 'material-ui/styles'
import {indigo, pink} from 'material-ui/colors'

const theme = createMuiTheme({
  palette: {
    primary: {
    light: '#757de8',
    main: '#3f51b5',
    dark: '#002984',
    contrastText: '#fff',
  },
  secondary: {
    light: '#ff79b0',
    main: '#ff4081',
    dark: '#c60055',
    contrastText: '#000',
  },
    openTitle: indigo['400'],
    protectedTitle: pink['400'],
    type: 'light'
  }
})
```

For the skeleton, we only apply minimal customization by setting some color values to be used in the UI. The theme variables generated here will be passed to, and available in, all the components we build.

Wrapping the root component with MUI theme and BrowserRouter

The custom React components that we create to make up the user interface will be accessed with frontend routes specified in the `MainRouter` component. Essentially, this component houses all the custom views developed for the application. When defining the root component in `App.js`, we wrap the `MainRouter` component with the `MuiThemeProvider` to give it access to the Material-UI theme, and `BrowserRouter` to enable frontend routing with React Router. The custom theme variables defined previously are passed as a prop to the `MuiThemeProvider`, making the theme available in all our custom React components.

`mern-skeleton/client/App.js`:

```
import React from 'react'
import MainRouter from './MainRouter'
import {BrowserRouter} from 'react-router-dom'

const App = () => (
  <BrowserRouter>
    <MuiThemeProvider theme={theme}>
      <MainRouter/>
    </MuiThemeProvider>
  </BrowserRouter>
)
```

Marking the root component as hot-exported

The last line of code in `App.js` to export the `App` component uses the `hot` module from `react-hot-loader` to mark the root component as `hot`. This will enable live reloading of the React components during development.

`mern-skeleton/client/App.js`:

```
import { hot } from 'react-hot-loader'
...
export default hot(module)(App)
```

For our MERN applications, we won't have to change the `main.js` and `App.js` code all that much after this point, and we can continue building out the rest of the React app by injecting new components in the `MainRouter` component.

Adding a home route to MainRouter

The `MainRouter.js` code will help render our custom React components with respect to routes or locations in the application. In this first version, we will only add the root route to render the `Home` component.

mern-skeleton/client/MainRouter.js:

```
import React, {Component} from 'react'
import {Route, Switch} from 'react-router-dom'
import Home from './core/Home'
class MainRouter extends Component {
  render() {
    return (<div>
      <Switch>
        <Route exact path="/" component={Home}/>
      </Switch>
    </div>)
  }
}
export default MainRouter
```

As we develop more view components, we will update the `MainRouter` to add routes for the new components inside the `Switch` component.

The `Switch` component in React Router renders a route exclusively. In other words, it only renders the first child that matches the requested route path. Whereas, without being nested in a `Switch`, every `Route` component renders inclusively when there is a path match. For example, a request at `'/'` also matches a route at `'/contact'`.

Home component

The `Home` component will be rendered on the browser when the user visits the root route, and we will compose it with Material-UI components. The following screenshot shows the `Home` component and the `Menu` component, which will be implemented later in the chapter as an individual component to provide navigation across the application:

The `Home` component and other view components that will be rendered in the browser for the user to interact with will follow a common code structure containing the following parts in the given order.

Imports

The component file will start with imports from React, Material-UI, React Router modules, images, CSS, API fetch, and auth helpers from our code as required by the specific component. For example, for the `Home` component code in `Home.js`, we use the following imports.

`mern-skeleton/client/core/Home.js`:

```
import React, {Component} from 'react'
import PropTypes from 'prop-types'
import {withStyles} from 'material-ui/styles'
import Card, {CardContent, CardMedia} from 'material-ui/Card'
import Typography from 'material-ui/Typography'
import seashellImg from './../assets/images/seashell.jpg'
```

The image file is kept in the `client/assets/images/` folder and imported/added to the `Home` component.

Style declarations

After the imports, we will define CSS styles utilizing the `Material-UI` theme variables as required to style the elements in the component. For the `Home` component in `Home.js`, we have the following styles.

`mern-skeleton/client/core/Home.js`:

```
const styles = theme => ({
  card: {
    maxWidth: 600,
    margin: 'auto',
    marginTop: theme.spacing.unit * 5
  },
  title: {
    padding:`${theme.spacing.unit * 3}px ${theme.spacing.unit * 2.5}px
    ${theme.spacing.unit * 2}px`,
    color: theme.palette.text.secondary
  },
  media: {
    minHeight: 330
  }
})
```

The JSS style objects defined here will be injected into the component and used to style the elements in the component, as shown in the following `Home` component definition.

 Material-UI uses JSS, which is a CSS-in-JS styling solution to add styles to the components. JSS uses JavaScript as a language to describe styles. This book will not cover CSS and styling implementations in detail. It will most rely on the default look and feel of Material-UI components. To learn more about JSS, visit `http://cssinjs.org/?v=v9.8.1`. For examples of how to customize the `Material-UI` component styles, check out the Material-UI documentation at `https://material-ui-next.com/`.

Component definition

In the component definition, we will compose the content and behavior of the component. The `Home` component will contain a Material-UI `Card` with a headline, an image, and a caption, all styled with the classes defined earlier and passed in as props.

`mern-skeleton/client/core/Home.js`:

```
class Home extends Component {
    render() {
      const {classes} = this.props
      return (
        <div>
          <Card className={classes.card}>
            <Typography type="headline" component="h2" className=
            {classes.title}>
              Home Page
            </Typography>
            <CardMedia className={classes.media} image={seashellImg}
            title="Unicorn Shells"/>
            <CardContent>
              <Typography type="body1" component="p">
                Welcome to the Mern Skeleton home page
              </Typography>
            </CardContent>
          </Card>
        </div>
      )
    }
  }
```

PropTypes validation

To validate the required injection of style declarations as props to the component, we add the `PropTypes` requirement validator to the defined component.

`mern-skeleton/client/core/Home.js`:

```
Home.propTypes = {
  classes: PropTypes.object.isRequired
}
```

Export component

Finally, in the last line of code in the component file, we will export the component with the defined styles passed in using `withStyles` from `Material-UI`. Using `withStyles` like this creates a **Higher-order component** (HOC) that has access to the defined style objects as props.

`mern-skeleton/client/core/Home.js`:

```
export default withStyles(styles)(Home)
```

The exported component can now be used for composition within other components, as we did with this `Home` component in a route in the `MainRouter` component discussed earlier.

The other view components to be implemented in our MERN applications will adhere to the same structure. In the rest of the book, we will focus mainly on the component definition, highlighting the unique aspects of the implemented component.

Bundling image assets

The static image file that we imported into the `Home` component view must also be included in the bundle with the rest of the compiled JS code so that the code can access and load it. To enable this, we need to update the Webpack configuration files to add a module rule to load, bundle, and emit image files to the output directory, which contains the compiled frontend and backend code.

Update the `webpack.config.client.js`, `webpack.config.server.js`, and `webpack.config.client.production.js` files to add the following module rule after the use of `babel-loader`:

```
[ ...
    {
        test: /\.(ttf|eot|svg|gif|jpg|png)(\?[\s\S]+)?$/,
        use: 'file-loader'
    }
]
```

This module rule uses the `file-loader` npm module for Webpack, which needs to be installed as a development dependency, as follows:

```
npm install --save-dev file-loader
```

Running and opening in the browser

The client code up to this point can be run to view the `Home` component in the browser at the root URL. To run the application, use the following command:

```
npm run development
```

Then, open the root URL (`http://localhost:3000`) in the browser to see the `Home` component.

The `Home` component developed here is a basic view component without interactive features and does not require the use of the backend APIs for user CRUD or auth. However, the remaining view components for our skeleton frontend will need the backend APIs and auth.

Backend API integration

Users should be able to use the frontend views to fetch and modify user data in the database based on authentication and authorization. To implement these functionalities, the React components will access the API endpoints exposed by the backend using the Fetch API.

 The Fetch API is a newer standard to make network requests similar to **XMLHttpRequest (XHR)** but using promises instead, enabling a simpler and cleaner API. To learn more about the Fetch API, visit `https://developer.mozilla.org/en-US/docs/Web/API/Fetch_API`.

Fetch for User CRUD

In the `client/user/api-user.js` file, we will add methods for accessing each of the user CRUD API endpoints, which the React components can use to exchange user data with the server and database as required.

Creating a user

The `create` method will take user data from the view component, use `fetch` to make a `POST` call to create a new user in the backend, and finally return the response from the server to the component as a promise.

`mern-skeleton/client/user/api-user.js`:

```
const create = (user) => {
  return fetch('/api/users/', {
      method: 'POST',
      headers: {
        'Accept': 'application/json',
        'Content-Type': 'application/json'
      },
```

```
      body: JSON.stringify(user)
    })
    .then((response) => {
      return response.json()
    }).catch((err) => console.log(err))
}
```

Listing users

The `list` method will use fetch to make a GET call to retrieve all the users in the database, and then return the response from the server as a promise to the component.

mern-skeleton/client/user/api-user.js:

```
const list = () => {
    return fetch('/api/users/', {
      method: 'GET',
    }).then(response => {
      return response.json()
    }).catch((err) => console.log(err))
}
```

Reading a user profile

The `read` method will use fetch to make a GET call to retrieve a specific user by ID. Since this is a protected route, besides passing the user ID as a parameter, the requesting component must also provide valid credentials, which in this case will be a valid JWT received after successful sign-in.

mern-skeleton/client/user/api-user.js:

```
const read = (params, credentials) => {
    return fetch('/api/users/' + params.userId, {
      method: 'GET',
      headers: {
        'Accept': 'application/json',
        'Content-Type': 'application/json',
        'Authorization': 'Bearer ' + credentials.t
      }
    }).then((response) => {
      return response.json()
    }).catch((err) => console.log(err))
}
```

The JWT is attached to the `GET` fetch call in the `Authorization` header using the `Bearer` scheme, and then the response from the server is returned to the component in a promise.

Updating a user's data

The `update` method will take changed user data from the view component for a specific user, then use `fetch` to make a `PUT` call to update the existing user in the backend. This is also a protected route that will require a valid JWT as credential.

mern-skeleton/client/user/api-user.js:

```
const update = (params, credentials, user) => {
  return fetch('/api/users/' + params.userId, {
    method: 'PUT',
    headers: {
      'Accept': 'application/json',
      'Content-Type': 'application/json',
      'Authorization': 'Bearer ' + credentials.t
    },
    body: JSON.stringify(user)
  }).then((response) => {
    return response.json()
  }).catch((err) => {
    console.log(err)
  })
}
```

Deleting a user

The `remove` method will allow the view component to delete a specific user from the database, using fetch to make a `DELETE` call. This, again, is a protected route that will require a valid JWT as a credential, similar to the `read` and `update` methods. The response from the server to the delete request will be returned to the component as a promise.

mern-skeleton/client/user/api-user.js:

```
const remove = (params, credentials) => {
  return fetch('/api/users/' + params.userId, {
    method: 'DELETE',
    headers: {
      'Accept': 'application/json',
      'Content-Type': 'application/json',
      'Authorization': 'Bearer ' + credentials.t
    }
  }).then((response) => {
```

```
      return response.json()
    }).catch((err) => {
      console.log(err)
    })
  }
```

Finally, export the user API helper methods to be imported and used by the React components as required.

`mern-skeleton/client/user/api-user.js`:

```
  export { create, list, read, update, remove }
```

Fetch for auth API

In order to integrate the auth API endpoints from the server with the frontend React components, we will add methods for fetching sign-in and sign-out API endpoints in the `client/auth/api-auth.js` file.

Sign-in

The `signin` method will take user sign-in data from the view component, then use `fetch` to make a `POST` call to verify the user with the backend. The response from the server will be returned to the component in a promise, which may contain the JWT if sign-in was successful.

`mern-skeleton/client/user/api-auth.js`:

```
  const signin = (user) => {
    return fetch('/auth/signin/', {
        method: 'POST',
        headers: {
          'Accept': 'application/json',
          'Content-Type': 'application/json'
        },
        credentials: 'include',
        body: JSON.stringify(user)
      })
      .then((response) => {
        return response.json()
      }).catch((err) => console.log(err))
  }
```

Sign-out

The `signout` method will use fetch to make a GET call to the signout API endpoint on the server.

`mern-skeleton/client/user/api-auth.js`:

```
const signout = () => {
  return fetch('/auth/signout/', {
    method: 'GET',
  }).then(response => {
      return response.json()
  }).catch((err) => console.log(err))
}
```

At the end of the `api-auth.js` file, export the `signin` and `signout` methods.

`mern-skeleton/client/user/api-auth.js`:

```
export { signin, signout }
```

With these API fetch methods, the React frontend has complete access to the endpoints available in the backend.

Auth in the frontend

As discussed in the previous chapter, implementing authentication with JWT relinquishes responsibility to the client side to manage and store user auth state. To this end, we need to write code that will allow the client-side to store the JWT received from the server on successful sign-in, make it available when accessing protected routes, delete or invalidate the token when the user signs out, and also restrict access to views and components on the frontend based on the user auth state.

Using examples of auth workflow from the React Router documentation, we will write helper methods to manage auth state across the components, and also use a custom `PrivateRoute` component to add protected routes to the frontend.

Managing auth state

In `client/auth/auth-helper.js`, we will define the following helper methods to store and retrieve JWT credentials from client-side `sessionStorage`, and also clear out the `sessionStorage` on user sign-out:

- `authenticate(jwt, cb)`: Save credentials on successful sign-in:

```
authenticate(jwt, cb) {
    if(typeof window !== "undefined")
        sessionStorage.setItem('jwt', JSON.stringify(jwt))
    cb()
}
```

- `isAuthenticated()`: Retrieve credentials if signed-in:

```
isAuthenticated() {
    if (typeof window == "undefined")
        return false

    if (sessionStorage.getItem('jwt'))
        return JSON.parse(sessionStorage.getItem('jwt'))
    else
        return false
}
```

- `signout(cb)`: Delete credentials and sign out:

```
signout(cb) {
    if(typeof window !== "undefined")
        sessionStorage.removeItem('jwt')
    cb()
    signout().then((data) => {
        document.cookie = "t=; expires=Thu, 01 Jan 1970 00:00:00
        UTC; path=/;"
    })
}
```

Using the methods defined here, the React components we build will be able to check and manage user auth state to restrict access in the frontend, as demonstrated in the following with the custom `PrivateRoute`.

PrivateRoute component

The `client/auth/PrivateRoute.js` defines the `PrivateRoute` component as shown in an auth flow example from `https://reacttraining.com/react-router/web/example/auth-workflow` in the React Router documentation. It will allow us to declare protected routes for the frontend to restrict view access based on user auth.

`mern-skeleton/client/auth/PrivateRoute.js`:

```
import React, { Component } from 'react'
import { Route, Redirect } from 'react-router-dom'
import auth from './auth-helper'

const PrivateRoute = ({ component: Component, ...rest }) => (
  <Route {...rest} render={props => (
    auth.isAuthenticated() ? (
      <Component {...props}/>
    ) : (
      <Redirect to={{
        pathname: '/signin',
        state: { from: props.location }
      }}/>
    )
  )}/>
)

export default PrivateRoute
```

Components to be rendered in this `PrivateRoute` will only load when the user is authenticated, otherwise the user will be redirected to the `Signin` component.

With the backend APIs integrated, and auth management helper methods ready for use in the components, we can start building the remaining view components.

User and auth components

The React components described in this section complete the interactive features defined for the skeleton by allowing users to view, create, and modify user data stored in the database with respect to auth restrictions. For each of the following components, we will go over the unique aspects of each component, and how to add the component to the application in the `MainRouter`.

Users component

The `Users` component in `client/user/Users.js`, shows the names of all the users fetched from the database, and links each name to the user profile. This component can be viewed by any visitor to the application and will render at the path `'/users'`:

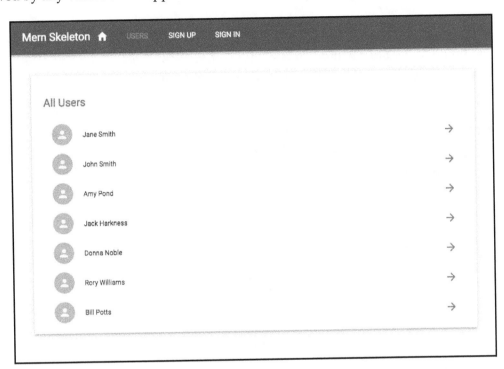

In the component definition, we first initialize the state with an empty array of users.

`mern-skeleton/client/user/Users.js`:

```
class Users extends Component {
  state = { users: [] }
...
```

Next, in `componentDidMount`, we use the `list` method from the `api-user.js` helper methods, to fetch the user list from the backend, and load the user data into the component by updating the state.

`mern-skeleton/client/user/Users.js`:

```
componentDidMount = () => {
```

```
            list().then((data) => {
              if (data.error)
                console.log(data.error)
              else
                this.setState({users: data})
            })
        }
```

The `render` function contains the actual view content of the `Users` component, and is composed with Material-UI components such as `Paper`, `List`, and `ListItems`. The elements are styled with the CSS defined and passed in as props.

`mern-skeleton/client/user/Users.js`:

```
    render() {
        const {classes} = this.props
        return (
          <Paper className={classes.root} elevation={4}>
            <Typography type="title" className={classes.title}>
              All Users
            </Typography>
            <List dense>
              {this.state.users.map(function(item, i) {
                  return <Link to={"/user/" + item._id} key={i}>
                    <ListItem button="button">
                      <ListItemAvatar>
                        <Avatar>
                          <Person/>
                        </Avatar>
                      </ListItemAvatar>
                      <ListItemText primary={item.name}/>
                      <ListItemSecondaryAction>
                        <IconButton>
                          <ArrowForward/>
                        </IconButton>
                      </ListItemSecondaryAction>
                    </ListItem>
                  </Link>
              })}
            </List>
          </Paper>
        )
    }
```

To generate each list item, we iterate through the array of users in the state using the map function.

To add this `Users` component to the React application, we need to update the `MainRouter` component with a `Route` that renders this component at the `'/users'` path. Add the `Route` inside the `Switch` component after the `Home` route.

`mern-skeleton/client/MainRouter.js`:

```
<Route path="/users" component={Users}/>
```

To see this view rendered in the browser, you can temporarily add a `Link` component in the `Home` component to route to the `Users` component:

```
<Link to="/users">Users</Link>
```

Signup component

The `Signup` component in `client/user/Signup.js`, presents a form with name, email, and password fields to the user for sign-up at the `'/signup'` path:

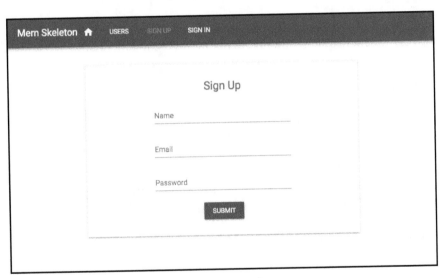

In the component definition, we first initialize the state with empty input field values, empty error message, and set the dialog open variable to false.

`mern-skeleton/client/user/Signup.js`:

```
constructor() {
    state = { name: '', password: '', email: '', open: false, error: '' }
    ...
```

We also define two handler functions to be called when the input value changes or the **submit** button is clicked. The `handleChange` function takes the new value entered in the input field and sets it to `state`.

`mern-skeleton/client/user/Signup.js`:

```
handleChange = name => event => {
    this.setState({[name]: event.target.value})
}
```

The `clickSubmit` function is called when the form is submitted. It takes the input values from state and calls the `create` fetch method to sign up the user with the backend. Then, depending on the response from the server, either an error message is shown or a success dialog is shown.

`mern-skeleton/client/user/Signup.js`:

```
clickSubmit = () => {
    const user = {
        name: this.state.name || undefined,
        email: this.state.email || undefined,
        password: this.state.password || undefined
    }
    create(user).then((data) => {
        if (data.error)
            this.setState({error: data.error})
        else
            this.setState({error: '', open: true})
    })
}
```

In the `render` function we compose and style the form components in the Sign-up view using components such as `TextField` from Material-UI.

`mern-skeleton/client/user/Signup.js`:

```
render() {
    const {classes} = this.props
    return (<div>
        <Card className={classes.card}>
            <CardContent>
                <Typography type="headline" component="h2"
                            className={classes.title}>
                    Sign Up
                </Typography>
                <TextField id="name" label="Name"
```

```
                className={classes.textField}
                    value={this.state.name}
                    onChange={this.handleChange('name')}
                    margin="normal"/> <br/>
        <TextField id="email" type="email" label="Email"
                    className={classes.textField} value=
                    {this.state.email}
                    onChange={this.handleChange('email')}
                    margin="normal"/><br/>
        <TextField id="password" type="password"
        label="Password" className={classes.textField}
                    value={this.state.password}
                    onChange={this.handleChange('password')}
                    margin="normal"/><br/>
        {this.state.error && ( <Typography component="p"
         color="error">
            <Icon color="error"
            className={classes.error}>error</Icon>
            {this.state.error}</Typography>) }
    </CardContent>
    <CardActions>
      <Button color="primary" raised="raised"
            onClick={this.clickSubmit}
       className={classes.submit}>Submit</Button>
    </CardActions>
  </Card>
  <Dialog> ... </Dialog>
</div>)
  }
```

The render also contains an error message block along with a `Dialog` component that is conditionally rendered depending on the sign up response from the server. The `Dialog` component in `Signup.js` is composed as follows.

`mern-skeleton/client/user/Signup.js`:

```
<Dialog open={this.state.open} disableBackdropClick={true}>
   <DialogTitle>New Account</DialogTitle>
   <DialogContent>
     <DialogContentText>
        New account successfully created.
     </DialogContentText>
   </DialogContent>
   <DialogActions>
      <Link to="/signin">
         <Button color="primary" autoFocus="autoFocus" variant="raised">
           Sign In
```

```
        </Button>
      </Link>
   </DialogActions>
 </Dialog>
```

On successful account creation, the user is given confirmation, and asked to sign in using this `Dialog` component, which links to the `Signin` component:

To add the `Signup` component to the app, add the following `Route` to the `MainRouter` in the `Switch` component.

`mern-skeleton/client/MainRouter.js`:

```
<Route path="/signup" component={Signup}/>
```

This will render the `Signup` view at `'/signup'`.

Signin component

The `Signin` component in `client/auth/Signin.js` is also a form with only email and password fields for signing in. This component is quite similar to the `Signup` component and will render at the `'/signin'` path. The key difference is in the implementation of redirection after successful sign-in and storing of the received JWT:

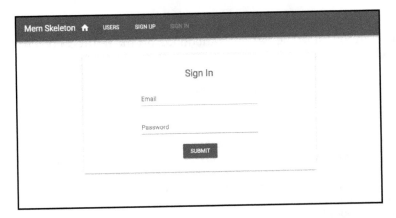

For redirection, we will use the `Redirect` component from React Router. First, initialize a `redirectToReferrer` value to `false` in the state with the other fields:

`mern-skeleton/client/auth/Signin.js:`

```
class Signin extends Component {
    state = { email: '', password: '', error: '', redirectToReferrer: false }
. . .
```

The `redirectToReferrer` should be set to `true` when the user successfully signs in after submitting the form and the received JWT is stored in the `sessionStorage`. To store the JWT and redirect afterwords, we will call the `authenticate()` method defined in `auth-helper.js`. This code will go in the `clickSubmit()` function to be called on form submit.

`mern-skeleton/client/auth/Signin.js:`

```
clickSubmit = () => {
    const user = {
        email: this.state.email || undefined,
        password: this.state.password || undefined
    }
    signin(user).then((data) => {
      if (data.error) {
        this.setState({error: data.error})
      } else {
        auth.authenticate(data, () => {
          this.setState({redirectToReferrer: true})
        })
      }
    })
}
```

The redirection will happen conditionally based on the `redirectToReferrer` value with the `Redirect` component in the `render` function. Add the redirect code in the render function before the return as follows:

`mern-skeleton/client/auth/Signin.js`:

```
render() {
    const {classes} = this.props
    const {from} = this.props.location.state || {
      from: {pathname: '/' }
    }
    const {redirectToReferrer} = this.state
    if (redirectToReferrer)
      return (<Redirect to={from}/>)
    return (...)
  }
}
```

The `Redirect` component, if rendered, will take the app to the last location or to the `Home` component at the root.

The return will contain the form elements similar to that of `Signup`, with just `email` and `password` fields, a conditional error message, and the `submit` button.

To add the `Signin` component to the app, add the following Route to the `MainRouter` in the `Switch` component.

`mern-skeleton/client/MainRouter.js`:

```
<Route path="/signin" component={Signin}/>
```

This will render the `Signin` component at `"/signin"`.

Profile component

The `Profile` component in `client/user/Profile.js` shows a single user's information in the view at the `'/user/:userId'` path, where the `userId` parameter represents the ID of the specific user:

This profile information can be fetched from the server only if the user is signed in, and to verify this, the component has to provide the JWT to the `read` fetch call, otherwise, the user should be redirected to the Sign In view.

In the `Profile` component definition, we first need to initialize the state with an empty user and set `redirectToSignin` to `false`.

`mern-skeleton/client/user/Profile.js`:

```
class Profile extends Component {
  constructor({match}) {
    super()
    this.state = { user: '', redirectToSignin: false }
    this.match = match
  } ...
```

We also need to get access to the match props passed by the `Route` component, which will contain `:userId` param value and can be accessed as `this.match.params.userId` when the component mounts.

The `Profile` component should fetch user information and render it when the `userId` parameter changes in the route. However, when the app goes from one profile view to the other, and it is just a param change in the route path, the React component does not re-mount. Rather, it passes the new props in `componentWillReceiveProps`. In order to make sure the component loads the relevant user's information when the route param updates, we will place the `read` fetch call in the `init()` function, which can then be called in both `componentDidMount` and `componentWillReceiveProps`.

`mern-skeleton/client/user/Profile.js`:

```
init = (userId) => {
    const jwt = auth.isAuthenticated()
    read({
      userId: userId
    }, {t: jwt.token}).then((data) => {
```

```
        if (data.error)
          this.setState({redirectToSignin: true})
        else
          this.setState({user: data})
      })
    }
```

The `init(userId)` function takes the `userId` value, and calls the read user fetch method. Since this method also requires credentials to authorize the signed-in user, the JWT is retrieved from `sessionStorage` using the `isAuthenticated` method from `auth-helper.js`. Once the server responds, either the state is updated with the user information or the view is redirected to the Sign-in view.

This `init` function is called in `componentDidMount` and `componentWillReceiveProps` with the relevant `userId` value passed in as a parameter so that the correct user information is fetched and loaded in the component.

mern-skeleton/client/user/Profile.js:

```
componentDidMount = () => {
  this.init(this.match.params.userId)
}
componentWillReceiveProps = (props) => {
  this.init(props.match.params.userId)
}
```

In the `render` function, we set up the conditional redirect to Signin view, and return the content of the `Profile` view:

mern-skeleton/client/user/Profile.js

```
render() {
  const {classes} = this.props
  const redirectToSignin = this.state.redirectToSignin
  if (redirectToSignin)
    return <Redirect to='/signin'/>
  return (...)
}
```

The `render` function will return the `Profile` view with the following elements if the user currently signed-in is viewing another user's profile.

mern-skeleton/client/user/Profile.js:

```
<div>
  <Paper className={classes.root} elevation={4}>
```

```
      <Typography type="title" className={classes.title}> Profile
</Typography>
        <List dense>
          <ListItem>
            <ListItemAvatar>
               <Avatar>
                 <Person/>
               </Avatar>
            </ListItemAvatar>
            <ListItemText primary={this.state.user.name}
                          secondary={this.state.user.email}/>
          </ListItem>
          <Divider/>
          <ListItem>
            <ListItemText primary={"Joined: " +
                (new Date(this.state.user.created)).toDateString()}/>
          </ListItem>
        </List>
    </Paper>
  </div>
```

However, if the user currently signed-in is viewing their own profile, they will be able to see an edit and delete option in the `Profile` component, as shown in the following screenshot:

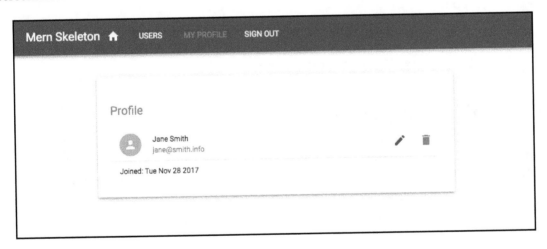

To implement this feature, in the first `ListItem` component in the `Profile`, add a `ListItemSecondaryAction` component containing the `Edit` button and a `DeleteUser` component, which will render conditionally based on whether the current user is viewing their own profile.

mern-skeleton/client/user/Profile.js:

```
{ auth.isAuthenticated().user && auth.isAuthenticated().user._id ==
this.state.user._id &&
    (<ListItemSecondaryAction>
        <Link to={"/user/edit/" + this.state.user._id}>
          <IconButton color="primary">
            <Edit/>
          </IconButton>
        </Link>
        <DeleteUser userId={this.state.user._id}/>
    </ListItemSecondaryAction>) }
```

The `Edit` button will route to the `EditProfile` component, and the custom `DeleteUser` component used here will handle the delete operation with the `userId` passed to it as a prop.

To add the `Profile` component to the app, add the `Route` to the `MainRouter` in the `Switch` component.

mern-skeleton/client/MainRouter.js:

```
<Route path="/user/:userId" component={Profile}/>
```

EditProfile component

The `EditProfile` component in `client/user/EditProfile.js` has similarities in implementation with both the `Signup` and `Profile` components. It will allow the authorized user to edit their own profile information in a form similar to the sign up form:

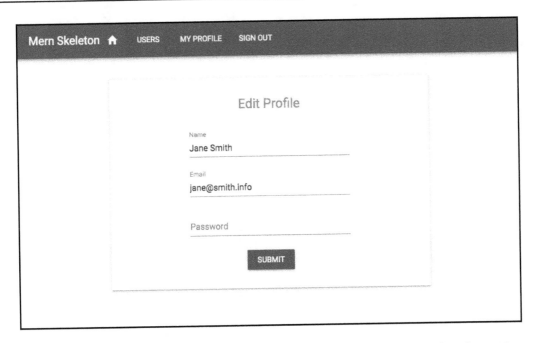

Upon load at `'/user/edit/:userId'`, the component will fetch the user's information with ID after verifying JWT for auth, then load the form with the received user information. The form will allow the user to edit and submit only the changed information to the `update` fetch call, and on successful update, redirect the user to the `Profile` view with updated information.

`EditProfile` will load the user information the same way as in the `Profile` component, by fetching with `read` in `componentDidMount` using the `userId` param from `this.match.params`, and credentials from `auth.isAuthenticated`. The form view will have the same elements as the `Signup` component with input values updated in the state on change.

On form submit, the component will call the `update` fetch method with the `userId`, JWT, and updated user data.

`mern-skeleton/client/user/EditProfile.js`:

```
clickSubmit = () => {
    const jwt = auth.isAuthenticated()
    const user = {
      name: this.state.name || undefined,
      email: this.state.email || undefined,
      password: this.state.password || undefined
```

```
      }
      update({
        userId: this.match.params.userId
      }, {
        t: jwt.token
      }, user).then((data) => {
        if (data.error) {
          this.setState({error: data.error})
        } else {
          this.setState({'userId': data._id, 'redirectToProfile': true})
        }
      })
    }
```

Depending on the response from the server, the user will either see an error message or be redirected to the updated Profile page with the following `Redirect` component in the render function.

`mern-skeleton/client/user/EditProfile.js`:

```
  if (this.state.redirectToProfile)
    return (<Redirect to={'/user/' + this.state.userId}/>)
```

To add the `EditProfile` component to the app, we will use a `PrivateRoute` this time, to restrict the component from loading at all if the user is not signed in. The order of placement in `MainRouter` will also be important.

`mern-skeleton/client/MainRouter.js`:

```
  <Switch>
    ...
    <PrivateRoute path="/user/edit/:userId" component={EditProfile}/><>
    <Route path="/user/:userId" component={Profile}/>
  </Switch>
```

The route with path `'/user/edit/:userId'` needs to be placed before the route with path `'/user/:userId'`, so that the edit path is matched first exclusively in the Switch component when this route is requested, and not confused with the `Profile` route.

DeleteUser component

The DeleteUser component in `client/user/DeleteUser.js` is basically a button that we will add to the Profile view, which when clicked opens a `Dialog` component asking the user to confirm the `delete` action:

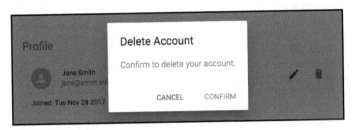

The component first initializes the state with `open` set to `false` for the `Dialog` component, and `redirect` also set to `false` so it isn't rendered first.

`mern-skeleton/client/user/DeleteUser.js`:

```
class DeleteUser extends Component {
    state = { redirect: false, open: false }
    ...
```

Next, we need handler methods to open and close the `dialog` button. The dialog is opened when the user clicks the `delete` button.

`mern-skeleton/client/user/DeleteUser.js`:

```
clickButton = () => {
    this.setState({open: true})
}
```

The dialog is closed when the user clicks `cancel` on the dialog.

`mern-skeleton/client/user/DeleteUser.js`:

```
handleRequestClose = () => {
    this.setState({open: false})
}
```

The component will have access to the `userId` passed in as a prop from the `Profile` component, which is needed to call the `remove` fetch method along with the JWT, after the user confirms the `delete` action in the dialog.

mern-skeleton/client/user/DeleteUser.js:

```
deleteAccount = () => {
    const jwt = auth.isAuthenticated()
    remove({
      userId: this.props.userId
    }, {t: jwt.token}).then((data) => {
      if (data.error) {
        console.log(data.error)
      } else {
        auth.signout(() => console.log('deleted'))
        this.setState({redirect: true})
      }
    })
  }
```

On confirmation, the `deleteAccount` function calls the `remove` fetch method with the `userId` from props and JWT from `isAuthenticated`. On successful deletion in the server, the user will be signed out and redirected to the Home view.

The render function contains the conditional `Redirect` to Home view and returns the `DeleteUser` component elements, a `DeleteIcon` button and the confirmation `Dialog`:

mern-skeleton/client/user/DeleteUser.js:

```
render() {
    const redirect = this.state.redirect
    if (redirect) {
      return <Redirect to='/'/>
    }
    return (<span>
      <IconButton aria-label="Delete" onClick={this.clickButton}
      color="secondary">
        <DeleteIcon/>
      </IconButton>
      <Dialog open={this.state.open} onClose={this.handleRequestClose}>
        <DialogTitle>{"Delete Account"}</DialogTitle>
        <DialogContent>
          <DialogContentText>
            Confirm to delete your account.
          </DialogContentText>
        </DialogContent>
        <DialogActions>
          <Button onClick={this.handleRequestClose} color="primary">
            Cancel
          </Button>
          <Button onClick={this.deleteAccount} color="secondary"
```

```
            autoFocus="autoFocus">
              Confirm
            </Button>
          </DialogActions>
        </Dialog>
      </span>)
  }
```

`DeleteUser` takes the `userId` as a prop to be used in the `delete` fetch call, so we add a `propType` check for the required prop `userId`.

`mern-skeleton/client/user/DeleteUser.js`:

```
DeleteUser.propTypes = {
  userId: PropTypes.string.isRequired
}
```

As we are using the `DeleteUser` component in the `Profile` component, it gets added to the application view when `Profile` is added in `MainRouter`.

Menu component

The `Menu` component will function as a navigation bar across the frontend application by providing links to all the available views, and also be indicating the current location in the application.

To implement these navigation bar functionalities, we will use the HOC `withRouter` from React Router to get access to the history object's properties. The following code in the `Menu` component adds just the title, the `Home` icon linked to the root Route, and `Users` button linked to the `'/users'` route.

`mern-skeleton/client/core/Menu.js`:

```
const Menu = withRouter(({history}) => (<div>
  <AppBar position="static">
    <Toolbar>
      <Typography type="title" color="inherit">
        MERN Skeleton
      </Typography>
      <Link to="/">
        <IconButton aria-label="Home" style={isActive(history, "/")}>
          <HomeIcon/>
        </IconButton>
      </Link>
      <Link to="/users">
```

```
            <Button style={isActive(history, "/users")}>Users</Button>
          </Link>
        </Toolbar>
      </AppBar>
    </div>))
```

To indicate the current location of the application on the Menu, we will highlight the link that matches with the current location path by changing the color conditionally.

mern-skeleton/client/core/Menu.js:

```
const isActive = (history, path) => {
  if (history.location.pathname == path)
    return {color: '#ff4081'}
  else
    return {color: '#ffffff'}
}
```

The isActive function is used to apply color to the buttons in the Menu as follows:

```
style={isActive(history, "/users")}
```

The remaining links such as **SIGN IN, SIGN UP, MY PROFILE,** and **SIGN OUT** will show up on the Menu based on whether the user is signed in or not:

For example, the links to **SIGN UP** and **SIGN IN** should only show on the menu when the user is not signed in. So we need to add it to the Menu component after the Users button with a condition.

mern-skeleton/client/core/Menu.js:

```
{!auth.isAuthenticated() && (<span>
    <Link to="/signup">
      <Button style={isActive(history, "/signup")}> Sign Up </Button>
    </Link>
    <Link to="/signin">
      <Button style={isActive(history, "/signin")}> Sign In </Button>
    </Link>
</span>)}
```

Similarly, the link to MY PROFILE and the SIGN OUT button should only show on the menu when the user is signed in, and should be added to the Menu component with this condition check.

`mern-skeleton/client/core/Menu.js`:

```
{auth.isAuthenticated() && (<span>
    <Link to={"/user/" + auth.isAuthenticated().user._id}>
        <Button style={isActive(history, "/user/" +
auth.isAuthenticated().user._id)}>
                My Profile
        </Button>
    </Link>
    <Button color="inherit"
            onClick={() => { auth.signout(() => history.push('/')) }}>
        Sign out
    </Button>
</span>)}
```

The MY PROFILE button uses the signed-in user's information to link to the user's own profile, and the SIGN OUT button calls the `auth.signout()` method when clicked. When the user is signed in, the Menu will look as follows:

To have the Menu navigation bar present in all the views, we need to add it to the MainRouter before all the other routes, and outside the Switch component.

`mern-skeleton/client/MainRouter.js`:

```
<Menu/>
<Switch>
...
</Switch>
```

This will make the Menu component render on top of all the other components when the component is accessed at a route.

The skeleton frontend is complete with all components necessary to enable a user to sign up, view, and modify user data on the backend with consideration to authentication and authorization restrictions. However, it is still not possible to visit the frontend routes directly in the browser address bar, and can only be accessed when linked from within the frontend view. To enable this functionality in the skeleton application, we need to implement basic server-side rendering.

Basic server-side rendering

Currently, when the React Router routes or pathnames are directly entered in the browser address bar or when a view that is not at the root path is refreshed, the URL does not work. This happens because the server does not recognize the React Router routes. We have to implement basic server-side rendering on the backend, so the server is able to respond when it receives a request to a frontend route.

To render relevant React components properly when the server receives requests to the frontend routes, we need to render the React components server side with regard to the React Router and Material-UI components.

The basic idea behind server-side rendering of React apps is to use the `renderToString` method from `react-dom` to convert the root React component to markup string, and attach it to the template that the server renders when it receives a request.

In `express.js`, we will replace the code that returns `template.js` in response to the `GET` request for `'/'`, with code, which on receiving any incoming GET request, generates server-side rendered markup of the relevant React components, and adds this markup to the template. This code will have the following structure:

```
app.get('*', (req, res) => {
    // 1. Prepare Material-UI styles
    // 2. Generate markup with renderToString
    // 3. Return template with markup and CSS styles in the response
})
```

Modules for server-side rendering

To implement basic server-side rendering, we will need to import the following React, React Router, and Material-UI-specific modules into the server code. In our code structure, these modules will be imported into `server/express.js`:

- **React modules**: Required to render the React components and use `renderToString`:

    ```
    import React from 'react'
    import ReactDOMServer from 'react-dom/server'
    ```

- **Router modules**: The `StaticRouter` is a stateless router that takes the requested URL to match the frontend route and the `MainRouter` component, which is the root component in our frontend:

```
import StaticRouter from 'react-router-dom/StaticRouter'
import MainRouter from './../client/MainRouter'
```

- **Material-UI modules**: The following modules will help generate the CSS styles for the frontend components based on the Material-UI theme used on the frontend:

```
import { SheetsRegistry } from 'react-jss/lib/jss'
import JssProvider from 'react-jss/lib/JssProvider'
import { MuiThemeProvider, createMuiTheme, createGenerateClassName
} from 'material-ui/styles'
import { indigo, pink } from 'material-ui/colors'
```

With these modules, we can prepare, generate, and return server-side rendered frontend code.

Preparing Material-UI styles for SSR

When the server receives any request, prior to responding with the generated markup containing the React view, we need to prepare the CSS styles that should also be added to the markup, so the UI does not break on initial render.

mern-skeleton/server/express.js:

```
const sheetsRegistry = new SheetsRegistry()
const theme = createMuiTheme({
    palette: {
      primary: {
      light: '#757de8',
      main: '#3f51b5',
      dark: '#002984',
      contrastText: '#fff',
    },
    secondary: {
      light: '#ff79b0',
      main: '#ff4081',
      dark: '#c60055',
      contrastText: '#000',
    },
      openTitle: indigo['400'],
```

```
            protectedTitle: pink['400'],
            type: 'light'
        },
    })
    const generateClassName = createGenerateClassName()
```

In order to inject the Material-UI styles, on every request we first generate a new
SheetsRegistry and MUI theme instance, matching what is used in the frontend code.

Generating markup

The purpose of using renderToString is to generate an HTML string version of the React
component that is to be shown to the user in response to the requested URL:

mern-skeleton/server/express.js:

```
    const context = {}
    const markup = ReactDOMServer.renderToString(
        <StaticRouter location={req.url} context={context}>
          <JssProvider registry={sheetsRegistry} generateClassName=
            {generateClassName}>
            <MuiThemeProvider theme={theme} sheetsManager={new Map()}>
              <MainRouter/>
            </MuiThemeProvider>
          </JssProvider>
        </StaticRouter>
    )
```

The client app's root component, MainRouter, is wrapped with the Material-UI theme and
JSS to provide the styling props needed by the MainRouter child components. The
stateless StaticRouter is used here instead of the BrowserRouter used on the client side,
to wrap MainRouter and provide the routing props used in implementing the client-side
components. Based on these values, such as the requested location route and theme
passed in as props to the wrapping components, the renderToString will return markup
containing the relevant view.

Sending a template with markup and CSS

Once the markup is generated, we first check if there was a `redirect` rendered in the component to be sent in the markup. If there was no redirect, then we generate the CSS string from the `sheetsRegistry`, and in the response send the template back with the markup and CSS injected.

`mern-skeleton/server/express.js`:

```
if (context.url) {
    return res.redirect(303, context.url)
}
const css = sheetsRegistry.toString()
res.status(200).send(Template({
    markup: markup,
    css: css
}))
```

An example of a case where redirect is rendered in the component is when trying to access a `PrivateRoute` via server-side render. As the server side cannot access the auth token from client-side `sessionStorage`, the redirect in the `PrivateRoute` will render. The `context.url`, in this case, will have the `'/signin'` route, and hence instead of trying to render the `PrivateRoute` component, it will redirect to the `'/signin'` route.

Updating template.js

The markup and CSS generated on the server must be added to the `template.js` HTML code as follows for it to be loaded when the server renders the template.

`mern-skeleton/template.js`:

```
export default ({markup, css}) => {
    return `...
            <div id="root">${markup}</div>
            <style id="jss-server-side">${css}</style>
            ...`
}
```

Updating MainRouter

Once the code rendered on the server side reaches the browser, and the frontend script takes over, we need to remove the server-side injected CSS when the main component mounts. This will give back full control over rendering the React app to the client side:

mern-skeleton/client/MainRouter.js:

```
componentDidMount() {
    const jssStyles = document.getElementById('jss-server-side')
    if (jssStyles && jssStyles.parentNode)
        jssStyles.parentNode.removeChild(jssStyles)
}
```

Hydrate instead of render

Now that the React components will be rendered on the server side, we can update the main.js code to use ReactDOM.hydrate() instead of ReactDOM.render():

```
import React from 'react'
import { hydrate } from 'react-dom'
import App from './App'

hydrate(<App/>, document.getElementById('root'))
```

The hydrate function hydrates a container that already has HTML content rendered by ReactDOMServer. This means the server-rendered markup is preserved and only event-handlers are attached when React takes over in the browser, allowing the initial load performance to be better.

With basic server-side rendering implemented, direct requests to the frontend routes from the browser address bar can now be handled properly by the server, making it possible to bookmark the React frontend views.

The skeleton MERN application developed here is now a completely functioning MERN web application with basic user features. We can extend the code in this skeleton to add a variety of features for different applications.

Summary

In this chapter, we completed the MERN skeleton application by adding a working React frontend, including frontend routing and basic server-side rendering of the React views.

We started off by updating the development flow to include client-side code bundling for the React views. We updated configuration for Webpack and Babel to compile the React code and discussed how to load the configured Webpack middleware from the Express app to initiate server-side and client-side code compilation from one place during development.

With the development flow updated and before building out the frontend, we added the relevant React dependencies along with React Router for frontend routing and Material-UI to use their existing components in the skeleton app's user interface.

Then, we implemented the top-level root React components, and integrated React Router that allowed us to add client-side routes for navigation. Using these routes, we loaded the custom React components that we developed using Material-UI components to make up the skeleton application's user interface.

To make these React views dynamic and interactive with data fetched from the backend, we used the Fetch API to connect to the backend user APIs. Then we incorporated authentication and authorization on the frontend views using `sessionStorage` to store user-specific details and JWT fetched from the server on successful sign-in, and also by limiting access to certain views using a `PrivateRoute` component.

Finally, we modified the server code to implement basic server-side rendering that allows loading the frontend routes directly in the browser with server-side rendered markup after the server recognizes that the incoming request is actually for a React route.

In the next chapter, we will use the concepts learned while developing this basic MERN application, and extend the skeleton application code to build a fully-featured social media application.

5
Starting with a Simple Social Media Application

Social media is an integral part of the web these days, and many of the user-centric web applications we build end up requiring a social component down the line to drive user engagement.

For our first real-world MERN application, we will modify and extend the MERN skeleton application developed in the previous chapter to build a simple social media application.

In this chapter, we will go over the implementation of the following social media-flavored features:

- User profile with a description and a photo
- Users following each other
- Who to follow suggestions
- Posting messages with photos
- News feed with posts from followed users
- Listing posts by user
- Liking posts
- Commenting on posts

MERN Social

MERN Social is a social media application with rudimentary features inspired by existing social media platforms such as Facebook and Twitter. The main purpose of this application is to demonstrate how to use the MERN stack technologies to implement features that allow users to connect and interact over content.You can extend these implementations further, as desired, for more complex features:

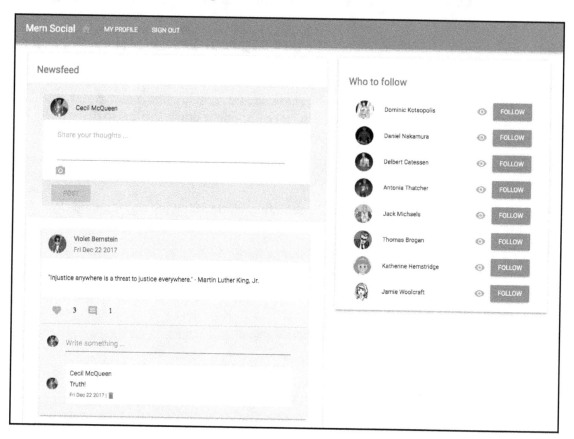

Code for the complete MERN Social application is available on GitHub in the repository at `github.com/shamahoque/mern-social`. You can clone this code and run the application as you go through the code explanations in the rest of this chapter.

The views needed for the MERN Social application will be developed by extending and modifying the existing React components in the MERN skeleton application. We will also add new custom components to compose views, including a Newsfeed view where the user can create a new post and also browse a list of all the posts from people they follow on MERN Social. The following component tree shows all the custom React components that make up the MERN Social frontend and also exposes the composition structure we will use to build out the views in the rest of the chapter:

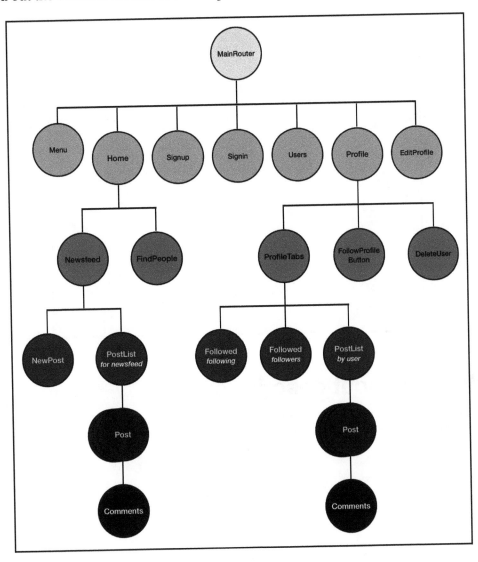

Updating the user profile

The skeleton application only has support for a user's name, email, and password. But in MERN Social we will allow users to add a description about themselves, and also upload a profile photo while editing the profile after signing up:

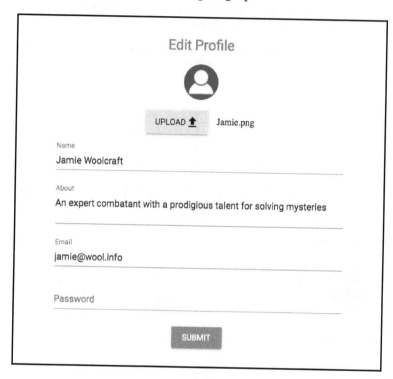

Adding an about description

In order to store the description entered in the about field by a user, we need to add an about field to the user model in server/models/user.model.js:

```
about: {
    type: String,
    trim: true
}
```

Then, to get the description as input from the user, we add a multiline `TextField` to the `EditProfile` form and handle the value change the same way we did for the user's name input.

`mern-social/client/user/EditProfile.js`:

```
<TextField
    id="multiline-flexible"
    label="About"
    multiline
    rows="2"
    value={this.state.about}
    onChange={this.handleChange('about')}
/>
```

Finally, to show the description text added to the `about` field on the user profile page, we can add it to the existing profile view.

`mern-social/client/user/Profile.js`:

```
<ListItem> <ListItemText primary={this.state.user.about}/> </ListItem>
```

With this modification to the user feature in the MERN skeleton code, users can now add and update a description about themselves to be displayed on their profiles.

Uploading a profile photo

Allowing a user to upload a profile photo will require that we store the uploaded image file, and retrieve it on request to load in the view. There are multiple ways of implementing this upload feature considering the different file storage options:

- **Server filesystem**: Upload and save files to a server filesystem and store the URL to MongoDB
- **External file storage**: Save files to external storage such as Amazon S3 and store the URL in MongoDB
- **Store as data in MongoDB**: Save files of a small size (less than 16 MB) to MongoDB as data of type Buffer

For MERN Social, we will assume that the photo files uploaded by the user will be of small sizes, and demonstrate how to store these files in MongoDB for the profile photo upload feature. In `Chapter 8`, *Building a Media Streaming Application*, we will discuss how to store larger files in MongoDB using GridFS.

Updating the user model to store a photo in MongoDB

In order to store the uploaded profile photo directly in the database, we will update the user model to add a `photo` field that stores the file as `data` of type `Buffer`, along with its `contentType`.

`mern-social/server/models/user.model.js`:

```
photo: {
    data: Buffer,
    contentType: String
}
```

Uploading a photo from the edit form

Users will be able to upload an image file from their local files when editing the profile. We will update the `EditProfile` component in `client/user/EditProfile.js` with an upload photo option, then attach the user selected file in the form data submitted to the server.

File input with Material-UI

We will utilize the HTML5 file input type to let the user select an image from their local files. The file input will return the filename in the change event when the user selects a file.

`mern-social/client/user/EditProfile.js`:

```
<input accept="image/*" type="file"
       onChange={this.handleChange('photo')}
       style={{display:'none'}}
       id="icon-button-file" />
```

To integrate this file `input` with Material-UI components, we apply `display:none` to hide the `input` element from view, then add a Material-UI button inside the label for this file input. This way, the view displays the Material-UI button instead of the HTML5 file input element.

`mern-social/client/user/EditProfile.js`:

```
<label htmlFor="icon-button-file">
  <Button variant="raised" color="default" component="span">
    Upload <FileUpload/>
  </Button>
</label>
```

With the `Button`'s component prop set to `span`, the `Button` component renders as a `span` element inside the `label` element. A click on the `Upload` span or label is registered by the file input with the same ID as the label, and as a result, the file select dialog is opened. Once the user selects a file, we can set it to state in the call to `handleChange(...)` and display the name in the view.

`mern-social/client/user/EditProfile.js`:

```
<span className={classes.filename}>
    {this.state.photo ? this.state.photo.name : ''}
</span>
```

Form submission with the file attached

Uploading files to the server with a form requires a multipart form submission in contrast to the `stringed` object sent in the previous implementation. We will modify the `EditProfile` component to use the `FormData` API to store the form data in the format needed for encoding type `multipart/form-data`.

First, we need to initialize `FormData` in `componentDidMount()`.

`mern-social/client/user/EditProfile.js`:

```
this.userData = new FormData()
```

Next, we will update the input `handleChange` function to store input values for both the text fields and the file input in `FormData`.

`mern-social/client/user/EditProfile.js`:

```
handleChange = name => event => {
  const value = name === 'photo'
    ? event.target.files[0]
    : event.target.value
  this.userData.set(name, value)
  this.setState({ [name]: value })
}
```

Then on submit, `this.userData` is sent with the fetch API call to update the user. As the content type of the data sent to the server is no longer `'application/json'`, we also need to modify the `update` fetch method in `api-user.js` to remove `Content-Type` from the headers in the `fetch` call.

`mern-social/client/user/api-user.js`:

```
const update = (params, credentials, user) => {
  return fetch('/api/users/' + params.userId, {
    method: 'PUT',
    headers: {
      'Accept': 'application/json',
      'Authorization': 'Bearer ' + credentials.t
    },
    body: user
  }).then((response) => {
    return response.json()
  }).catch((e) => {
    console.log(e)
  })
}
```

Now if the user chooses to upload a profile photo when editing profile, the server will receive a request with the file attached along with the other field values.

 Learn more about the FormData API at `developer.mozilla.org/en-US/docs/Web/API/FormData`.

Processing a request containing a file upload

On the server, to process the request to the update API that may now contain a file, we will use the `formidable` npm module:

```
npm install --save formidable
```

Formidable will allow us to read the `multipart` form data, giving access to the fields and the file, if any. If there is a file, `formidable` will store it temporarily in the filesystem. We will read it from the filesystem, using the `fs` module to retrieve the file type and data, and store it to the photo field in the user model. The `formidable` code will go in the `update` controller in `user.controller.js` as follows.

`mern-social/server/controllers/user.controller.js`:

```
import formidable from 'formidable'
import fs from 'fs'
const update = (req, res, next) => {
  let form = new formidable.IncomingForm()
  form.keepExtensions = true
```

```
form.parse(req, (err, fields, files) => {
  if (err) {
    return res.status(400).json({
      error: "Photo could not be uploaded"
    })
  }
  let user = req.profile
  user = _.extend(user, fields)
  user.updated = Date.now()
  if(files.photo){
    user.photo.data = fs.readFileSync(files.photo.path)
    user.photo.contentType = files.photo.type
  }
  user.save((err, result) => {
    if (err) {
      return res.status(400).json({
        error: errorHandler.getErrorMessage(err)
      })
    }
    user.hashed_password = undefined
    user.salt = undefined
    res.json(user)
  })
})
}
```

This will store the uploaded file as data in the database. Next, we will set up file retrieval to be able to access and display the photo uploaded by the user in the frontend views.

Retrieving a profile photo

The simplest option to retrieve the file stored in the database and show it in a view is to set up a route that will fetch the data and return it as an image file to the requesting client.

Profile photo URL

We will set up a route to the photo stored in the database for each user, and also add another route that will fetch a default photo if the given user has not uploaded a profile photo.

`mern-social/server/routes/user.routes.js`:

```
router.route('/api/users/photo/:userId')
  .get(userCtrl.photo, userCtrl.defaultPhoto)
router.route('/api/users/defaultphoto')
  .get(userCtrl.defaultPhoto)
```

We will look for the photo in the `photo` controller method and if found, send it in the response to the request at the photo route, otherwise we call `next()` to return the default photo.

`mern-social/server/controllers/user.controller.js`:

```
const photo = (req, res, next) => {
  if(req.profile.photo.data){
    res.set("Content-Type", req.profile.photo.contentType)
    return res.send(req.profile.photo.data)
  }
  next()
}
```

The default photo is retrieved and sent from the server's file system.

`mern-social/server/controllers/user.controller.js`:

```
import profileImage from './../../client/assets/images/profile-pic.png'
const defaultPhoto = (req, res) => {
  return res.sendFile(process.cwd()+profileImage)
}
```

Showing a photo in a view

With the photo URL routes set up to retrieve the photo, we can simply use these in the `img` element's `src` attribute to load the photo in the view. For example, in the `Profile` component, we get the user ID from state and use it to construct the photo URL.

`mern-social/client/user/Profile.js`:

```
const photoUrl = this.state.user._id
        ? `/api/users/photo/${this.state.user._id}?${new
Date().getTime()}`
        : '/api/users/defaultphoto'
```

To ensure the `img` element reloads in the `Profile` view after the photo is updated in the edit, we also add a time value to the photo URL to bypass the browser's default image caching behavior.

Then, we can set the `photoUrl` to the Material-UI `Avatar` component, which renders the linked image in the view:

```
<Avatar src={photoUrl}/>
```

The updated user profile in MERN Social can now display a user uploaded profile photo and an `about` description:

Following users in MERN Social

In MERN Social, the users will be able to follow each other. Each user will have a list of followers and a list of people they follow. Users will also be able to see a list of users they can follow; in other words, the users in MERN Social they are not already following.

Follow and unfollow

In order to keep track of which user is following which other users, we will have to maintain two lists for each user. When one user follows or unfollows another user, we will update one's `following` list and the other's `followers` list.

Updating the user model

To store the list of `following` and `followers` in the database, we will update the user model with two arrays of user references.

`mern-social/server/models/user.model.js`:

```
following: [{type: mongoose.Schema.ObjectId, ref: 'User'}],
followers: [{type: mongoose.Schema.ObjectId, ref: 'User'}]
```

These references will point to the users in the collection being followed by or following the given user.

Updating the userByID controller method

When a single user is retrieved from the backend, we want the `user` object to include the names and IDs of the users referenced in the `following` and `followers` arrays. To retrieve these details, we need to update the `userByID` controller method to populate the returned user object.

`mern-social/server/controllers/user.controller.js`:

```
const userByID = (req, res, next, id) => {
  User.findById(id)
    .populate('following', '_id name')
    .populate('followers', '_id name')
    .exec((err, user) => {
    if (err || !user) return res.status('400').json({
      error: "User not found"
    })
    req.profile = user
    next()
  })
}
```

We use the Mongoose `populate` method to specify that the user object returned from the query should contain the name and ID of the users referenced in the `following` and `followers` lists. This will give us the names and IDs of the user references in the `followers` and `following` lists when we fetch the user with the read API call.

API to follow and unfollow

When a user follows or unfollows another user from the view, both users' records in the database will be updated in response to the `follow` or `unfollow` requests.

We will set up `follow` and `unfollow` routes in `user.routes.js` as follows.

`mern-social/server/routes/user.routes.js`:

```
router.route('/api/users/follow')
  .put(authCtrl.requireSignin, userCtrl.addFollowing, userCtrl.addFollower)
router.route('/api/users/unfollow')
  .put(authCtrl.requireSignin, userCtrl.removeFollowing,
userCtrl.removeFollower)
```

The `addFollowing` controller method in the user controller will update the `'following'` array for the current user by pushing the followed user's reference into the array.

`mern-social/server/controllers/user.controller.js`:

```
const addFollowing = (req, res, next) => {
  User.findByIdAndUpdate(req.body.userId, {$push: {following:
req.body.followId}}, (err, result) => {
    if (err) {
      return res.status(400).json({
        error: errorHandler.getErrorMessage(err)
      })
    }
    next()
  })
}
```

On successful update of the following array, the `addFollower` method is executed to add the current user's reference to the followed user's `'followers'` array.

`mern-social/server/controllers/user.controller.js`:

```
const addFollower = (req, res) => {
  User.findByIdAndUpdate(req.body.followId, {$push: {followers:
req.body.userId}}, {new: true})
  .populate('following', '_id name')
  .populate('followers', '_id name')
  .exec((err, result) => {
    if (err) {
      return res.status(400).json({
        error: errorHandler.getErrorMessage(err)
      })
    }
    result.hashed_password = undefined
    result.salt = undefined
    res.json(result)
  })
}
```

For unfollowing, the implementation is similar. The `removeFollowing` and `removeFollower` controller methods update the respective `'following'` and `'followers'` arrays by removing the user references with `$pull` instead of `$push`.

mern-social/server/controllers/user.controller.js:

```
const removeFollowing = (req, res, next) => {
  User.findByIdAndUpdate(req.body.userId, {$pull: {following:
req.body.unfollowId}}, (err, result) => {
    if (err) {
      return res.status(400).json({
        error: errorHandler.getErrorMessage(err)
      })
    }
    next()
  })
}
const removeFollower = (req, res) => {
  User.findByIdAndUpdate(req.body.unfollowId, {$pull: {followers:
req.body.userId}}, {new: true})
  .populate('following', '_id name')
  .populate('followers', '_id name')
  .exec((err, result) => {
    if (err) {
      return res.status(400).json({
        error: errorHandler.getErrorMessage(err)
      })
    }
    result.hashed_password = undefined
    result.salt = undefined
    res.json(result)
  })
}
```

Accessing follow and unfollow APIs in views

In order to access these API calls in the views, we will update `api-user.js` with `follow` and `unfollow` fetch methods. The `follow` and `unfollow` methods will be similar, making calls to the respective routes with the current user's ID and credentials, and the followed or unfollowed user's ID. The `follow` method will be as follows.

`mern-social/client/user/api-user.js:`

```
const follow = (params, credentials, followId) => {
  return fetch('/api/users/follow/', {
    method: 'PUT',
    headers: {
      'Accept': 'application/json',
      'Content-Type': 'application/json',
      'Authorization': 'Bearer ' + credentials.t
    },
    body: JSON.stringify({userId:params.userId, followId: followId})
  }).then((response) => {
    return response.json()
  }).catch((err) => {
    console.log(err)
  })
}
```

The `unfollow` fetch method is similar, it takes the unfollowed user's ID and calls the `unfollow` API.

`mern-social/client/user/api-user.js:`

```
const unfollow = (params, credentials, unfollowId) => {
  return fetch('/api/users/unfollow/', {
    method: 'PUT',
    headers: {
      'Accept': 'application/json',
      'Content-Type': 'application/json',
      'Authorization': 'Bearer ' + credentials.t
    },
    body: JSON.stringify({userId:params.userId, unfollowId: unfollowId})
  }).then((response) => {
    return response.json()
  }).catch((err) => {
    console.log(err)
  })
}
```

Follow and unfollow buttons

The button that will allow a user to `follow` or `unfollow` another user will appear conditionally depending on whether the user is already followed or not by the current user:

FollowProfileButton component

We will create a separate component for the follow button called `FollowProfileButton`, which will be added to the `Profile` component. This component will show either `Follow` or `Unfollow` buttons depending on whether the current user is already a follower of the user in the profile. The `FollowProfileButton` component will be as follows.

`mern-social/client/user/FollowProfileButton.js`:

```
class FollowProfileButton extends Component {
  followClick = () => {
    this.props.onButtonClick(follow)
  }
  unfollowClick = () => {
    this.props.onButtonClick(unfollow)
  }
  render() {
    return (<div>
      { this.props.following
        ? (<Button variant="raised" color="secondary" onClick=
        {this.unfollowClick}>Unfollow</Button>)
        : (<Button variant="raised" color="primary" onClick=
        {this.followClick}>Follow</Button>)
      }
    </div>)
  }
}
FollowProfileButton.propTypes = {
  following: PropTypes.bool.isRequired,
  onButtonClick: PropTypes.func.isRequired
}
```

When the `FollowProfileButton` is added to the profile, the `'following'` value will be determined and sent from the `Profile` component as a prop to the `FollowProfileButton`, along with the click handler that takes the specific `follow` or `unfollow` fetch API to be called as a parameter:

Update Profile component

In the `Profile` view, the `FollowProfileButton` should only be shown when the user views the profile of other users, so we need to modify the condition for showing `Edit` and `Delete` buttons when viewing a profile as follows:

```
{auth.isAuthenticated().user && auth.isAuthenticated().user._id ==
this.state.user._id
    ? (edit and delete buttons)
    : (follow button)
}
```

In the `Profile` component, after the user data is successfully fetched on `componentDidMount`, we will check if the signed in user is already following the user in the profile or not, and set the `following` value to the state.

`mern-social/client/user/Profile.js`:

```
let following = this.checkFollow(data)
this.setState({user: data, following: following})
```

To determine the value to set in `following`, the `checkFollow` method will check if the signed-in user exists in the fetched user's followers list, then return the `match` if found, otherwise return `undefined` if a match is not found.

mern-social/client/user/Profile.js:

```
checkFollow = (user) => {
    const jwt = auth.isAuthenticated()
    const match = user.followers.find((follower)=> {
      return follower._id == jwt.user._id
    })
    return match
}
```

The `Profile` component will also define the click handler for `FollowProfileButton`, so the state of the `Profile` can be updated when the follow or unfollow action completes.

mern-social/client/user/Profile.js:

```
clickFollowButton = (callApi) => {
    const jwt = auth.isAuthenticated()
    callApi({
      userId: jwt.user._id
    }, {
      t: jwt.token
    }, this.state.user._id).then((data) => {
      if (data.error) {
        this.setState({error: data.error})
      } else {
        this.setState({user: data, following: !this.state.following})
      }
    })
}
```

The click handler definition takes the fetch API call as a parameter and is passed as a prop to the `FollowProfileButton` along with the `following` value when it is added to the `Profile` view.

mern-social/client/user/Profile.js:

```
<FollowProfileButton following={this.state.following}
onButtonClick={this.clickFollowButton}/>
```

Listing followings and followers

In each user's profile, we will add a list of their followers and the people they are following:

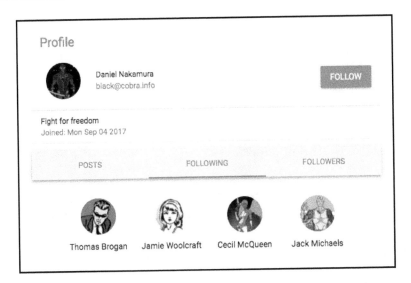

The details of the users referenced in the `following` and `followers` lists are already in the user object fetched using the `read` API when the profile is loaded. In order to render these separate lists of followers and followings, we will create a new component called `FollowGrid`.

FollowGrid component

The `FollowGrid` component will take a list of users as props, display the avatars of the users with their names, and link to each user's profile. We can add this component as desired to the `Profile` view to display `followings` or `followers`.

`mern-social/client/user/FollowGrid.js`:

```
class FollowGrid extends Component {
  render() {
    const {classes} = this.props
    return (<div className={classes.root}>
      <GridList cellHeight={160} className={classes.gridList} cols={4}>
        {this.props.people.map((person, i) => {
          return <GridListTile style={{'height':120}} key={i}>
            <Link to={"/user/" + person._id}>
              <Avatar src={'/api/users/photo/'+person._id} className=
              {classes.bigAvatar}/>
              <Typography className={classes.tileText}>{person.name}
              </Typography>
            </Link>
          </GridListTile>
```

```
            </GridListTile>
        })}
      </GridList>
    </div>)
  }
}

FollowGrid.propTypes = {
  classes: PropTypes.object.isRequired,
  people: PropTypes.array.isRequired
}
```

To add the `FollowGrid` component to the `Profile` view, we can place it as desired in the view and pass the list of `followers` or `followings` as the `people` prop:

```
<FollowGrid people={this.state.user.followers}/>
<FollowGrid people={this.state.user.following}/>
```

As pictured previously, in MERN Social we chose to display the `FollowGrid` components in tabs within the `Profile` component. We created a separate `ProfileTabs` component using Material-UI tab components and added that to the `Profile` component. This `ProfileTabs` component contains the two `FollowGrid` components with following and followers lists, along with a `PostList` component that shows the posts by the user. This will be discussed later in the chapter.

Finding people to follow

The **Who to follow** feature will show the signed in user a list of people in MERN Social that they are not currently following, giving the option to follow them or view their profiles:

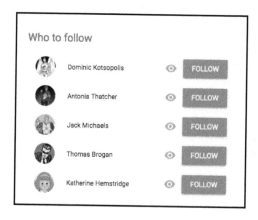

Fetching users not followed

We will implement a new API on the server to query the database and fetch this list of users the current user is not following.

`mern-social/server/routes/user.routes.js`:

```
router.route('/api/users/findpeople/:userId')
    .get(authCtrl.requireSignin, userCtrl.findPeople)
```

In the `findPeople` controller method, we will query the User collection in the database to find the users not in the current user's `following` list.

`mern-social/server/controllers/user.controller.js`:

```
const findPeople = (req, res) => {
  let following = req.profile.following
  following.push(req.profile._id)
  User.find({ _id: { $nin : following } }, (err, users) => {
    if (err) {
      return res.status(400).json({
        error: errorHandler.getErrorMessage(err)
      })
    }
    res.json(users)
  }).select('name')
}
```

To use this list of users in the frontend, we will update the `api-user.js` to add a fetch for this find people API.

`mern-social/client/user/api-user.js`:

```
const findPeople = (params, credentials) => {
  return fetch('/api/users/findpeople/' + params.userId, {
    method: 'GET',
    headers: {
      'Accept': 'application/json',
      'Content-Type': 'application/json',
      'Authorization': 'Bearer ' + credentials.t
    }
  }).then((response) => {
    return response.json()
  }).catch((err) => console.log(err))
}
```

FindPeople component

To display the *who to follow* feature, we will create a component called `FindPeople`, which can be added to any of the views or rendered on its own. In this component, we will first fetch the users not followed by calling the `findPeople` method in `componentDidMount`.

`mern-social/client/user/FindPeople.js`:

```
componentDidMount = () => {
    const jwt = auth.isAuthenticated()
    findPeople({
      userId: jwt.user._id
    }, {
      t: jwt.token
    }).then((data) => {
      if (data.error) {
        console.log(data.error)
      } else {
        this.setState({users: data})
      }
    })
}
```

The fetched list of users will be iterated over and rendered in a Material-UI `List` component, with each list item containing the user's avatar, name, a link to the profile page, and a `Follow` button.

`mern-social/client/user/FindPeople.js`:

```
<List>{this.state.users.map((item, i) => {
        return <span key={i}>
            <ListItem>
                <ListItemAvatar className={classes.avatar}>
                    <Avatar src={'/api/users/photo/'+item._id}/>
                </ListItemAvatar>
                <ListItemText primary={item.name}/>
                <ListItemSecondaryAction className={classes.follow}>
                  <Link to={"/user/" + item._id}>
                    <IconButton variant="raised" color="secondary"
                     className={classes.viewButton}>
                      <ViewIcon/>
                    </IconButton>
                  </Link>
                  <Button aria-label="Follow" variant="raised"
                    color="primary"
                    onClick={this.clickFollow.bind(this, item, i)}>
                    Follow
```

```
            </Button>
          </ListItemSecondaryAction>
        </ListItem>
      </span>
    })
  }
</List>
```

Clicking the `Follow` button will make a call to the follow API, and update the list of users to follow by splicing out the newly followed user.

`mern-social/client/user/FindPeople.js`:

```
clickFollow = (user, index) => {
    const jwt = auth.isAuthenticated()
    follow({
      userId: jwt.user._id
    }, {
      t: jwt.token
    }, user._id).then((data) => {
      if (data.error) {
        this.setState({error: data.error})
      } else {
        let toFollow = this.state.users
        toFollow.splice(index, 1)
        this.setState({users: toFollow, open: true, followMessage:
        `Following ${user.name}!`})
      }
    })
  }
```

We will also add a Material-UI `Snackbar` component that will open temporarily when the user is successfully followed, to tell the user that they started following this new user.

`mern-social/client/user/FindPeople.js`:

```
<Snackbar
  anchorOrigin={{ vertical: 'bottom', horizontal: 'right'}}
  open={this.state.open}
  onClose={this.handleRequestClose}
  autoHideDuration={6000}
  message={<span
className={classes.snack}>{this.state.followMessage}</span>}
/>
```

The `Snackbar` will display the message in the bottom-right corner of the page, and auto-hide after the set duration:

MERN Social users can now follow each other, view lists of followings and followers for each user, and also see a list of people they can follow. The main purpose of following another user in MERN Social is to track their social posts, so next we will look at the implementation of the post feature.

Posts

The posting feature in MERN Social will allow users to share content on the MERN Social application platform and also interact with each other over the content by commenting on or liking a post:

Mongoose schema model for Post

To store each post, we will first define the Mongoose Schema in
`server/models/post.model.js`. The Post schema will store a post's text content, a
photo, a reference to the user who posted, time of creation, likes on the post from users, and
comments on the post by users:

- **Post text**: The `text` will be a required field to be provided by the user on new
  post creation from the view:

  ```
  text: {
    type: String,
    required: 'Name is required'
  }
  ```

- **Post photo**: The `photo` will be uploaded from the user's local files during post
  creation, and stored in MongoDB similar to the user profile photo upload feature.
  The photo will be optional for each post:

  ```
  photo: {
    data: Buffer,
    contentType: String
  }
  ```

- **Post by**: Creating a post will require a user to be signed in first, so we can store a
  reference to the user who is posting in the `postedBy` field:

  ```
  postedBy: {type: mongoose.Schema.ObjectId, ref: 'User'}
  ```

- **Created time**: The `created` time will be generated automatically at the time of
  post creation in the database:

  ```
  created: { type: Date, default: Date.now }
  ```

- **Likes**: References to the users who liked a specific post will be stored in a `likes`
  array:

  ```
  likes: [{type: mongoose.Schema.ObjectId, ref: 'User'}]
  ```

- **Comments**: Each comment on a post will contain text content, the time of creation, and a reference to the user who posted the comment. Each post will have an array of `comments`:

```
comments: [{
    text: String,
    created: { type: Date, default: Date.now },
    postedBy: { type: mongoose.Schema.ObjectId, ref: 'User'}
}]
```

This schema definition will enable us to implement all the post-related features in MERN Social.

Newsfeed component

Before delving further into the implementations of the posting features in MERN Social, we will look at the composition of the **Newsfeed** view to showcase a basic example of how to design nested UI components that share state. The `Newsfeed` component will contain two main child components—a new post form and a list of posts from followed users:

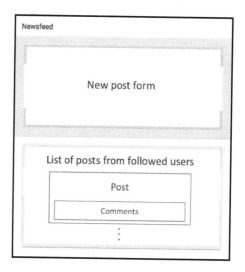

The basic structure of the `Newsfeed` component will be as follows, with the `NewPost` component and the `PostList` component.

`mern-social/client/post/Newsfeed.js`:

```
<Card>
    <Typography type="title"> Newsfeed </Typography>
    <Divider/>
    <NewPost addUpdate={this.addPost}/>
    <Divider/>
    <PostList removeUpdate={this.removePost} posts={this.state.posts}/>
</Card>
```

As the parent component, `Newsfeed` will control the state of the posts' data rendered in the child components. It will provide a way to update the state of posts across the components when the post data is modified within the child components, such as the addition of a new post in the `NewPost` component, or removal of a post from the `PostList` component.

Here specifically, a `loadPosts` function in `Newsfeed` makes the call to the server initially to fetch a list of posts from people the currently signed in user follows and sets it to the state to be rendered in the `PostList` component. The `Newsfeed` component provides the `addPost` and `removePost` functions to `NewPost` and `PostList`, which will be used when a new post is created or an existing post is deleted to update the list of posts in `Newsfeed`'s state and ultimately reflect it in the `PostList`.

The `addPost` function defined in the `Newsfeed` component will take the new post created in the `NewPost` component and add it to the posts in the state.

`mern-social/client/post/Newsfeed.js`:

```
addPost = (post) => {
    const updatedPosts = this.state.posts
    updatedPosts.unshift(post)
    this.setState({posts: updatedPosts})
}
```

The `removePost` function defined in the `Newsfeed` component will take the deleted post from the `Post` component in `PostList`, and remove it from the posts in the state.

`mern-social/client/post/Newsfeed.js`:

```
removePost = (post) => {
    const updatedPosts = this.state.posts
    const index = updatedPosts.indexOf(post)
    updatedPosts.splice(index, 1)
    this.setState({posts: updatedPosts})
}
```

As the posts are updated in `Newsfeed`'s state this way, the `PostList` will render the changed list of posts to the viewer. This mechanism of relaying state updates from parent to child components and back will be applied across other features, such as comment updates in a post and also when a `PostList` is rendered for an individual user in the `Profile` component.

Listing posts

In MERN Social, we will list posts in the `Newsfeed` and in the profile of each user. We will create a generic `PostList` component that will render any list of posts provided to it, and we can use it in both the `Newsfeed` and the `Profile` component.

`mern-social/client/post/PostList.js`:

```
class PostList extends Component {
  render() {
    return (
      <div style={{marginTop: '24px'}}>
        {this.props.posts.map((item, i) => {
          return <Post post={item} key={i}
                       onRemove={this.props.removeUpdate}/>
        })
        }
      </div>
    )
  }
}
PostList.propTypes = {
  posts: PropTypes.array.isRequired,
  removeUpdate: PropTypes.func.isRequired
}
```

The `PostList` component will iterate through the list of posts passed to it as props from the `Newsfeed` or the `Profile`, and pass the data of each post to a `Post` component that will render details of the post. The `PostList` will also pass the `removeUpdate` function that was sent as a prop from the parent component to the `Post` component, so the state can be updated when a single post is deleted.

List in Newsfeed

We will set up an API on the server that queries the Post collection, and returns posts from the people a specified user is following. So these posts may be displayed in the `PostList` in `Newsfeed`.

Newsfeed API for posts

This Newsfeed-specific API will receive a request at the following route to be defined in `server/routes/post.routes.js`:

```
router.route('/api/posts/feed/:userId')
  .get(authCtrl.requireSignin, postCtrl.listNewsFeed)
```

We are using the `:userID` param in this route to specify the currently signed-in user, and we will utilize the `userByID` controller method in the `user.controller` to fetch the user details as we did before and append them to the request object that is accessed in the `listNewsFeed` post controller method. So, also add the following to the `mern-social/server/routes/post.routes.js`:

```
router.param('userId', userCtrl.userByID)
```

The `post.routes.js` file will be very similar to the `user.routes.js` file, and to load these new routes in the Express app we need to mount the post routes in `express.js` like we did for the auth and user routes.

`mern-social/server/express.js`:

```
app.use('/', postRoutes)
```

The `listNewsFeed` controller method in `post.controller.js` will query the Post collection in the database to get the matching posts.

`mern-social/server/controllers/post.controller.js`:

```
const listNewsFeed = (req, res) => {
  let following = req.profile.following
  following.push(req.profile._id)
  Post.find({postedBy: { $in : req.profile.following } })
    .populate('comments', 'text created')
    .populate('comments.postedBy', '_id name')
    .populate('postedBy', '_id name')
    .sort('-created')
    .exec((err, posts) => {
      if (err) {
```

```
      return res.status(400).json({
        error: errorHandler.getErrorMessage(err)
      })
    }
    res.json(posts)
  })
}
```

In the query to the Post collection, we find all the posts that have `postedBy` user references that match the current user's followings and the current user.

Fetching Newsfeed posts in the view

To use this API in the frontend, we will add a fetch method to `client/post/api-post.js`:

```
const listNewsFeed = (params, credentials) => {
  return fetch('/api/posts/feed/'+ params.userId, {
    method: 'GET',
    headers: {
      'Accept': 'application/json',
      'Content-Type': 'application/json',
      'Authorization': 'Bearer ' + credentials.t
    }
  }).then(response => {
    return response.json()
  }).catch((err) => console.log(err))
}
```

This is the fetch method that will load the posts rendered in the `PostList`, which is added as a child component to the `Newsfeed` component. So this fetch needs to be called in the `loadPosts` method in the `Newsfeed` component.

`mern-social/client/post/Newsfeed.js`:

```
loadPosts = () => {
  const jwt = auth.isAuthenticated()
  listNewsFeed({
    userId: jwt.user._id
  }, {
    t: jwt.token
  }).then((data) => {
    if (data.error) {
      console.log(data.error)
    } else {
      this.setState({posts: data})
```

```
        }
    })
}
```

The `loadPosts` method will be called in the `componentDidMount` of the `Newsfeed` component to initially load the state with posts that are rendered in the `PostList` component:

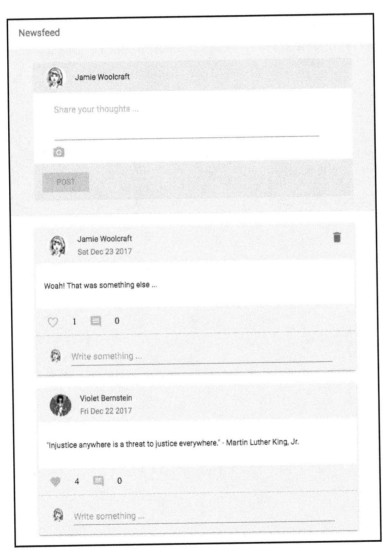

Listing by user in Profile

The implementation for getting a list of posts created by a specific user and showing it in the `Profile` will be similar to the discussion in the previous section. We will set up an API on the server that queries the Post collection, and returns posts from a specific user to the `Profile` view.

API for posts by a user

The route that will receive a query to return posts by a specific user will be added in `mern-social/server/routes/post.routes.js`:

```
router.route('/api/posts/by/:userId')
    .get(authCtrl.requireSignin, postCtrl.listByUser)
```

The `listByUser` controller method in `post.controller.js` will query the Post collection to find posts that have a matching reference in the `postedBy` field to the user specified in the `userId` param in the route.

`mern-social/server/controllers/post.controller.js`:

```
const listByUser = (req, res) => {
  Post.find({postedBy: req.profile._id})
  .populate('comments', 'text created')
  .populate('comments.postedBy', '_id name')
  .populate('postedBy', '_id name')
  .sort('-created')
  .exec((err, posts) => {
    if (err) {
      return res.status(400).json({
        error: errorHandler.getErrorMessage(err)
      })
    }
    res.json(posts)
  })
}
```

Fetching user posts in the view

To use this API in the frontend, we will add a fetch method to `mern-social/client/post/api-post.js`:

```
const listByUser = (params, credentials) => {
  return fetch('/api/posts/by/'+ params.userId, {
    method: 'GET',
    headers: {
      'Accept': 'application/json',
      'Content-Type': 'application/json',
      'Authorization': 'Bearer ' + credentials.t
    }
  }).then(response => {
    return response.json()
  }).catch((err) => console.log(err))
}
```

This `fetch` method will load the required posts for the `PostList` that is added to the `Profile` view. We will update the `Profile` component to define a `loadPosts` method that calls the `listByUser` fetch method.

`mern-social/client/user/Profile.js`:

```
loadPosts = (user) => {
  const jwt = auth.isAuthenticated()
  listByUser({
    userId: user
  }, {
    t: jwt.token
  }).then((data) => {
    if (data.error) {
      console.log(data.error)
    } else {
      this.setState({posts: data})
    }
  })
}
```

In the `Profile` component, the `loadPosts` method will be called with the user ID of the user whose profile is being loaded, after the user details have been fetched from the server in the `init()` function. The posts loaded for the specific user are set to state and rendered in the `PostList` component that is added to the `Profile` component. The `Profile` component also provides a `removePost` function, similar to the `Newsfeed` component, as a prop to the `PostList` component, so the list of posts can be updated if a post is removed:

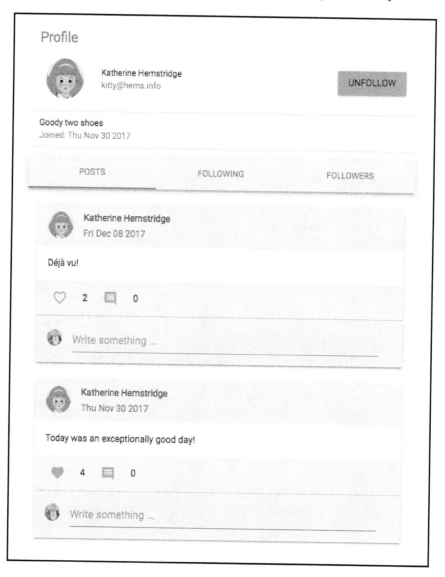

Creating a new post

The create new post feature will allow a signed in user to post a message and optionally add an image to the post by uploading it from their local files.

Creating post API

On the server, we will define an API to create the post in the database, starting with declaring a route to accept a POST request at /api/posts/new/:userId in mern-social/server/routes/post.routes.js:

```
router.route('/api/posts/new/:userId')
  .post(authCtrl.requireSignin, postCtrl.create)
```

The create method in the post.controller.js will use the formidable module to access the fields and the image file, if any, as we did for the user profile photo update.

mern-social/server/controllers/post.controller.js:

```
const create = (req, res, next) => {
  let form = new formidable.IncomingForm()
  form.keepExtensions = true
  form.parse(req, (err, fields, files) => {
    if (err) {
      return res.status(400).json({
        error: "Image could not be uploaded"
      })
    }
    let post = new Post(fields)
    post.postedBy= req.profile
    if(files.photo){
      post.photo.data = fs.readFileSync(files.photo.path)
      post.photo.contentType = files.photo.type
    }
    post.save((err, result) => {
      if (err) {
        return res.status(400).json({
          error: errorHandler.getErrorMessage(err)
        })
      }
      res.json(result)
    })
  })
}
```

Retrieving a post's photo

To retrieve the uploaded photo, we will also set up a `photo` route URL that returns the photo with a specific post.

`mern-social/server/routes/post.routes.js`:

```
router.route('/api/posts/photo/:postId').get(postCtrl.photo)
```

The `photo` controller will return the `photo` data stored in MongoDB as an image file.

`mern-social/server/controllers/post.controller.js`:

```
const photo = (req, res, next) => {
    res.set("Content-Type", req.post.photo.contentType)
    return res.send(req.post.photo.data)
}
```

As the photo route uses the `:postID` parameter, we will set up a `postByID` controller method to fetch the specific post by its ID before returning to the photo request. We will add the param call to `post.routes.js`.

`mern-social/server/routes/post.routes.js`:

```
router.param('postId', postCtrl.postByID)
```

The `postByID` will be similar to the `userByID` method, and it will attach the post retrieved from the database to the request object, to be accessed by the `next` method. The attached post data in this implementation will also contain the ID and name of the `postedBy` user reference.

`mern-social/server/controllers/post.controller.js`:

```
const postByID = (req, res, next, id) => {
  Post.findById(id).populate('postedBy', '_id name').exec((err, post) => {
    if (err || !post)
      return res.status('400').json({
        error: "Post not found"
      })
    req.post = post
    next()
  })
}
```

Fetching the create post API in the view

We will update the `api-post.js` to add a `create` method to make a `fetch` call to the create API.

`mern-social/client/post/api-post.js`:

```
const create = (params, credentials, post) => {
  return fetch('/api/posts/new/'+ params.userId, {
    method: 'POST',
    headers: {
      'Accept': 'application/json',
      'Authorization': 'Bearer ' + credentials.t
    },
    body: post
  }).then((response) => {
    return response.json()
  }).catch((err) => {
    console.log(err)
  })
}
```

This method, like the user `edit` fetch, will send a multipart form submission using a `FormData` object that can contain the text field and the image file.

NewPost component

The `NewPost` component added in the `Newsfeed` component will allow users to write a new post containing a text message and optionally an image:

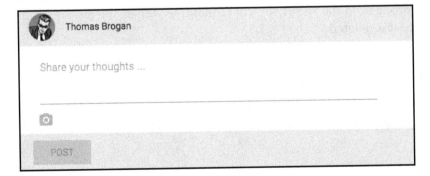

The NewPost component will be a standard form with a Material-UI TextField and a file upload button as implemented in EditProfile, that takes the values and sets them in a FormData object to be passed in the call to the create fetch method on post submission.

mern-social/client/post/NewPost.js:

```
clickPost = () => {
    const jwt = auth.isAuthenticated()
    create({
      userId: jwt.user._id
    }, {
      t: jwt.token
    }, this.postData).then((data) => {
      if (data.error) {
        this.setState({error: data.error})
      } else {
        this.setState({text:'', photo: ''})
        this.props.addUpdate(data)
      }
    })
}
```

The NewPost component is added as a child component in the Newsfeed, and given the addUpdate method as a prop. On successful post creation, the form view is emptied and addUpdate is executed so the post list in the Newsfeed is updated with the new post.

Post component

Post details in each post will be rendered in the Post component, which will receive the post data as props from the PostList component, as well as the onRemove prop to be applied if a post is deleted.

Layout

The Post component layout will have a header showing details of the poster, content of the post, an actions bar with likes and comment count, and the *Comments* section:

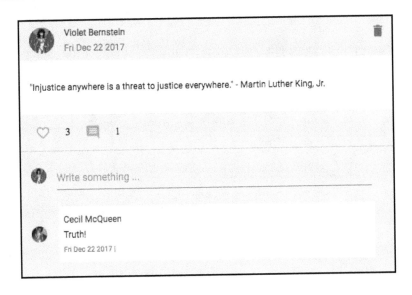

Header

The header will contain information such as the name, avatar, link to the profile of the user who posted, and the date the post was created.

`mern-social/client/post/Post.js`:

```
<CardHeader
  avatar={<Avatar src={'/api/users/photo/'+this.props.post.postedBy._id}/>}
      action={this.props.post.postedBy._id ===
          auth.isAuthenticated().user._id &&
          <IconButton onClick={this.deletePost}>
            <DeleteIcon />
          </IconButton>
        }
      title={<Link to={"/user/" + this.props.post.postedBy._id}>
          {this.props.post.postedBy.name}
        </Link>}
    subheader={(new Date(this.props.post.created)).toDateString()}
  className={classes.cardHeader}
/>
```

The header will also conditionally show a `delete` button if the signed-in user is viewing their own post.

Content

The content section will show the text of the post and the image if the post contains a photo.

`mern-social/client/post/Post.js`:

```
<CardContent className={classes.cardContent}>
  <Typography component="p" className={classes.text}>
    {this.props.post.text}
  </Typography>
  {this.props.post.photo &&
    (<div className={classes.photo}>
       <img className={classes.media}
            src={'/api/posts/photo/'+this.props.post._id}/>
    </div>)
  }
</CardContent>
```

Actions

The actions section will contain an interactive `"like"` option with the total number of likes on the post and a comment icon with the total number of comments on the post.

`mern-social/client/post/Post.js`:

```
<CardActions>
  { this.state.like
    ? <IconButton onClick={this.like} className={classes.button}
    aria-label="Like" color="secondary">
       <FavoriteIcon />
      </IconButton>
    :<IconButton onClick={this.like} className={classes.button}
    aria-label="Unlike" color="secondary">
       <FavoriteBorderIcon />
      </IconButton>
  } <span> {this.state.likes} </span>
  <IconButton className={classes.button}
   aria-label="Comment" color="secondary">
     <CommentIcon/>
  </IconButton> <span>{this.state.comments.length}</span>
</CardActions>
```

Comments

The comments section will contain all the comment related elements in the `Comments` component and will get `props` such as the `postId`, and the `comments` data, along with a `state` updating method that can be called when a comment is added or deleted in the `Comments` component.

mern-social/client/post/Post.js:

```
<Comments postId={this.props.post._id}
          comments={this.state.comments}
          updateComments={this.updateComments}/>
```

Deleting a post

The `delete` button is only visible if the signed-in user and `postedBy` user are the same for the specific post being rendered. For the post to be deleted from the database, we will have to set up a delete post API that will also have a fetch method in the frontend to be applied when `delete` is clicked.

mern-social/server/routes/post.routes.js:

```
router.route('/api/posts/:postId')
    .delete(authCtrl.requireSignin,
            postCtrl.isPoster,
                postCtrl.remove)
```

The delete route will check for authorization before calling `remove` on the post, by ensuring the authenticated user and `postedBy` user are the same users. The `isPoster` method checks if the signed-in user is the original creator of the post before executing the `next` method.

mern-social/server/controllers/post.controller.js:

```
const isPoster = (req, res, next) => {
  let isPoster = req.post && req.auth &&
  req.post.postedBy._id == req.auth._id
  if(!isPoster){
    return res.status('403').json({
      error: "User is not authorized"
    })
  }
  next()
}
```

The rest of the implementation for the delete API with a `remove` controller method and fetch method for the frontend are the same as other API implementations. The important difference here, in the delete post feature, is the call to the `onRemove` update method in the `Post` component when delete succeeds. The `onRemove` method is sent as a prop from either `Newsfeed` or `Profile`, to update the list of posts in the state when the delete is successful.

The following `deletePost` method defined in the `Post` component is called when the `delete` button is clicked on a post.

mern-social/client/post/Post.js:

```
deletePost = () => {
    const jwt = auth.isAuthenticated()
    remove({
      postId: this.props.post._id
    }, {
      t: jwt.token
    }).then((data) => {
      if (data.error) {
        console.log(data.error)
      } else {
        this.props.onRemove(this.props.post)
      }
    })
}
```

This method makes a fetch call to the delete post API, and on success updates the list of posts in the state by executing the `onRemove` method received as a prop from the parent component.

Likes

The like option in the `Post` component's action bar section will allow the user to like or unlike a post, and also show the total number of likes for the post. To record a like, we will have to set up like and unlike APIs that can be called in the view.

Like API

The like API will be a PUT request to update the `likes` array in the `Post` document. The request will be received at the route `api/posts/like`.

`mern-social/server/routes/post.routes.js`:

```
router.route('/api/posts/like')
  .put(authCtrl.requireSignin, postCtrl.like)
```

In the `like` controller method, the post ID received in the request body will be used to find the Post document and update it by pushing the current user's ID to the `likes` array.

`mern-social/server/controllers/post.controller.js`:

```
const like = (req, res) => {
  Post.findByIdAndUpdate(req.body.postId,
  {$push: {likes: req.body.userId}}, {new: true})
  .exec((err, result) => {
    if (err) {
      return res.status(400).json({
        error: errorHandler.getErrorMessage(err)
      })
    }
    res.json(result)
  })
}
```

To use this API, a fetch method called `like` will be added to `api-post.js`, which will be used when the user clicks the `like` button.

`mern-social/client/post/api-post.js`:

```
const like = (params, credentials, postId) => {
  return fetch('/api/posts/like/', {
    method: 'PUT',
    headers: {
      'Accept': 'application/json',
      'Content-Type': 'application/json',
      'Authorization': 'Bearer ' + credentials.t
    },
    body: JSON.stringify({userId:params.userId, postId: postId})
  }).then((response) => {
    return response.json()
  }).catch((err) => {
    console.log(err)
  })
}
```

Unlike API

The `unlike` API will be implemented similar to the like API, with its own route at `mern-social/server/routes/post.routes.js`:

```
router.route('/api/posts/unlike')
    .put(authCtrl.requireSignin, postCtrl.unlike)
```

The `unlike` method in the controller will find the post by its ID and update the `likes` array by removing the current user's ID using `$pull` instead of `$push`.

`mern-social/server/controllers/post.controller.js`:

```
const unlike = (req, res) => {
  Post.findByIdAndUpdate(req.body.postId, {$pull: {likes:
req.body.userId}}, {new: true})
  .exec((err, result) => {
    if (err) {
      return res.status(400).json({
        error: errorHandler.getErrorMessage(err)
      })
    }
    res.json(result)
  })
}
```

The unlike API will also have a corresponding fetch method similar to the `like` method in `api-post.js`.

Checking if liked and counting likes

When the `Post` component is rendered, we need to check if the currently signed in user has liked the post or not, so the appropriate `like` option can be shown.

`mern-social/client/post/Post.js`:

```
checkLike = (likes) => {
    const jwt = auth.isAuthenticated()
    let match = likes.indexOf(jwt.user._id) !== -1
    return match
}
```

The checkLike function can be called during componentDidMount and componentWillReceiveProps of the Post component, to set the like state for the post after checking if the current user is referenced in the post's likes array:

The like value set in the state using the checkLike method can be used to render a heart outline button or a full heart button. A heart outline button will render if the user has not liked the post, and clicking which will make a call to the like API, show the full heart button, and increment the likes count. The full heart button will indicate the current user has already liked this post, and clicking this will call the unlike API, render the heart outline button, and decrement the likes count.

The likes count is also set initially when the Post component mounts and props are received by setting the likes value to state with this.props.post.likes.length.

mern-social/client/post/Post.js:

```
componentDidMount = () => {
    this.setState({like:this.checkLike(this.props.post.likes),
                   likes: this.props.post.likes.length,
                   comments: this.props.post.comments})
}
componentWillReceiveProps = (props) => {
    this.setState({like:this.checkLike(props.post.likes),
                   likes: props.post.likes.length,
                   comments: props.post.comments})
}
```

The likes related values are updated again when a like or unlike action takes place, and the updated post data is returned from the API call.

Handling like clicks

To handle clicks on the like and unlike buttons, we will set up a like method that will call the appropriate fetch method based on whether it is a like or unlike action, and update the state of like and likes count for the post.

`mern-social/client/post/Post.js:`

```
like = () => {
    let callApi = this.state.like ? unlike : like
    const jwt = auth.isAuthenticated()
    callApi({
      userId: jwt.user._id
    }, {
      t: jwt.token
    }, this.props.post._id).then((data) => {
      if (data.error) {
        console.log(data.error)
      } else {
        this.setState({like: !this.state.like, likes:
       data.likes.length})
      }
    })
  }
```

Comments

The Comments section in each post will allow signed in users to add comments, see the list of comments, and delete their own comments. Any changes to the comment list, such as a new addition or a removal, will update the comments and also the comment count in the action bar section of the `Post` component:

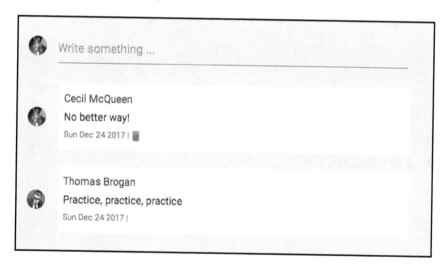

Adding a comment

When a user adds a comment, the post document will be updated in the database with the new comment.

Comment API

To implement the add comment API, we will set up a PUT route as follows to update the post.

`mern-social/server/routes/post.routes.js`:

```
router.route('/api/posts/comment')
    .put(authCtrl.requireSignin, postCtrl.comment)
```

The comment controller method will find the relevant post to be updated by its ID, and push the comment object received in the request body to the comments array of the post.

`mern-social/server/controllers/post.controller.js`:

```
const comment = (req, res) => {
  let comment = req.body.comment
  comment.postedBy = req.body.userId
  Post.findByIdAndUpdate(req.body.postId,
  {$push: {comments: comment}}, {new: true})
  .populate('comments.postedBy', '_id name')
  .populate('postedBy', '_id name')
  .exec((err, result) => {
    if (err) {
      return res.status(400).json({
        error: errorHandler.getErrorMessage(err)
      })
    }
    res.json(result)
  })
}
```

In the response, the updated post object will be sent back with details of the postedBy users populated in the post and in the comments.

To use this API in the view, we will set up a fetch method in `api-post.js` that takes the current user's ID, the post ID, and the `comment` object from the view, to send with the add comment request.

`mern-social/client/post/api-post.js`:

```
const comment = (params, credentials, postId, comment) => {
  return fetch('/api/posts/comment/', {
    method: 'PUT',
    headers: {
      'Accept': 'application/json',
      'Content-Type': 'application/json',
      'Authorization': 'Bearer ' + credentials.t
    },
    body: JSON.stringify({userId:params.userId, postId: postId,
    comment: comment})
  }).then((response) => {
    return response.json()
  }).catch((err) => {
    console.log(err)
  })
}
```

Writing something in the view

The *add comment* section in the `Comments` component will allow the signed-in user to type in the comment text:

It will contain an avatar with the user's photo and a text field, which will add the comment when the user presses the *Enter* key.

`mern-social/client/post/Comments.js`:

```
<CardHeader
  avatar={<Avatar className={classes.smallAvatar}
            src={'/api/users/photo/'+auth.isAuthenticated().user._id}/>}
  title={<TextField
          onKeyDown={this.addComment}
          multiline
          value={this.state.text}
          onChange={this.handleChange('text')}
          placeholder="Write something ..."
```

```
               className={classes.commentField}
               margin="normal"/>}
      className={classes.cardHeader}
  />
```

The text will be stored in state when the value changes, and on the onKeyDown event the addComment method will call the comment fetch method if the *Enter* key is pressed.

`mern-social/client/post/Comments.js`:

```
addComment = (event) => {
    if(event.keyCode == 13 && event.target.value){
      event.preventDefault()
      const jwt = auth.isAuthenticated()
      comment({
        userId: jwt.user._id
      }, {
        t: jwt.token
      }, this.props.postId, {text: this.state.text}).then((data) => {
        if (data.error) {
          console.log(data.error)
        } else {
          this.setState({text: ''})
          this.props.updateComments(data.comments)
        }
      })
    }
  }
```

The Comments component receives the updateComments method (discussed in the last section) as a prop from the Post component. This will be executed when the new comment is added, in order to update the comments and the comment count in the Post view.

Listing comments

The Comments component receives the list of comments for the specific post as props from the Post component, then iterates over the individual comments to render the details of the commenter and the comment content.

`mern-social/client/post/Comments.js:`

```
{this.props.comments.map((item, i) => {
            return <CardHeader
                    avatar={
                      <Avatar src=
                    {'/api/users/photo/'+item.postedBy._id}/>
                      }
                    title={commentBody(item)}
                    className={classes.cardHeader}
                    key={i}/>
          })
    }
```

The `commentBody` renders the content including the name of the commenter linked to their profile, the comment text, and the date of comment creation.

`mern-social/client/post/Comments.js:`

```
const commentBody = item => {
   return (
      <p className={classes.commentText}>
         <Link to={"/user/" + item.postedBy._id}>{item.postedBy.name}
         </Link><br/>
         {item.text}
         <span className={classes.commentDate}>
           {(new Date(item.created)).toDateString()} |
           {auth.isAuthenticated().user._id === item.postedBy._id &&
             <Icon onClick={this.deleteComment(item)}
                   className={classes.commentDelete}>delete</Icon> }
         </span>
      </p>
   )
}
```

The `commentBody` will also render a delete option for the comment if the `postedBy` reference of the comment matches the currently signed-in user.

Deleting a comment

Clicking the delete button in a comment will update the post in the database by removing the comment from the `comments` array:

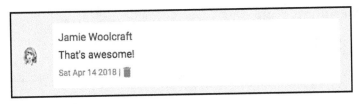

Uncomment API

We will implement an `uncomment` API at the following PUT route.

`mern-social/server/routes/post.routes.js`:

```
router.route('/api/posts/uncomment')
    .put(authCtrl.requireSignin, postCtrl.uncomment)
```

The `uncomment` controller method will find the relevant post by ID, then pull the comment with the deleted comment's ID from the `comments` array in the post.

`mern-social/server/controllers/post.controller.js`:

```
const uncomment = (req, res) => {
  let comment = req.body.comment
  Post.findByIdAndUpdate(req.body.postId, {$pull: {comments: {_id:
comment._id}}}, {new: true})
    .populate('comments.postedBy', '_id name')
    .populate('postedBy', '_id name')
    .exec((err, result) => {
      if (err) {
        return res.status(400).json({
          error: errorHandler.getErrorMessage(err)
        })
      }
      res.json(result)
    })
}
```

The updated post will be returned in the response as in the comment API.

To use this API in the view, we will also set up a fetch method in `api-post.js`, similar to the add `comment` fetch method, that takes the current user's ID, the post ID, and the deleted `comment` object to send with the `uncomment` request.

Removing a comment from view

When a comment's delete button is clicked by the commenter, the `Comments` component will call the `deleteComment` method to fetch the `uncomment` API, and update the comments along with the comment count when the comment is successfully removed from the server.

`mern-social/client/post/Comments.js`:

```
deleteComment = comment => event => {
    const jwt = auth.isAuthenticated()
    uncomment({
      userId: jwt.user._id
    }, {
      t: jwt.token
    }, this.props.postId, comment).then((data) => {
      if (data.error) {
        console.log(data.error)
      } else {
        this.props.updateComments(data.comments)
      }
    })
  }
```

Comment count update

The `updateComments` method, which will enable the `comments` and comment count to be updated when a comment is added or deleted, is defined in the `Post` component and passed as a prop to the `Comments` component.

`mern-social/client/post/Post.js`:

```
updateComments = (comments) => {
    this.setState({comments: comments})
  }
```

This method takes the updated list of comments as a parameter and updates the state that holds the list of comments rendered in the view. The initial state of comments in the Post component is set when the `Post` component mounts, and receives the post data as props. The comments set here are sent as props to the `Comments` component, and also used to render the comment count next to the likes action in the action bar of the Post layout, as follows.

`mern-social/client/post/Post.js`:

```
<IconButton aria-label="Comment" color="secondary">
  <CommentIcon/>
</IconButton> <span>{this.state.comments.length}</span>
```

This relation between the comment count in the `Post` component, and the comments rendered and updated in the `Comments` component, once again gives a simple demonstration of how changing data is shared among nested components in React to create dynamic and interactive user interfaces.

The MERN Social application is complete with the set of features we defined earlier for the application. Users are able to update their profiles with a photo and description, follow each other on the application, and create posts with photos and text, as well as like and comment on posts. The implementations shown here can be tuned and extended further to add more features, utilizing the revealed mechanisms of working with the MERN stack.

Summary

The MERN Social application developed in this chapter demonstrated how the MERN stack technologies can be used together to build out a fully-featured and functioning web application with social media features.

We began by updating the user feature in the skeleton application to allow anyone with an account on MERN Social to add a description about themselves, and also to upload a profile picture from their local files. In the implementation of uploading a profile picture, we explored how to upload multipart form data from the client, then receive it on the server to store the file data directly in the MongoDB database, and then be able to retrieve it back for viewing.

Next, we updated the user feature further, to allow users to follow each other on the MERN Social platform. In the user model, we added the capability to maintain arrays of user references to represent lists of followers and followings for each user. Extending this capability, we incorporated follow and unfollow options in the view, and displayed lists of followers, followings, and even lists of users not followed yet.

Then, we added the ability to allow users to post content and interact over the content by liking or commenting on the post. On the backend, we set up the Post model and corresponding APIs, capable of storing the post content that may or may not include an image, and maintaining records of likes and comments incurred on a post by any user.

Finally, while implementing the views for posting, liking, and commenting features, we explored how to use component composition and share changing state values across the components to create complex and interactive views.

In the next chapter, we will expand further on these abilities in the MERN stack, and unlock new possibilities as we develop an online marketplace application by extending the MERN skeleton application.

6
Exercising New MERN Skills with an Online Marketplace

As more businesses continue to move to the web, the ability to buy and sell in an online marketplace setting has become a core requirement for many web platforms. In this and the next chapter, we will utilize the MERN stack technologies to develop an online marketplace application complete with features that enable users to buy and sell.

In this chapter, we will start building the online marketplace by extending the MERN skeleton with the following features:

- Users with seller accounts
- Shop management
- Product management
- Product search by name and category

MERN Marketplace

The MERN Marketplace application will allow users to become sellers, who can manage multiple shops, and add the products they want to sell in each shop. Users who visit MERN Marketplace will be able to search for and browse products they want to buy, and add products to their shopping cart to place an order:

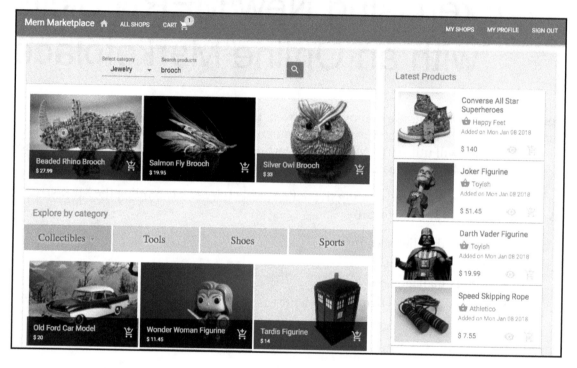

The code for the complete MERN Marketplace application is available on GitHub: `github.com/shamahoque/mern-marketplace`. The implementations discussed in this chapter can be accessed in the seller-shops-products branch of the repository. You can clone this code and run the application as you go through the code explanations in the rest of this chapter.

The views needed for the features related to seller accounts, shops, and products will be developed by extending and modifying the existing React components in the MERN skeleton application. The component tree pictured next shows all the custom React components that make up the MERN Marketplace frontend developed in this chapter:

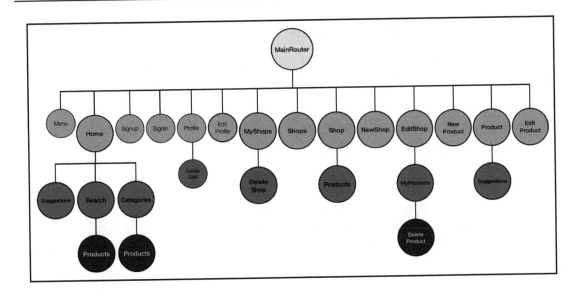

Users as sellers

Any user that signs up on the MERN Marketplace can choose to become a seller by updating their profile:

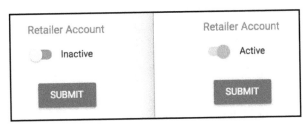

In contrast to being a regular user, becoming sellers will allow users to create and manage their own shops where they can manage products:

To add this seller feature, we need to update the user model, the Edit Profile view, and add a **MY SHOPS** link to the menu that will only be visible to sellers.

Updating the user model

The user model will need a seller value that will be set to `false` by default to represent regular users, and can be set to `true` to represent users who are also sellers.

`mern-marketplace/server/models/user.model.js`:

```
seller: {
    type: Boolean,
    default: false
}
```

 The seller value must be sent to the client with the user details received on successful sign-in, so the view can be rendered accordingly to show information relevant to the seller.

Updating the Edit Profile view

A signed-in user will see a toggle in the Edit Profile view, to either activate or deactivate the seller feature. We will update the `EditProfile` component to add a `Material-UI Switch` component in `FormControlLabel`.

`mern-marketplace/client/user/EditProfile.js`:

```
<Typography type="subheading" component="h4"
className={classes.subheading}>
    Seller Account
</Typography>
<FormControlLabel
    control = { <Switch classes={{ checked: classes.checked, bar:
classes.bar}}
                    checked={this.state.seller}
                    onChange={this.handleCheck}
                /> }
    label={this.state.seller? 'Active' : 'Inactive'}
/>
```

Any changes to the switch will be set to the value of the `seller` in state by calling the `handleCheck` method.

mern-marketplace/client/user/EditProfile.js:

```
handleCheck = (event, checked) => {
    this.setState({'seller': checked})
}
```

On submit, the `seller` value is added to details sent in the update to the server.

mern-marketplace/client/user/EditProfile.js:

```
clickSubmit = () => {
    const jwt = auth.isAuthenticated()
    const user = {
      name: this.state.name || undefined,
      email: this.state.email || undefined,
      password: this.state.password || undefined,
      seller: this.state.seller
    }
    update({
      userId: this.match.params.userId
    }, {
      t: jwt.token
    }, user).then((data) => {
      if (data.error) {
        this.setState({error: data.error})
      } else {
        auth.updateUser(data, ()=> {
        this.setState({'userId':data._id, 'redirectToProfile':true})
        })
      }
    })
}
```

On successful update, the user details stored in `sessionStorage` for auth purposes should also be updated. The `auth.updateUser` method is called to do this `sessionStorage` update. It is defined with the other `auth-helper.js` methods, and passed the updated user data and a callback function that updates the view, as parameters.

mern-marketplace/client/auth/auth-helper.js:

```
updateUser(user, cb) {
    if(typeof window !== "undefined"){
      if(sessionStorage.getItem('jwt')){
        let auth = JSON.parse(sessionStorage.getItem('jwt'))
```

```
        auth.user = user
        sessionStorage.setItem('jwt', JSON.stringify(auth))
        cb()
    }
  }
}
```

Updating the menu

In the navigation bar, to conditionally display a link to *My Shops*, which is only visible to the signed-in users who are also sellers, we will update the Menu component, as follows, within the previous code that only renders when a user is signed in.

`mern-marketplace/client/core/Menu.js`:

```
{auth.isAuthenticated().user.seller &&
  (<Link to="/seller/shops">
   <Button color = {isPartActive(history, "/seller/")}> My Shops </Button>
   </Link>)
}
```

Shops in the Marketplace

Sellers on MERN Marketplace can create shops and add products to each shop. To store the shop data and enable shop management, we will implement a Mongoose Schema for shops, backend APIs to access and modify the shop data, and frontend views for the shop owner and buyers browsing through the marketplace.

Shop model

The Shop schema defined in `server/models/shop.model.js` will have simple fields to store shop details, along with a logo image, and a reference to the user who owns the shop.

- **Shop name and description**: Name and description fields will be string types, with name as a required field:

```
name: {
    type: String,
    trim: true,
    required: 'Name is required'
},
```

```
description: {
    type: String,
    trim: true
},
```

- **Shop logo image**: The `image` field will store the logo image file to be uploaded by the user, as data in the MongoDB database:

```
image: {
    data: Buffer,
    contentType: String
},
```

- **Shop owner**: The owner field will reference the user who is creating the shop:

```
owner: {
    type: mongoose.Schema.ObjectId,
    ref: 'User'
}
```

- **Created and updated at times**: The `created` and `updated` fields will be `Date` types, with `created` generated when a new shop is added, and `updated` changed when any shop details are modified:

```
updated: Date,
created: {
    type: Date,
    default: Date.now
},
```

The fields in this schema definition will enable us to implement all shop-related features in MERN Marketplace.

Create a new shop

In MERN Marketplace, a user who is signed in and also a seller will be able to create new shops.

Create shop API

In the backend, we will add a POST route that verifies that the current user is a seller and creates a new shop with the shop data passed in the request.

mern-marketplace/server/routes/shop.routes.js:

```
router.route('/api/shops/by/:userId')
    .post(authCtrl.requireSignin, authCtrl.hasAuthorization,
        userCtrl.isSeller, shopCtrl.create)
```

The `shop.routes.js` file will be very similar to the `user.routes` file, and to load these new routes in the Express app, we need to mount the shop routes in `express.js`, like we did for the auth and user routes.

mern-marketplace/server/express.js:

```
app.use('/', shopRoutes)
```

We will update the user controller to add the `isSeller` method, this will ensure the current user is actually a seller before creating the new shop.

mern-marketplace/server/controllers/user.controller.js:

```
const isSeller = (req, res, next) => {
  const isSeller = req.profile && req.profile.seller
  if (!isSeller) {
    return res.status('403').json({
      error: "User is not a seller"
    })
  }
  next()
}
```

The `create` method, in the shop controller, uses the `formidable` npm module to parse the multipart request that may contain an image file uploaded by the user for the shop logo. If there is a file, `formidable` will store it temporarily in the filesystem, and we will read it using the `fs` module to retrieve the file type and data to store it to the `image` field in the shop document.

mern-marketplace/server/controllers/shop.controller.js:

```
const create = (req, res, next) => {
  let form = new formidable.IncomingForm()
  form.keepExtensions = true
  form.parse(req, (err, fields, files) => {
```

```
    if (err) {
      res.status(400).json({
        message: "Image could not be uploaded"
      })
    }
    let shop = new Shop(fields)
    shop.owner= req.profile
    if(files.image){
      shop.image.data = fs.readFileSync(files.image.path)
      shop.image.contentType = files.image.type
    }
    shop.save((err, result) => {
      if (err) {
        return res.status(400).json({
          error: errorHandler.getErrorMessage(err)
        })
      }
      res.status(200).json(result)
    })
  })
}
```

The logo image file for the shop is uploaded by the user and stored in MongoDB as data. Then, in order to be shown in the views, it is retrieved from the database as an image file at a separate GET API. The GET API is set up as an Express route at /api/shops/logo/:shopId, which gets the image data from MongoDB and sends it as a file in the response. The implementation steps for file upload, storage, and retrieval are outlined in detail in the *Upload profile photo* section in Chapter 5, *Starting with a Simple Social Media Application*.

Fetch the create API in the view

In the frontend, to use this create API, we will set up a fetch method in client/shop/api-shop.js to make a post request to the create API by passing the multipart form data:

```
const create = (params, credentials, shop) => {
  return fetch('/api/shops/by/'+ params.userId, {
      method: 'POST',
      headers: {
        'Accept': 'application/json',
        'Authorization': 'Bearer ' + credentials.t
      },
      body: shop
```

```
      })
      .then((response) => {
        return response.json()
      }).catch((err) => console.log(err))
  }
```

NewShop component

In the NewShop component, we will render a form that allows a seller to create a shop by entering a name and description, and uploading a logo image file from their local filesystem:

We will add the file upload elements using a Material-UI button and an HTML5 file input element.

mern-marketplace/client/shop/NewShop.js:

```
<input accept="image/*" onChange={this.handleChange('image')}
       style={display:'none'} id="icon-button-file" type="file" />
<label htmlFor="icon-button-file">
   <Button raised color="secondary" component="span">
     Upload Logo <FileUpload/>
   </Button>
</label>
<span> {this.state.image ? this.state.image.name : ''} </span>
```

The name and description form fields will be added with the `TextField` components.

mern-marketplace/client/shop/NewShop.js:

```
<TextField
    id="name"
    label="Name"
    value={this.state.name}
    onChange={this.handleChange('name')}/> <br/>
<TextField
    id="multiline-flexible"
    label="Description"
    multiline rows="2"
    value={this.state.description}
    onChange={this.handleChange('description')}/>
```

These form field changes will be tracked with the `handleChange` method.

mern-marketplace/client/shop/NewShop.js:

```
handleChange = name => event => {
    const value = name === 'image'
      ? event.target.files[0]
      : event.target.value
    this.shopData.set(name, value)
    this.setState({ [name]: value })
}
```

The `handleChange` method updates the state with the new values and populates `shopData`, which is a `FormData` object that ensures the data is stored in the correct format needed for the `multipart/form-data` encoding type. The `shopData` object is initialized in `componentDidMount`.

mern-marketplace/client/shop/NewShop.js:

```
componentDidMount = () => {
  this.shopData = new FormData()
}
```

On form submit, the `create` fetch method is called in the `clickSubmit` function.

mern-marketplace/client/shop/NewShop.js:

```
clickSubmit = () => {
  const jwt = auth.isAuthenticated()
  create({
    userId: jwt.user._id
```

```
    }, {
      t: jwt.token
    }, this.shopData).then((data) => {
      if (data.error) {
        this.setState({error: data.error})
      } else {
        this.setState({error: '', redirect: true})
      }
    })
  }
```

On successful shop creation, the user is redirected back to the MyShops view.

mern-marketplace/client/shop/NewShop.js:

```
if (this.state.redirect) {
    return (<Redirect to={'/seller/shops'}/>)
}
```

The NewShop component can only be viewed by a signed-in user who is also a seller. So we will add a PrivateRoute in the MainRouter component, that will render this form only for authorized users at /seller/shop/new.

mern-marketplace/client/MainRouter.js:

```
<PrivateRoute path="/seller/shop/new" component={NewShop}/>
```

This link can be added to any of the view components that may be accessed by the seller.

List shops

In MERN Marketplace, regular users will be able to browse through a list of all the shops on the platform, and a shop owner will manage a list of their own shops.

List all shops

A list of all the shops will be fetched from the backend and displayed to the end user.

Shops list API

In the backend, we will add a route in `server/routes/shop.routes.js` to retrieve all the shops stored in the database when the server receives a GET request at `'/api/shops'`:

```
router.route('/api/shops')
    .get(shopCtrl.list)
```

The `list` controller method in `shop.controller.js` will query the Shop collection in the database to return all the shops.

mern-marketplace/server/controllers/shop.controller.js:

```
const list = (req, res) => {
  Shop.find((err, shops) => {
    if (err) {
      return res.status(400).json({
        error: errorHandler.getErrorMessage(err)
      })
    }
    res.json(shops)
  })
}
```

Fetch all shops for the view

In the frontend, to fetch the shops using this list API, we will set up a `fetch` method in `client/shop/api-shop.js`:

```
const list = () => {
  return fetch('/api/shops', {
    method: 'GET',
  }).then(response => {
    return response.json()
  }).catch((err) => console.log(err))
}
```

Shops component

In the Shops component, we will render the list of shops in a Material-UI List, after fetching the data when the component mounts and setting the data to state:

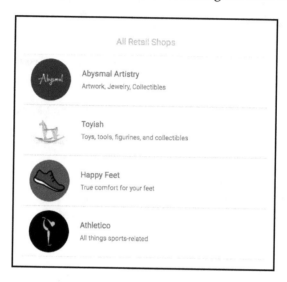

The loadShops method is called in componentDidMount to load the shops when the component mounts.

mern-marketplace/client/shop/Shops.js:

```
componentDidMount = () => {
    this.loadShops()
}
```

It uses the list fetch method to retrieve the shop list and sets the data to state.

mern-marketplace/client/shop/Shops.js:

```
loadShops = () => {
    list().then((data) => {
        if (data.error) {
            console.log(data.error)
        } else {
            this.setState({shops: data})
        }
    })
}
```

In the `Shops` component, the retrieved shops array is iterated over using `map`, with each shop's data rendered in the view in a Material-UI `ListItem`, and each `ListItem` is also linked to the individual shop's view.

`mern-marketplace/client/shop/Shops.js`:

```
{this.state.shops.map((shop, i) => {
   return <Link to={"/shops/"+shop._id} key={i}>
           <Divider/>
           <ListItem button>
             <ListItemAvatar>
             <Avatar src={'/api/shops/logo/'+shop._id+"?" + new
             Date().getTime()}/>
             </ListItemAvatar>
             <div>
               <Typography type="headline" component="h2"
              color="primary">
                 {shop.name}
               </Typography>
               <Typography type="subheading" component="h4">
                 {shop.description}
               </Typography>
             </div>
           </ListItem><Divider/>
        </Link>})}
```

The `Shops` component will be accessed by the end user at `/shops/all`, set up with React Router and declared in `MainRouter.js`.

`mern-marketplace/client/MainRouter.js`:

```
<Route path="/shops/all" component={Shops}/>
```

List shops by owner

Authorized sellers will see a list of the shops they created, which they can manage by editing or deleting any shop on the list.

Shops by owner API

We will add a GET route to retrieve the shops owned by a specific user to the shop routes declared in the backend.

`mern-marketplace/server/routes/shop.routes.js`:

```
router.route('/api/shops/by/:userId')
    .get(authCtrl.requireSignin, authCtrl.hasAuthorization,
shopCtrl.listByOwner)
```

To process the `:userId` param and retrieve the associated user from the database, we will utilize the `userByID` method in user controller. We will add the following to the `Shop` routes in `shop.routes.js`, so the user is available in the `request` object as `profile`.

`mern-marketplace/server/routes/shop.routes.js`:

```
router.param('userId', userCtrl.userByID)
```

The `listByOwner` controller method in `shop.controller.js` will query the `Shop` collection in the database to get the matching shops.

`mern-marketplace/server/controllers/shop.controller.js`:

```
const listByOwner = (req, res) => {
  Shop.find({owner: req.profile._id}, (err, shops) => {
    if (err) {
      return res.status(400).json({
        error: errorHandler.getErrorMessage(err)
      })
    }
    res.json(shops)
  }).populate('owner', '_id name')
}
```

In the query to the Shop collection, we find all the shops where the `owner` field matches the user specified with the `userId` param.

Fetch all shops owned by a user for the view

In the frontend, to fetch the shops for a specific user using this list by owner API, we will add a fetch method in `client/shop/api-shop.js`:

```
const listByOwner = (params, credentials) => {
  return fetch('/api/shops/by/'+params.userId, {
    method: 'GET',
    headers: {
      'Accept': 'application/json',
      'Authorization': 'Bearer ' + credentials.t
    }
  }).then((response) => {
```

```
        return response.json()
    }).catch((err) => {
        console.log(err)
    })
}
```

MyShops component

The `MyShops` component is similar to the `Shops` component, it fetches the list of shops owned by the current user in `componentDIdMount`, and renders each shop in a `ListItem`:

Additionally, each shop has an `edit` and a `delete` option, unlike the list of items in `shops`.

`mern-marketplace/client/shop/MyShops.js`:

```
<ListItemSecondaryAction>
    <Link to={"/seller/shop/edit/" + shop._id}>
        <IconButton aria-label="Edit" color="primary">
            <Edit/>
        </IconButton>
    </Link>
    <DeleteShop shop={shop} onRemove={this.removeShop}/>
</ListItemSecondaryAction>
```

The `Edit` button links to the Edit Shop view. The `DeleteShop` component handles the delete action, and updates the list by calling the `removeShop` method passed from `MyShops`, to update the state with the modified list of shops for the current user.

`mern-marketplace/client/shop/MyShops.js`:

```
removeShop = (shop) => {
    const updatedShops = this.state.shops
    const index = updatedShops.indexOf(shop)
    updatedShops.splice(index, 1)
    this.setState({shops: updatedShops})
}
```

The `MyShops` component can only be viewed by a signed-in user who is also a seller. So we will add a `PrivateRoute` in the `MainRouter` component, which will render this component only for authorized users, at `/seller/shops`.

`mern-marketplace/client/MainRouter.js`:

```
<PrivateRoute path="/seller/shops" component={MyShops}/>
```

Display a shop

Any users browsing MERN Marketplace will be able to browse each individual shop.

Read a shop API

In the backend, we will add a `GET` route that queries the `Shop` collection with an ID and returns the shop in the response.

`mern-marketplace/server/routes/shop.routes.js`:

```
router.route('/api/shop/:shopId')
    .get(shopCtrl.read)
router.param('shopId', shopCtrl.shopByID)
```

The `:shopId` param in the route URL will call the `shopByID` controller method, which is similar to the `userByID` controller method, retrieves the shop from the database, and attaches it to the request object to be used in the `next` method.

`mern-marketplace/server/controllers/shop.controller.js:`

```
const shopByID = (req, res, next, id) => {
  Shop.findById(id).populate('owner', '_id name').exec((err, shop) => {
    if (err || !shop)
      return res.status('400').json({
        error: "Shop not found"
      })
    req.shop = shop
    next()
  })
}
```

The `read` controller method then returns this `shop` object in the response to the client.

`mern-marketplace/server/controllers/shop.controller.js:`

```
const read = (req, res) => {
  return res.json(req.shop)
}
```

Fetch the shop in the view

In `api-shop.js`, we will add a `fetch` method to use this read API in the frontend.

`mern-marketplace/client/shop/api-shop.js:`

```
const read = (params, credentials) => {
  return fetch('/api/shop/' + params.shopId, {
    method: 'GET'
  }).then((response) => {
    return response.json()
  }).catch((err)  => console.log(err) )
}
```

Shop component

The Shop component will render the shop details and also a list of products in the specified shop using a product list component, which will be discussed in the *Products* section:

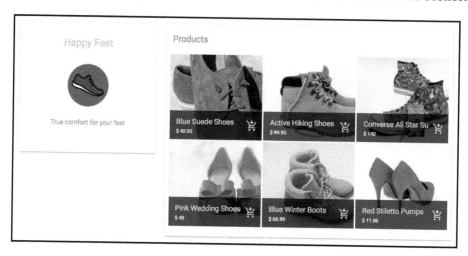

The Shop component can be accessed in the browser at the /shops/:shopId route, which is defined in MainRouter as follows.

mern-marketplace/client/MainRouter.js:

```
<Route path="/shops/:shopId" component={Shop}/>
```

In componentDidMount, the shop details are fetched using the read method from api-shop.js.

mern-marketplace/client/shop/Shop.js:

```
componentDidMount = () => {
    read({
      shopId: this.match.params.shopId
    }).then((data) => {
      if (data.error) {
        this.setState({error: data.error})
      } else {
        this.setState({shop: data})
      }
    })
  }
```

The retrieved shop data is set to state and rendered in the view to display the shop's name, logo, and description.

mern-marketplace/client/shop/Shop.js:

```
<CardContent>
    <Typography type="headline" component="h2">
        {this.state.shop.name}
    </Typography><br/>
    <Avatar src={logoUrl}/><br/>
    <Typography type="subheading" component="h2">
        {this.state.shop.description}
    </Typography><br/>
</CardContent>
```

The `logoUrl` points to the route that retrieves the logo image from the database if it exists, and it's defined as follows.

mern-marketplace/client/shop/Shop.js:

```
const logoUrl = this.state.shop._id
  ? `/api/shops/logo/${this.state.shop._id}?${new Date().getTime()}`
  : '/api/shops/defaultphoto'
```

Edit a shop

Authorized sellers will also be able to edit the details of the shops they own.

Edit shop API

In the backend, we will add a PUT route that allows an authorized seller to edit one of their shops.

mern-marketplace/server/routes/shop.routes.js:

```
router.route('/api/shops/:shopId')
    .put(authCtrl.requireSignin, shopCtrl.isOwner, shopCtrl.update)
```

The `isOwner` controller method ensures that the signed-in user is actually the owner of the shop being edited.

mern-marketplace/server/controllers/shop.controller.js:

```
const isOwner = (req, res, next) => {
  const isOwner = req.shop && req.auth && req.shop.owner._id ==
  req.auth._id
  if(!isOwner){
    return res.status('403').json({
      error: "User is not authorized"
    })
  }
  next()
}
```

The update controller method will use formidable and fs modules as in the create controller method discussed earlier, to parse the form data and update the existing shop in the database.

mern-marketplace/server/controllers/shop.controller.js:

```
const update = (req, res, next) => {
  let form = new formidable.IncomingForm()
  form.keepExtensions = true
  form.parse(req, (err, fields, files) => {
    if (err) {
      res.status(400).json({
        message: "Photo could not be uploaded"
      })
    }
    let shop = req.shop
    shop = _.extend(shop, fields)
    shop.updated = Date.now()
    if(files.image){
      shop.image.data = fs.readFileSync(files.image.path)
      shop.image.contentType = files.image.type
    }
    shop.save((err) => {
      if (err) {
        return res.status(400).send({
          error: errorHandler.getErrorMessage(err)
        })
      }
      res.json(shop)
    })
  })
}
```

Fetch the edit API in the view

The edit API is called in the view using a `fetch` method that takes the form data and sends the multipart request to the backend.

`mern-marketplace/client/shop/api-shop.js`:

```
const update = (params, credentials, shop) => {
  return fetch('/api/shops/' + params.shopId, {
    method: 'PUT',
    headers: {
      'Accept': 'application/json',
      'Authorization': 'Bearer ' + credentials.t
    },
    body: shop
  }).then((response) => {
    return response.json()
  }).catch((err) => {
    console.log(err)
  })
}
```

EditShop component

The `EditShop` component will show a form similar to the create new shop form, pre-populated with the existing shop details. This component will also show a list of the products in this shop, to be discussed in the *Products* section:

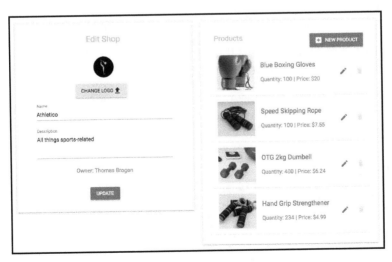

The form part is similar to the form in the `NewShop` component, with the same form fields and a `formData` object that holds the multipart form data sent with the `update` fetch method.

The `EditShop` component is only accessible by authorized shop owners. So we will add a `PrivateRoute` in the `MainRouter` component, which will render this component only for authorized users at `/seller/shop/edit/:shopId`.

mern-marketplace/client/MainRouter.js:

```
<PrivateRoute path="/seller/shop/edit/:shopId" component={EditShop}/>
```

This link is added with an edit icon for each shop in the `MyShops` component.

Delete a shop

An authorized seller can delete any of their own shops from the `MyShops` list.

Delete shop API

In the backend, we will add a `DELETE` route that allows an authorized seller to delete one of their own shops.

mern-marketplace/server/routes/shop.routes.js:

```
router.route('/api/shops/:shopId')
    .delete(authCtrl.requireSignin, shopCtrl.isOwner, shopCtrl.remove)
```

The `remove` controller method deletes the specified shop from the database, if `isOwner` confirms that the signed-in user is the owner of the shop.

mern-marketplace/server/controllers/shop.controller.js:

```
const remove = (req, res, next) => {
  let shop = req.shop
  shop.remove((err, deletedShop) => {
    if (err) {
      return res.status(400).json({
        error: errorHandler.getErrorMessage(err)
```

```
        })
      }
      res.json(deletedShop)
    })
  }
```

Fetch the delete API in the view

We will add a corresponding method in the frontend to make a delete request to the delete API.

`mern-marketplace/client/shop/api-shop.js`:

```
const remove = (params, credentials) => {
  return fetch('/api/shops/' + params.shopId, {
    method: 'DELETE',
    headers: {
      'Accept': 'application/json',
      'Content-Type': 'application/json',
      'Authorization': 'Bearer ' + credentials.t
    }
  }).then((response) => {
    return response.json()
  }).catch((err) => {
    console.log(err)
  })
}
```

DeleteShop component

The `DeleteShop` component is added to the `MyShops` component for each shop in the list. It takes the `shop` object and a `onRemove` method as props from `MyShops`:

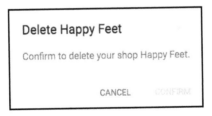

This component is basically an icon button that, on click, opens a confirm dialog to ask the user whether they are sure they want to delete their shop.

`mern-marketplace/client/shop/DeleteShop.js:`

```
<IconButton aria-label="Delete" onClick={this.clickButton}
color="secondary">
    <DeleteIcon/>
</IconButton>
<Dialog open={this.state.open} onRequestClose={this.handleRequestClose}>
    <DialogTitle>{"Delete "+this.props.shop.name}</DialogTitle>
        <DialogContent>
            <DialogContentText>
                Confirm to delete your shop {this.props.shop.name}.
            </DialogContentText>
        </DialogContent>
        <DialogActions>
            <Button onClick={this.handleRequestClose} color="primary">
                Cancel
            </Button>
            <Button onClick={this.deleteShop} color="secondary"
             autoFocus="autoFocus">
                Confirm
            </Button>
        </DialogActions>
</Dialog>
```

On delete confirmation from the user in the dialog, the `delete` fetch method is called in `deleteShop`.

`mern-marketplace/client/shop/DeleteShop.js:`

```
deleteShop = () => {
  const jwt = auth.isAuthenticated()
  remove({
    shopId: this.props.shop._id
  }, {t: jwt.token}).then((data) => {
    if (data.error) {
      console.log(data.error)
    } else {
      this.setState({open: false}, () => {
        this.props.onRemove(this.props.shop)
      })
    }
  })
}
```

On successful deletion, the dialog is closed and the shop list in MyShops is updated by calling the onRemove prop, which gets the removeShop method passed in as a prop from MyShops.

These shop views will allow both buyers and sellers to interact with the shops. The shops will also have products, discussed next, which the owners will manage and the buyers will browse through with an option to add to their cart.

Products

Products are the most crucial aspect in a marketplace application. In the MERN Marketplace, sellers can manage products in their shops, and visitors can search for and browse products.

Product model

Products will be stored in a product collection in the database, with a schema defined using Mongoose. For MERN Marketplace, we will keep the product schema simple with support for fields such as product name, description, image, category, quantity, price, created at, updated at, and a reference to the shop.

- **Product name and description**: The name and description fields will be String types, with name as a required field:

```
name: {
    type: String,
    trim: true,
    required: 'Name is required'
},
description: {
    type: String,
    trim: true
},
```

- **Product image**: The image field will store an image file to be uploaded by the user as data in the MongoDB database:

```
image: {
    data: Buffer,
    contentType: String
},
```

- **Product category**: The `category` value will allow grouping products of the same type together:

```
category: {
    type: String
},
```

- **Product quantity**: The `quantity` field will represent the amount available for selling in the shop:

```
quantity: {
    type: Number,
    required: "Quantity is required"
},
```

- **Product price**: The `price` field will hold the unit price this product will cost the buyer:

```
price: {
    type: Number,
    required: "Price is required"
},
```

- **Product shop**: The `shop` field will reference the shop in which the product was added:

```
shop: {
    type: mongoose.Schema.ObjectId,
    ref: 'Shop'
}
```

- **Created and updated at times**: The `created` and `updated` fields will be `Date` types, with `created` generated when a new product is added, and the `updated` time changed when the same product's details are modified:

```
updated: Date,
created: {
    type: Date,
    default: Date.now
},
```

The fields in this schema definition will enable us to implement all product-related features in MERN Marketplace.

Create a new product

Sellers in MERN Marketplace will be able to add new products to the shops they own and create on the platform.

Create product API

In the backend, we will add a route at `/api/products/by/:shopId`, which accepts a `POST` request containing product data, to create a new product associated with the shop identified by the `:shopId` param. The code to handle this request will first check that the current user is the owner of the shop in which the new product will be added, before creating the new product in the database.

This create product API route is declared in the `product.routes.js` file, and it utilizes the `shopByID` and `isOwner` methods from the shop controller to process the `:shopId` param, and to verify the current user as the shop owner.

`mern-marketplace/server/routes/product.routes.js`:

```
router.route('/api/products/by/:shopId')
  .post(authCtrl.requireSignin,
          shopCtrl.isOwner,
              productCtrl.create)
router.param('shopId', shopCtrl.shopByID)
```

The `product.routes.js` file will be very similar to the `shop.routes.js` file, and to load these new routes in the Express app, we need to mount the product routes in `express.js`, like we did for the shop routes.

`mern-marketplace/server/express.js`:

```
app.use('/', productRoutes)
```

The `create` method, in the product controller, uses the `formidable` npm module to parse the multipart request that may contain an image file uploaded by the user along with the product fields. The parsed data is then saved to the `Product` collection as a new product.

`mern-marketplace/server/controllers/product.controller.js:`

```
const create = (req, res, next) => {
  let form = new formidable.IncomingForm()
  form.keepExtensions = true
  form.parse(req, (err, fields, files) => {
    if (err) {
      return res.status(400).json({
        message: "Image could not be uploaded"
      })
    }
    let product = new Product(fields)
    product.shop= req.shop
    if(files.image){
      product.image.data = fs.readFileSync(files.image.path)
      product.image.contentType = files.image.type
    }
    product.save((err, result) => {
      if (err) {
        return res.status(400).json({
          error: errorHandler.getErrorMessage(err)
        })
      }
      res.json(result)
    })
  })
}
```

Fetching the create API in the view

In the frontend, to use this create API, we will set up a `fetch` method in
`client/product/api-product.js` to make a post request to the create API by passing
the multipart form data from the view.

`mern-marketplace/client/product/api-product.js:`

```
const create = (params, credentials, product) => {
  return fetch('/api/products/by/'+ params.shopId, {
    method: 'POST',
    headers: {
      'Accept': 'application/json',
      'Authorization': 'Bearer ' + credentials.t
    },
    body: product
  })
  .then((response) => {
```

```
      return response.json()
    }).catch((err) => console.log(err))
}
```

The NewProduct component

The NewProduct component will be similar to the NewShop component. It will contain a form that allows a seller to create a product by entering a name, description, category, quantity, and price, and uploading a product image file from their local filesystem:

This NewProduct component will only load at a route that is associated with a specific shop, so only signed-in users who are sellers can add a product to a shop they own. To define this route, we add a PrivateRoute in the MainRouter component, which will render this form only for authorized users at /seller/:shopId/products/new.

mern-marketplace/client/MainRouter.js:

```
<PrivateRoute path="/seller/:shopId/products/new" component={NewProduct}/>
```

List products

In MERN Marketplace, products will be presented to users in multiple ways, the two main distinctions will be in the way products are listed for sellers and the way they are listed for buyers.

List by shop

Visitors to the marketplace will browse products in each shop, and sellers will manage a list of products in each of their shops.

Products by shop API

To retrieve products from a specific shop in the database, we will set up a GET route at `/api/products/by/:shopId`, as follows.

`mern-marketplace/server/routes/product.routes.js`:

```
router.route('/api/products/by/:shopId')
    .get(productCtrl.listByShop)
```

The `listByShop` controller method executed in response to this request will query the Product collection to return the products matching the given shop's reference.

`mern-marketplace/server/controllers/product.controller.js`:

```
const listByShop = (req, res) => {
  Product.find({shop: req.shop._id}, (err, products) => {
    if (err) {
      return res.status(400).json({
        error: errorHandler.getErrorMessage(err)
      })
    }
    res.json(products)
  }).populate('shop', '_id name').select('-image')
}
```

In the frontend, to fetch the products in a specific shop using this list by shop API, we will add a fetch method in `api-product.js`.

`mern-marketplace/client/product/api-product.js`:

```
const listByShop = (params) => {
  return fetch('/api/products/by/'+params.shopId, {
    method: 'GET'
  }).then((response) => {
    return response.json()
  }).catch((err) => {
    console.log(err)
  })
}
```

Products component for buyers

The `Products` component is mainly for displaying the products to visitors who may buy the products. We will use this component to render product lists relevant to the buyer. It will receive the product list as props from a parent component displaying a list of products:

The list of products in a shop will be displayed to the user in an individual `Shop` view. So this `Products` component is added to the `Shop` component and given the list of relevant products as props. The `searched` prop relays whether this list is a result of a product search, so appropriate messages can be rendered.

`mern-marketplace/client/shop/Shop.js`:

```
<Products products={this.state.products} searched={false}/></Card>
```

In the `Shop` component, we need to add a call to the `listByShop` fetch method on `componentDidMount` to retrieve the relevant products and set it to state.

```
mern-marketplace/client/shop/Shop.js:
```

```
    listByShop({
        shopId: this.match.params.shopId
      }).then((data)=>{
        if (data.error) {
          this.setState({error: data.error})
        } else {
          this.setState({products: data})
        }
    })
```

In the `Products` component, if the product lists sent in the props contains products, the list is iterated over and the relevant details of each product are rendered in a Material-UI `GridListTile`, with a link to the individual product view and an `AddToCart` component (implementation for which is discussed in Chapter 7, *Extending the Marketplace for Orders and Payments*).

```
mern-marketplace/client/product/Products.js:
```

```
  {this.props.products.length > 0 ?
     (<div><GridList cellHeight={200} cols={3}>
        {this.props.products.map((product, i) => (
          <GridListTile key={i}>
            <Link to={"/product/"+product._id}>
              <img src={'/api/product/image/'+product._id}
            alt= {product.name} />
            </Link>
            <GridListTileBar
              title={<Link to={"/product/"+product._id}>{product.name}
            </Link>}
              subtitle={<span>$ {product.price}</span>}
              actionIcon={<AddToCart item={tile}/>}
            />
          </GridListTile>
        ))}
     </GridList></div>) : this.props.searched &&
      (<Typography type="subheading" component="h4">
                        No products found! :(</Typography>) }
```

This `Products` component is used to render products in a shop, products by category, and products in search results.

MyProducts component for shop owners

In contrast to the `Products` component, the `MyProducts` component in `client/product/MyProducts.js` is only for displaying products to sellers so they can manage the products in each shop:

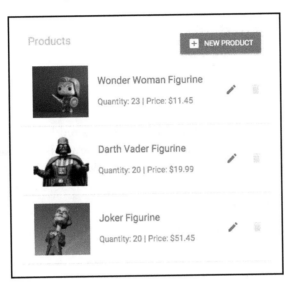

The `MyProducts` component is added to the `EditShop` view, so sellers can manage a shop and its contents in one place. It is provided the shop's ID in a prop, so relevant products can be fetched.

`mern-marketplace/client/shop/EditShop.js`:

```
<MyProducts shopId={this.match.params.shopId}/>
```

In `MyProducts`, the relevant products are first loaded in `componentDidMount`.

`mern-marketplace/client/product/MyProducts.js`:

```
componentDidMount = () => {
    this.loadProducts()
}
```

The `loadProducts` method uses the same `listByShop` fetch method to retrieve the products in the shop and sets it to state.

`mern-marketplace/client/product/MyProducts.js:`

```
loadProducts = () => {
    listByShop({
      shopId: this.props.shopId
    }).then((data)=>{
      if (data.error) {
        this.setState({error: data.error})
      } else {
        this.setState({products: data})
      }
    })
}
```

This list of products is iterated over and each product is rendered in `ListItem` along with an edit and delete option, similar to the `MyShops` list view. The edit button links to the Edit Product view. The `DeleteProduct` component handles the delete action, and reloads the list by calling an `onRemove` method passed from `MyProducts`, to update the state with the updated list of products for the current shop.

The `removeProduct` method, defined in `MyProducts`, is provided as the `onRemove` prop to the `DeleteProduct` component.

`mern-marketplace/client/product/MyProducts.js:`

```
removeProduct = (product) => {
    const updatedProducts = this.state.products
    const index = updatedProducts.indexOf(product)
    updatedProducts.splice(index, 1)
    this.setState({shops: updatedProducts})
}
...
<DeleteProduct
        product={product}
        shopId={this.props.shopId}
        onRemove={this.removeProduct}/>
```

List product suggestions

Visitors to MERN Marketplace will see product suggestions, such as the latest products added to the marketplace and products related to the product they are currently viewing.

Latest products

On the homepage of the MERN Marketplace, we will display five of the latest products added to the marketplace. To fetch the latest products, we will set up an API that will receive a GET request at /api/products/latest.

mern-marketplace/server/routes/product.routes.js:

```
router.route('/api/products/latest')
    .get(productCtrl.listLatest)
```

The listLatest controller method will sort the list of products in the database with the created date from newest to oldest and return the first five from the sorted list in the response.

mern-marketplace/server/controllers/product.controller.js:

```
const listLatest = (req, res) => {
  Product.find({}).sort('-created').limit(5).populate('shop', '_id
  name').exec((err, products) => {
    if (err) {
      return res.status(400).json({
        error: errorHandler.getErrorMessage(err)
      })
    }
    res.json(products)
  })
}
```

In the frontend, we will set up a corresponding fetch method in api-product.js for this latest products API, similar to the fetch for retrieving the list by shop. This retrieved list will then be rendered in the Suggestions component added to the homepage.

Related products

In each individual product view, we will show five related products as suggestions. To retrieve these related products, we will set up an API that accepts a request at /api/products/related.

mern-marketplace/server/routes/product.routes.js:

```
router.route('/api/products/related/:productId')
              .get(productCtrl.listRelated)
router.param('productId', productCtrl.productByID)
```

The `:productId` param in the route URL route will call the `productByID` controller method, which is similar to the `shopByID` controller method, and retrieves the product from the database and attaches it to the request object to be used in the `next` method.

`mern-marketplace/server/controllers/product.controller.js`:

```
const productByID = (req, res, next, id) => {
  Product.findById(id).populate('shop', '_id name').exec((err, product) =>
{
    if (err || !product)
      return res.status('400').json({
        error: "Product not found"
      })
    req.product = product
    next()
  })
}
```

The `listRelated` controller method queries the `Product` collection to find other products with the same category as the given product, excluding the given product, and returns the first five products in the resulting list.

`mern-marketplace/server/controllers/product.controller.js`:

```
const listRelated = (req, res) => {
  Product.find({ "_id": { "$ne": req.product },
              "category": req.product.category}).limit(5)
        .populate('shop', '_id name')
        .exec((err, products) => {
          if (err) {
            return res.status(400).json({
            error: errorHandler.getErrorMessage(err)
          })
        }
    res.json(products)
  })
}
```

In order to utilize this related-products API in the frontend, we will set up a corresponding fetch method in `api-product.js`. The fetch method will be called in the `Product` component with the product ID to populate the `Suggestions` component rendered in the product view.

Suggestions component

The `Suggestions` component will be rendered on the homepage and on an individual product page to show the latest products and related products, respectively:

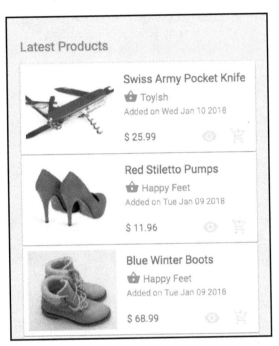

It will receive the relevant list of products from the parent component as props, along with a title for the list:

```
<Suggestions  products={this.state.suggestions}
title={this.state.suggestionTitle}/>
```

In the `Suggestions` component, the received list is iterated over and individual products rendered with relevant details, a link to the individual product page, and an `AddToCart` component.

`mern-marketplace/client/product/Suggestions.js:`

```
<Typography type="title"> {this.props.title} </Typography>
{this.props.products.map((item, i) => {
  return <span key={i}>
          <Card>
            <CardMedia image={'/api/product/image/'+item._id}
                       title={item.name}/>
```

```
<CardContent>
  <Link to={'/product/'+item._id}>
    <Typography type="title" component="h3">
    {item.name}</Typography>
  </Link>
  <Link to={'/shops/'+item.shop._id}>
    <Typography type="subheading">
        <Icon>shopping_basket</Icon> {item.shop.name}
    </Typography>
  </Link>
  <Typography component="p">
    Added on {(new
    Date(item.created)).toDateString()}
  </Typography>
</CardContent>
<Typography type="subheading" component="h3">$
{item.price}</Typography>
<Link to={'/product/'+item._id}>
  <IconButton color="secondary" dense="dense">
    <ViewIcon className={classes.iconButton}/>
  </IconButton>
</Link>
<AddToCart item={item}/>
      </Card>
    </span>})}
```

Display a product

Visitors to the MERN Marketplace will be able to browse each product with more details displayed in a separate view.

Read a product API

In the backend, we will add a GET route that queries the `Product` collection with an ID and returns the product in the response.

`mern-marketplace/server/routes/product.routes.js`:

```
router.route('/api/products/:productId')
    .get(productCtrl.read)
```

The `:productId` param invokes the `productByID` controller method, which retrieves the product from the database and appends it to the request object. The product in the request object is used by the `read` controller method to respond to the `read` request.

`mern-marketplace/server/controllers/product.controller.js`:

```
const read = (req, res) => {
  req.product.image = undefined
  return res.json(req.product)
}
```

In `api-product.js`, we will add a fetch method to use this read API in the frontend.

`mern-marketplace/client/product/api-product.js`:

```
const read = (params) => {
  return fetch('/api/products/' + params.productId, {
    method: 'GET'
  }).then((response) => {
    return response.json()
  }).catch((err) => console.log(err))
}
```

Product component

The `Product` component will render the product details, include an **add to cart** option, and also show a list of related products:

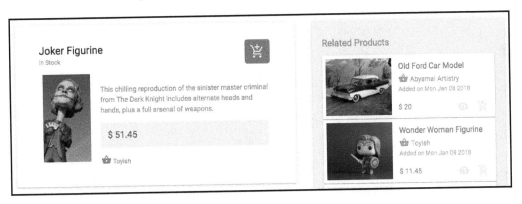

The `Product` component can be accessed in the browser at the `/product/:productID` route, which is defined in `MainRouter` as follows.

`mern-marketplace/client/MainRouter.js`:

```
<Route path="/product/:productId" component={Product}/>
```

The product details and the related list data will be fetched when the component mounts or will receive new props when the `productId` changes in the frontend route path after the user clicks on another product in the related list.

`mern-marketplace/client/product/Product.js`:

```
componentDidMount = () => {
  this.loadProduct(this.match.params.productId)
}
componentWillReceiveProps = (props) => {
  this.loadProduct(props.match.params.productId)
}
```

The `loadProduct` method calls the `read` and `listRelated` fetch methods to get the product and related list data, then sets the data to state.

`mern-marketplace/client/product/Product.js`:

```
loadProduct = (productId) => {
    read({productId: productId}).then((data) => {
      if (data.error) {
        this.setState({error: data.error})
      } else {
        this.setState({product: data})
        listRelated({
          productId: data._id}).then((data) => {
          if (data.error) {
            console.log(data.error)
          } else {
            this.setState({suggestions: data})
          }
        })
      }
    })
}
```

The product details part of the component displays relevant information about the product and an `AddToCart` component in a Material-UI `Card` component.

`mern-marketplace/client/product/Product.js`:

```
<Card>
  <CardHeader
    action={<AddToCart cartStyle={classes.addCart}
    item= {this.state.product}/>}
    title={this.state.product.name}
    subheader={this.state.product.quantity > 0? 'In Stock': 'Out of
```

```
  Stock'}
  />
  <CardMedia image={imageUrl} title={this.state.product.name}/>
  <Typography component="p" type="subheading">
    {this.state.product.description}<br/>
    $ {this.state.product.price}
    <Link to={'/shops/'+this.state.product.shop._id}>
      <Icon>shopping_basket</Icon> {this.state.product.shop.name}
    </Link>
  </Typography>
</Card>
...
<Suggestions  products={this.state.suggestions} title='Related Products'/>
```

The `Suggestions` component is added in the Product view with the related list data
passed as a prop.

Edit and delete a product

Implementations to edit and delete products in the application are similar to editing and
deleting shops, as covered in previous sections. These functionalities will require
corresponding APIs in the backend, fetch methods in the frontend, and React component
views with forms and actions.

Edit

The edit functionality is very similar to create product and the `EditProduct` form
component is also only accessible by verified sellers at
`/seller/:shopId/:productId/edit`.

`mern-marketplace/client/MainRouter.js`:

```
<PrivateRoute path="/seller/:shopId/:productId/edit"
component={EditProduct}/>
```

The `EditProduct` component contains the same form as `NewProduct` with populated
values of the product retrieved using the read product API, and it uses a fetch method to
send multipart form data with a PUT request to the edit product API in the backend at
`/api/products/by/:shopId`.

```
mern-marketplace/server/routes/product.routes.js:
```

```
router.route('/api/product/:shopId/:productId')
      .put(authCtrl.requireSignin, shopCtrl.isOwner, productCtrl.update)
```

The `update` controller is similar to the product `create` method and shop `update` method; it handles the multipart form data using `formidable` and extends the product details to save the updates.

Delete

The `DeleteProduct` component is added to the `MyProducts` component for each product in the list, as discussed earlier. It takes the `product` object, `shopID`, and a `loadProducts` method as a prop from `MyProducts`. The component is similar to `DeleteShop`, and when the delete intent is confirmed by the user, it calls the fetch method for delete, which makes the DELETE request to the server at `/api/product/:shopId/:productId`.

```
mern-marketplace/server/routes/product.routes.js:
```

```
router.route('/api/product/:shopId/:productId')
      .delete(authCtrl.requireSignin, shopCtrl.isOwner, productCtrl.remove)
```

Product search with category

In MERN Marketplace, visitors will be able to search for specific products by name and also in a specific category.

Categories API

To allow users to select a specific category to search in, we will set up an API that retrieves all the distinct categories present in the `Product` collection in the database. A GET request to `/api/products/categories` will return an array of unique categories.

```
mern-marketplace/server/routes/product.routes.js:
```

```
router.route('/api/products/categories')
      .get(productCtrl.listCategories)
```

The `listCategories` controller method queries the `Product` collection with a `distinct` call against the `category` field.

mern-marketplace/server/controllers/product.controller.js:

```
const listCategories = (req, res) => {
  Product.distinct('category',{},(err, products) => {
    if (err) {
      return res.status(400).json({
        error: errorHandler.getErrorMessage(err)
      })
    }
    res.json(products)
  })
}
```

This categories API can be used in the frontend with a corresponding fetch method to retrieve the array of distinct categories and display in the view.

Search products API

The search products API will take a GET request at `/api/products?search=value&category=value`, with query parameters in the URL to query the `Product` collection with provided search text and category values.

mern-marketplace/server/routes/product.routes.js:

```
router.route('/api/products')
    .get(productCtrl.list)
```

The `list` controller method will first process the query parameters in the request, then find products in the given category, if any, with names that partially match with the provided search text.

mern-marketplace/server/controllers/product.controller.js:

```
const list = (req, res) => {
  const query = {}
  if(req.query.search)
    query.name = {'$regex': req.query.search, '$options': "i"}
  if(req.query.category && req.query.category != 'All')
    query.category = req.query.category
  Product.find(query, (err, products) => {
    if (err) {
      return res.status(400).json({
```

```
    error: errorHandler.getErrorMessage(err)
  })
}
res.json(products)
}).populate('shop', '_id name').select('-image')
}
```

Fetch search results for the view

To utilize this search API in the frontend, we will set up a method that constructs the URL with query parameters and calls a fetch to the API.

`mern-marketplace/client/product/api-product.js`:

```
import queryString from 'query-string'
const list = (params) => {
  const query = queryString.stringify(params)
  return fetch('/api/products?'+query, {
    method: 'GET',
  }).then(response => {
    return response.json()
  }).catch((err) => console.log(err))
}
```

In order to construct the query parameters in the correct format, we will use the `query-string` npm module, which will help stringify the params object into a query string that can be attached to the request route.

Search component

The first use case for applying the categories API and search API is the `Search` component:

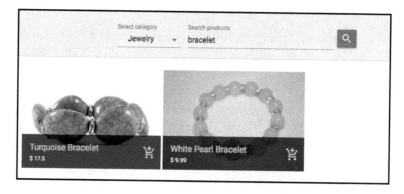

The `Search` component provides the user with a simple form containing a search `input` text field and a dropdown of the category options received from a parent component that will retrieve the list using the distinct categories API.

`mern-marketplace/client/product/Search.js`:

```
<TextField id="select-category" select label="Select category"
value={this.state.category}
    onChange={this.handleChange('category')}
    SelectProps={{ MenuProps: { className: classes.menu, } }}>
  <MenuItem value="All"> All </MenuItem>
  {this.props.categories.map(option => (
    <MenuItem key={option} value={option}> {option} </MenuItem>
      ))}
</TextField>
<TextField id="search" label="Search products" type="search"
onKeyDown={this.enterKey}
    onChange={this.handleChange('search')}
/>
<Button raised onClick={this.search}> Search </Button>
<Products products={this.state.results} searched={this.state.searched}/>
```

Once the user enters a search text and hits *Enter,* a call is made to the search API to retrieve the results.

`mern-marketplace/client/product/Search.js`:

```
search = () => {
    if(this.state.search){
      list({
        search: this.state.search || undefined, category:
      this.state.category
      }).then((data) => {
        if (data.error) {
          console.log(data.error)
        } else {
          this.setState({results: data, searched:true})
        }
      })
    }
  }
```

Then the results array is passed as a prop to the `Products` component to render the matching products below the search form.

Categories component

The Categories component is the second use case for the distinct categories and search APIs. For this component, we first fetch the list of categories in a parent component and send it as props to display the categories to the user:

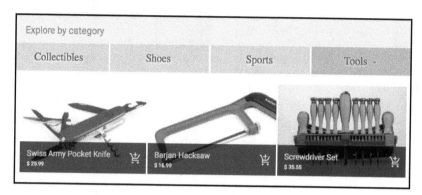

When the user selects a category in the displayed list, a call is made to the Search API with just a category value, and the backend returns all the products in the selected category. The returned products are then rendered in a Products component.

In this first version of the MERN Marketplace, users can become sellers to create shops and add products, and visitors can browse shops and search for products, while the application also suggests products to the visitor.

Summary

In this chapter, we started building an online marketplace application using the MERN stack. The MERN skeleton was extended to add a seller role to users, so they can create shops and add products to each shop intended for selling to other users. We also explored how to utilize the stack to implement features such as product browsing, searching, and suggestions for regular users who are interesting in buying. But a marketplace application is incomplete without a shopping cart for checkout, order management, and payments processing.

In the next chapter, we will grow our application to add these features and learn more about how the MERN stack can be used to implement these core aspects of an e-commerce application.

7
Extending the Marketplace for Orders and Payments

Processing payments from customers when they place orders and allowing sellers to manage these orders are key aspects of e-commerce applications. In this chapter, we'll extend the online marketplace built in the previous chapter by introducing the following capabilities:

- Shopping cart
- Payment processing with Stripe
- Order management

The MERN Marketplace with a cart, payments, and orders

The MERN Marketplace application developed in Chapter 6, *Exercising New MERN Skills with an Online Marketplace* will be extended to include a shopping cart feature, Stripe integration for processing credit card payments, and a basic order-management flow. The implementations that follow are kept simple to serve as starting points for developing more complex versions of these features.

The following component-tree diagram shows all the custom components that make up the MERN Marketplace frontend. The features discussed in this chapter modify some of the existing components, such as `Profile`, `MyShops`, `Products`, and `Suggestions`, and also add new components, such as `AddToCart`, `MyOrders`, `Cart`, and `ShopOrders`:

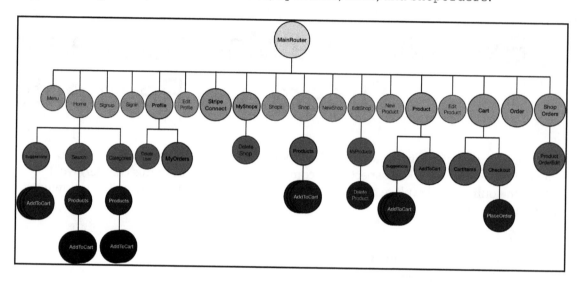

The code for the complete MERN Marketplace application is available on GitHub `github.com/shamahoque/mern-marketplace`. You can clone this code and run the application as you go through the code explanations in the rest of this chapter. To get the code for Stripe payments working, you will need to create your own Stripe account and update the `config/config.js` file with your testing values for the Stripe API key, secret key, and Stripe Connect client ID.

Shopping cart

Visitors to the MERN Marketplace can add products they wish to buy to a shopping cart by clicking the `add to cart` button on each product. A cart icon in the menu will indicate the number of products already added to their cart as the user continues to browse through the marketplace. They can also update the cart contents and begin the checkout by opening the cart view. But to complete checkout and place an order, users will be required to sign in.

The shopping cart is mainly a frontend feature, so the cart details will be stored locally on the client side until the user places the order at checkout. To implement the shopping cart features, we will set up helper methods in `client/cart/cart-helper.js` to help manipulate the cart details with relevant React components.

Adding to cart

The `AddToCart` component in `client/Cart/AddToCart.js` takes a `product` object and a CSS styles object as props from the parent component it is added to. For example, in MERN Marketplace, it is added to a Product view as follows:

```
<AddToCart cartStyle={classes.addCart} item={this.state.product}/>
```

The `AddToCart` component itself displays a cart icon button depending on whether the passed item is in stock or not:

For example, if the item quantity is more than 0, the `AddCartIcon` is displayed, otherwise the `DisabledCartIcon` is rendered.

`mern-marketplace/client/cart/AddToCart.js`:

```
{this.props.item.quantity >= 0 ?
    <IconButton color="accent" dense="dense" onClick={this.addToCart}>
      <AddCartIcon className={this.props.cartStyle ||
    classes.iconButton}/>
    </IconButton> :
    <IconButton disabled={true} color="accent" dense="dense"
      <DisabledCartIcon className={this.props.cartStyle ||
    classes.disabledIconButton}/>
    </IconButton>}
```

The `AddCartIcon` button calls an `addToCart` method when clicked.

`mern-marketplace/client/cart/AddToCart.js`:

```
addToCart = () => {
    cart.addItem(this.props.item, () => {
      this.setState({redirect:true})
    })
}
```

The `addItem` helper method defined in `cart-helper.js`, takes the `product` item and the state-updating `callback` function as parameters, then stores the updated cart details in `localStorage` and executes the callback passed.

`mern-marketplace/client/cart/cart-helper.js`:

```
addItem(item, cb) {
    let cart = []
    if (typeof window !== "undefined") {
      if (localStorage.getItem('cart')) {
        cart = JSON.parse(localStorage.getItem('cart'))
      }
      cart.push({
        product: item,
        quantity: 1,
        shop: item.shop._id
      })
      localStorage.setItem('cart', JSON.stringify(cart))
      cb()
    }
}
```

The cart data stored in `localStorage` contains an array of cart item objects, each containing product details, the quantity of the product added to cart (which is set to 1 by default), and the ID of the shop the product belongs to.

Cart icon on the menu

In the menu, we will add a link to the Cart view, and also add a badge that displays the length of the cart array stored in `localStorage`, in order to visually inform the user of how many items are currently in their cart:

The link for the cart will be similar to the other links in the Menu, with the exception of the Material-UI `Badge` component that displays the cart length.

`mern-marketplace/client/core/Menu.js`:

```
<Link to="/cart">
    <Button color={isActive(history, "/cart")}>
        Cart
        <Badge color="accent" badgeContent={cart.itemTotal()} >
            <CartIcon />
        </Badge>
    </Button>
</Link>
```

The cart length is returned by the `itemTotal` helper method in `cart-helper.js`, which reads the cart array stored in `localStorage` and returns the length of the array.

`mern-marketplace/client/cart/cart-helper.js`:

```
itemTotal() {
    if (typeof window !== "undefined") {
      if (localStorage.getItem('cart')) {
         return JSON.parse(localStorage.getItem('cart')).length
      }
    }
    return 0
}
```

Cart view

The Cart view will contain the cart items and checkout details, but initially only the cart details will be displayed until the user is ready to check out.

`mern-marketplace/client/cart/Cart.js`:

```
<Grid container spacing={24}>
    <Grid item xs={6} sm={6}>
        <CartItems checkout={this.state.checkout}
            setCheckout={this.setCheckout}/>
    </Grid>
  {this.state.checkout &&
    <Grid item xs={6} sm={6}>
      <Checkout/>
    </Grid>}
</Grid>
```

The `CartItems` component is passed a `checkout` Boolean value, and a state update method for this checkout value, so that the `Checkout` component and options can be rendered based on user interaction.

`mern-marketplace/client/cart/Cart.js`:

```
setCheckout = val =>{
    this.setState({checkout: val})
}
```

The `Cart` component will be accessed at the `/cart` route, so we need to add a `Route` to the `MainRouter` component as follows.

`mern-marketplace/client/MainRouter.js`:

```
<Route path="/cart" component={Cart}/>
```

The CartItems component

The `CartItems` component will allow the user to view and update the items currently in their cart. It will also give them the option to start the checkout process if they are signed in:

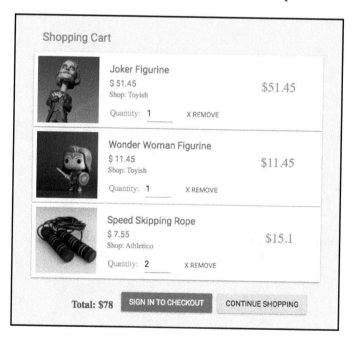

If the cart contains items, the `CartItems` component iterates over the items and renders the products in the cart. It there are no items added, the cart view just displays a message that the cart is empty.

mern-marketplace/client/cart/CartItems.js:

```
{this.state.cartItems.length > 0 ? <span>
      {this.state.cartItems.map((item, i) => {
         ...
            ... Product details
            ... Edit quantity
            ... Remove product option
         ...
      })
   }
   ... Show total price and Checkout options ...
   </span> :
   <Typography type="subheading" component="h3" color="primary">
      No items added to your cart.
   </Typography>
}
```

Each product item shows the details of the product and an editable quantity text field, along with a remove item option. Finally, it shows the total price of the items in the cart and the option to start checkout.

Retrieving cart details

The `getCart` helper method in `cart-helper.js` retrieves and returns the cart details from `localStorage`.

mern-marketplace/client/cart/cart-helper.js:

```
getCart() {
    if (typeof window !== "undefined") {
      if (localStorage.getItem('cart')) {
        return JSON.parse(localStorage.getItem('cart'))
      }
    }
    return []
}
```

In the `CartItems` component, we will retrieve the cart items using the `getCart` helper method in `componentDidMount` and set it to state.

`mern-marketplace/client/cart/CartItems.js`:

```
componentDidMount = () => {
    this.setState({cartItems: cart.getCart()})
}
```

Then the `cartItems` array retrieved from `localStorage` is iterated over using the `map` function to render the details of each item.

`mern-marketplace/client/cart/CartItems.js`:

```
<span key={i}>
  <Card>
    <CardMedia image={'/api/product/image/'+item.product._id}
          title={item.product.name}/>
        <CardContent>
                <Link to={'/product/'+item.product._id}>
                    <Typography type="title" component="h3"
                    color="primary">
                      {item.product.name}</Typography>
                </Link>
                <Typography type="subheading" component="h3"
                color="primary">
                    $ {item.product.price}
                </Typography>
                <span>${item.product.price * item.quantity}</span>
                <span>Shop: {item.product.shop.name}</span>
        </CardContent>
        <div>
         ... Editable quantity ...
         ... Remove item option ...
        </div>
  </Card>
  <Divider/>
</span>
```

Modifying quantity

The editable quantity `TextField` rendered for each cart item allows the user to update the quantity for each product they are buying, and sets a minimum allowed value of 1.

`mern-marketplace/client/cart/CartItems.js:`

```
Quantity: <TextField
            value={item.quantity}
            onChange={this.handleChange(i)}
            type="number"
            inputProps={{ min:1 }}
            InputLabelProps={{
              shrink: true,
            }}
         />
```

When the user updates this value, the `handleChange` method is called to enforce the minimum value validation, update the `cartItems` in state, and update the cart in `localStorage` using the helper method.

`mern-marketplace/client/cart/CartItems.js:`

```
handleChange = index => event => {
    let cartItems = this.state.cartItems
    if(event.target.value == 0){
      cartItems[index].quantity = 1
    }else{
      cartItems[index].quantity = event.target.value
    }
    this.setState({cartItems: cartItems})
    cart.updateCart(index, event.target.value)
}
```

The `updateCart` helper method takes the index of the product being updated in the cart array and the new quantity value as parameters, and updates the details stored in `localStorage`.

`mern-marketplace/client/cart/cart-helper.js:`

```
updateCart(itemIndex, quantity) {
    let cart = []
    if (typeof window !== "undefined") {
      if (localStorage.getItem('cart')) {
        cart = JSON.parse(localStorage.getItem('cart'))
      }
      cart[itemIndex].quantity = quantity
      localStorage.setItem('cart', JSON.stringify(cart))
    }
}
```

Removing item

The remove item option rendered for each item in the cart is a button, which, when clicked, passes the array index of the item to the `removeItem` method so that it can be removed from the array.

mern-marketplace/client/cart/CartItems.js:

```
<Button color="primary" onClick={this.removeItem(i)}>x Remove</Button>
```

The `removeItem` click handler method uses the `removeItem` helper method to remove the item from the cart in `localStorage`, then updates the `cartItems` in state. This method also checks whether the cart has been emptied, so checkout can be hidden by using the `setCheckout` function passed as a prop from the `Cart` component.

mern-marketplace/client/cart/CartItems.js:

```
removeItem = index => event =>{
    let cartItems = cart.removeItem(index)
    if(cartItems.length == 0){
      this.props.setCheckout(false)
    }
    this.setState({cartItems: cartItems})
}
```

The `removeItem` helper method in `cart-helper.js` takes the index of the product to be removed from the array, then splices it out, and updates the `localStorage` before returning the updated `cart` array.

mern-marketplace/client/cart/cart-helper.js:

```
removeItem(itemIndex) {
    let cart = []
    if (typeof window !== "undefined") {
      if (localStorage.getItem('cart')) {
        cart = JSON.parse(localStorage.getItem('cart'))
      }
      cart.splice(itemIndex, 1)
      localStorage.setItem('cart', JSON.stringify(cart))
    }
    return cart
}
```

Showing total price

At the bottom of the `CartItems` component, we will display the total price of the items in the cart.

mern-marketplace/client/cart/CartItems.js:

```
<span className={classes.total}>Total: ${this.getTotal()}</span>
```

The `getTotal` method will calculate the total price taking into consideration the unit price and quantity of each item in the `cartItems` array.

mern-marketplace/client/cart/CartItems.js:

```
getTotal(){
    return this.state.cartItems.reduce( function(a, b){
        return a + (b.quantity*b.product.price)
    }, 0)
}
```

Option to check out

The user will see the option to perform the checkout depending on whether they are signed in and whether the checkout has already been opened.

mern-marketplace/client/cart/CartItems.js:

```
{!this.props.checkout && (auth.isAuthenticated() ?
    <Button onClick={this.openCheckout}>
        Checkout
    </Button> :
    <Link to="/signin">
        <Button>Sign in to checkout</Button>
    </Link>)
}
```

When the checkout button is clicked, the `openCheckout` method will use the `setCheckout` method passed as a prop to set the checkout value to `true` in the `Cart` component:

```
openCheckout = () => {
    this.props.setCheckout(true)
}
```

Once the checkout value is set to `true` in the Cart view, the `Checkout` component will be rendered to allow the user to enter the checkout details and place an order.

Using Stripe for payments

Payment processing is required across implementations of the checkout, order creation, and order management processes. It also involves updates to both the buyer's and seller's user data. Before we delve into the implementations of the checkout and order features, we will briefly discuss payment processing options and considerations using Stripe, and see how it is to be integrated in MERN Marketplace.

Stripe

Stripe provides an extensive set of tools necessary to integrate payments in any web application. These tools can be selected and used in different ways depending on the specific type of the application and the payment use case being implemented.

In case of the MERN Marketplace setup, the application itself will have a platform on Stripe and will expect sellers to have connected Stripe accounts on the platform, so the application can charge users who enter their credit card details at checkout on behalf of the sellers. In MERN Marketplace, a user can add products from different shops to their shopping cart, so charges on their cards will only be created by the application for the specific product ordered when it is processed by the seller. Additionally, sellers will have complete control over the charges created on their behalf from their own Stripe dashboards. We will demonstrate how to use the tools provided by Stripe to get this payment setup working.

Stripe provides a complete set of documentations and guidelines for each tool, and also exposes testing data for accounts and platforms set up on Stripe. For the purpose of implementing payments in MERN Marketplace, we will be using testing keys and leave it up to you to extend the implementation for live payments.

Stripe-connected account for each seller

In order to create charges on behalf of sellers, the application will let a user, who is a seller, connect their Stripe account to their MERN Marketplace user account.

Updating user model

To store the Stripe OAuth credentials after a user's Stripe account is successfully connected, we will update the user model with the following field.

`mern-marketplace/server/models/user.model.js`:

```
stripe_seller: {}
```

The `stripe_seller` field will store the seller's Stripe account credential, and this will be used when a charge needs to be processed via Stripe for a product they sold from their shop.

Button to connect with Stripe

In the user profile page of a seller, if the user has not connected their Stripe account yet, we will show a button that will take the user to Stripe to authenticate and connect their Stripe account:

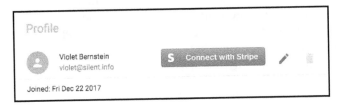

If the user has successfully connected their Stripe account already, we will show a disabled **STRIPE CONNECTED** button instead:

The code added to the `Profile` component will first check whether the user is a seller before rendering any STRIPE CONNECTED button. Then, a second check will confirm whether Stripe credentials already exist in the `stripe_seller` field for the given user. If Stripe credentials already exist for the user, then the disabled STRIPE CONNECTED button is shown, otherwise a link to connect to Stripe using their OAuth link is displayed instead.

`mern-marketplace/client/user/Profile.js:`

```
{this.state.user.seller &&
    (this.state.user.stripe_seller ?
        (<Button variant="raised" disabled>
            Stripe connected
        </Button>) :
        (<a
href={"https://connect.stripe.com/oauth/authorize?response_type=code&client
_id="+config.stripe_connect_test_client_id+"&scope=read_write"}}>
            <img src={stripeButton}/>
        </a>)
    )}
```

The OAuth link takes the platform's client ID, which we will set in a `config` variable, and other option values as query parameters. This link takes the user to Stripe and allows the user to connect an existing Stripe account or create a new one. Then once Stripe's auth process completes, it returns to our application using a Redirect URL set in the Platform's Connect settings in the dashboard on Stripe. Stripe attaches either an auth code or error message as query parameters to the Redirect URL.

The MERN Marketplace redirect URI is set at `/seller/stripe/connect`, which will render the `StripeConnect` component.

`mern-marketplace/client/MainRouter.js:`

```
<Route path="/seller/stripe/connect" component={StripeConnect}/>
```

The StripeConnect component

The `StripeConnect` component will basically complete the remaining auth process steps with Stripe, and render relevant messages based on whether the Stripe connection was successful:

Connect your Stripe Account

Your Stripe account successfully connected!

When the `StripeConnect` component loads, in `componentDidMount`, we will first parse the query parameters attached to the URL from the Stripe redirect. For parsing, we use the same `query-string` npm module that we used previously for the product search. Then, if the URL `query` parameter contains an auth code, we make an API call necessary to complete the Stripe OAuth from our server.

`mern-marketplace/client/user/StripeConnect.js`:

```
componentDidMount = () => {
  const parsed = queryString.parse(this.props.location.search)
  if(parsed.error){
    this.setState({error: true})
  }
  if(parsed.code){
    this.setState({connecting: true, error: false})
    const jwt = auth.isAuthenticated()
    stripeUpdate({
      userId: jwt.user._id
    }, {
      t: jwt.token
    }, parsed.code).then((data) => {
      if (data.error) {
        this.setState({error: true, connected: false,
        connecting:false})
      } else {
        this.setState({connected: true, connecting: false,
        error:false})
      }
    })
  }
}
```

The `stripeUpdate` fetch method is defined in `api-user.js`, and it passes the auth code retrieved from Stripe to an API we will set up in our server at `'/api/stripe_auth/:userId'`.

`mern-marketplace/client/user/api-user.js`:

```
const stripeUpdate = (params, credentials, auth_code) => {
  return fetch('/api/stripe_auth/'+params.userId, {
    method: 'PUT',
    headers: {
      'Accept': 'application/json',
      'Content-Type': 'application/json',
      'Authorization': 'Bearer ' + credentials.t
    },
```

```
    body: JSON.stringify({stripe: auth_code})
  }).then((response)=> {
    return response.json()
  }).catch((err) => {
    console.log(err)
  })
}
```

Stripe auth update API

Once the Stripe account connection is successful, in order to complete the OAuth process, we need to use the retrieved auth code to make a POST API call to Stripe OAuth from our server and retrieve the credentials to be stored in the seller's user account for processing charges. The Stripe auth update API receives a request at /api/stripe_auth/:userId and initiates the POST API call to retrieve the credentials from Stripe.

The route for this Stripe auth update API will be declared on the server in user routes as follows.

mern-marketplace/server/routes/user.routes.js:

```
router.route('/api/stripe_auth/:userId')
  .put(authCtrl.requireSignin, authCtrl.hasAuthorization,
    userCtrl.stripe_auth, userCtrl.update)
```

A request to this route uses the stripe_auth controller method to retrieve the credentials from Stripe and passes it to the existing user update method to be stored in the database.

In order to make a POST request to the Stripe API from our server, we will use the request npm module:

npm install request --save

The stripe_auth controller method in the user controller will be as follows.

mern-marketplace/server/controllers/user.controller.js:

```
const stripe_auth = (req, res, next) => {
  request({
    url: "https://connect.stripe.com/oauth/token",
    method: "POST",
    json: true,
    body:
    {client_secret:config.stripe_test_secret_key,code:req.body.stripe,
    grant_type:'authorization_code'}
```

```
    }, (error, response, body) => {
      if(body.error){
        return res.status('400').json({
          error: body.error_description
        })
      }
      req.body.stripe_seller = body
      next()
    })
  }
```

The POST API call to Stripe takes the platform's secret key and the retrieved auth code to complete the authorization and returns the credentials for the connected account, which is then appended to the request body so the user can be updated in the next() method.

With these credentials, the application can create charges on customer credit cards on behalf of the seller.

Stripe Card Elements for checkout

During checkout, to collect credit card details from the user, we will use Stripe's Card Elements to add the credit card field in the checkout form. To integrate the Card Elements with our React interface, we will utilize the react-stripe-elements npm module:

```
npm install --save react-stripe-elements
```

We will also need to inject the Stripe.js code in template.js to access Stripe in the frontend code:

```
<script id="stripe-js" src="https://js.stripe.com/v3/" async></script>
```

For MERN Marketplace, Stripe will only be required in the Cart view, where the Checkout component needs it to render the Card Elements and process card detail input. Hence, we will initialize the Stripe instance with the application's Stripe API key, after the Cart component mounts, in its componentDidMount.

mern-marketplace/client/cart/Cart.js:

```
componentDidMount = () => {
    if (window.Stripe) {
      this.setState({stripe:
      window.Stripe(config.stripe_test_api_key)})
    } else {
```

```
        document.querySelector('#stripe-js')
        .addEventListener('load', ()
        => {
           this.setState({stripe:
        window.Stripe(config.stripe_test_api_key)})
         })
       }
   }
```

The `Checkout` component added in `Cart.js` should be wrapped with the `StripeProvider` component from `react-stripe-elements`, so the `Elements` in `Checkout` have access to the Stripe instance.

`mern-marketplace/client/cart/Cart.js`:

```
<StripeProvider stripe={this.state.stripe}>
    <Checkout/>
</StripeProvider>
```

Then, within the `Checkout` component, we will use Stripe's `Elements` components. Using Stripe's `Card Elements` will enable the application to collect the user's credit card details and use the Stripe instance to tokenize card information rather than handling it on our own servers. Implementation for this part of collecting the card details and generating the card token during the checkout process will be discussed in the *Checkout* and *Creating new order* sections.

Stripe Customer to record card details

When an order is being placed at the end of the checkout process, the generated card token will be used to create or update a Stripe Customer (https://stripe.com/docs/api#customers) representing our user, which is a good way to store credit card information (https://stripe.com/docs/saving-cards) with Stripe for further usage, such as creating charges for specific products in the cart only when a seller processes the ordered product from their shop. This eliminates the complications of having to store user credit card details securely on your own server.

Updating user model

To keep track of the corresponding Stripe `Customer` information for a user in our database, we will update the user model with the following field:

```
stripe_customer: {},
```

Updating user controller

We will create a new, or update an existing, Stripe Customer when the user places an order after entering their credit card details. To implement this, we will update the user controllers with a `stripeCustomer` method that will be called before the order is created when our server receives a request to the create order API (discussed in the *Creating new order* section).

In the `stripeCustomer` controller method, we will need to use the `stripe` npm module:

```
npm install stripe --save
```

After installing the `stripe` module, it needs to be imported into the user controller file and the `stripe` instance initialized with the application's Stripe secret key.

mern-marketplace/server/controllers/user.controller.js:

```
import stripe from 'stripe'
const myStripe = stripe(config.stripe_test_secret_key)
```

The `stripeCustomer` controller method will first check whether the current user already has a corresponding Stripe Customer stored in the database, and then use the card token received from the frontend to either create a new Stripe Customer or update the existing one.

Creating a new Stripe Customer

If the current user does not have a corresponding Stripe `Customer`, in other words, a value is not stored for the `stripe_customer` field, we will use the create a Customer API (https://stripe.com/docs/api#create_customer) from Stripe.

mern-marketplace/server/controllers/user.controller.js:

```
myStripe.customers.create({
        email: req.profile.email,
        source: req.body.token
    }).then((customer) => {
        User.update({'_id':req.profile._id},
          {'$set': { 'stripe_customer': customer.id }},
          (err, order) => {
            if (err) {
              return res.status(400).send({
                error: errorHandler.getErrorMessage(err)
              })
            }
```

```
                    req.body.order.payment_id = customer.id
                    next()
                })
        })
```

If the Stripe Customer is successfully created, we will update the current user's data by storing the Stripe Customer ID reference in the `stripe_customer` field. We will also add this Customer ID to the order being placed, so it is simpler to create a charge related to the order.

Updating an existing Stripe Customer

For an existing Stripe Customer, in other words, the current user has a value stored for the `stripe_customer` field, we will use the Stripe API to update a Stripe Customer.

`mern-marketplace/server/controllers/user.controller.js`:

```
myStripe.customers.update(req.profile.stripe_customer, {
    source: req.body.token
},
    (err, customer) => {
      if(err){
        return res.status(400).send({
          error: "Could not update charge details"
        })
      }
      req.body.order.payment_id = customer.id
      next()
    })
```

Once the Stripe Customer is successfully updated, we will add the Customer ID to the order being created in the `next()` call.

Though not covered here, the Stripe Customer feature can be used further to allow users to store and update their credit card information from the application.

Creating a charge for each product processed

When a seller updates an order by processing the product ordered in their shop, the application will create a charge on behalf of the seller on the Customer's credit card for the cost of the product ordered. To implement this, we will update the `user.controller.js` file, with a `createCharge` controller method that will use Stripe's create a charge API, and need the seller's Stripe account ID along with the buyer's Stripe Customer ID.

`mern-marketplace/server/controllers/user.controller.js:`

```
const createCharge = (req, res, next) => {
  if(!req.profile.stripe_seller){
    return res.status('400').json({
      error: "Please connect your Stripe account"
    })
  }
  myStripe.tokens.create({
    customer: req.order.payment_id,
  }, {
    stripe_account: req.profile.stripe_seller.stripe_user_id,
  }).then((token) => {
      myStripe.charges.create({
        amount: req.body.amount * 100, //amount in cents
        currency: "usd",
        source: token.id,
      }, {
        stripe_account: req.profile.stripe_seller.stripe_user_id,
      }).then((charge) => {
        next()
      })
  })
}
```

If the seller has not connected their Stripe account yet, the `createCharge` method will return a 400 error response to indicate that a connected Stripe account is required.

To be able to charge the Stripe Customer on behalf of the seller's Stripe account, we first need to generate a Stripe token with the Customer ID and the seller's Stripe account ID, and then use that token to create a charge.

The `createCharge` controller method will be called when the server receives a request to update an order with a product status change to **Processing** (the API implementation for this order update request will be discussed in the *Orders by shop* section).

This covers all the Stripe-related concepts relevant to the implementation of payments processing for the specific use cases of MERN Marketplace. Now we will move on to allowing a user to complete checkout and place their order.

Checkout

Users who are signed in and have added items to the cart will be able to start the checkout process. The **Checkout** form will collect customer details, delivery address information, and credit card information:

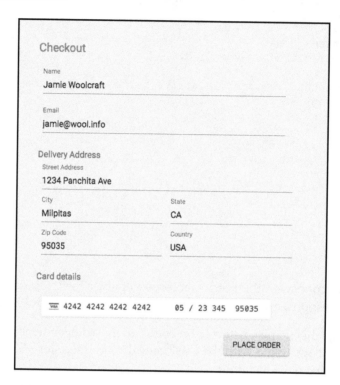

Initializing checkout details

In the `Checkout` component, we will initialize the `checkoutDetails` object in state before collecting the details from the form.

`mern-marketplace/client/cart/Checkout.js`:

```
state = {
    checkoutDetails: {customer_name: '', customer_email:'',
                    delivery_address: {street: '', city: '', state:
                        '', zipcode: '', country:''}},
    }
```

After the component mounts, we will prepopulate the customer details based on the current user's details and also add the current cart items to `checkoutDetails`.

`mern-marketplace/client/cart/Checkout.js`:

```
componentDidMount = () => {
    let user = auth.isAuthenticated().user
    let checkoutDetails = this.state.checkoutDetails
    checkoutDetails.products = cart.getCart()
    checkoutDetails.customer_name = user.name
    checkoutDetails.customer_email = user.email
    this.setState({checkoutDetails: checkoutDetails})
}
```

Customer information

In the checkout form, we will add text fields to collect the customer name and email.

`mern-marketplace/client/cart/Checkout.js`:

```
<TextField id="name" label="Name"
value={this.state.checkoutDetails.customer_name}
onChange={this.handleCustomerChange('customer_name')}/>
<TextField id="email" type="email" label="Email"
value={this.state.checkoutDetails.customer_email}
onChange={this.handleCustomerChange('customer_email')}/><br/>
```

When the user updates the values, the `handleCustomerChange` method will update the relevant details in the state:

```
handleCustomerChange = name => event => {
    let checkoutDetails = this.state.checkoutDetails
    checkoutDetails[name] = event.target.value || undefined
    this.setState({checkoutDetails: checkoutDetails})
}
```

Delivery address

To collect the delivery address from the user, we will add the following text fields to the checkout form to collect street address, city, zip code, state, and country.

`mern-marketplace/client/cart/Checkout.js`:

```
<TextField id="street" label="Street Address"
value={this.state.checkoutDetails.delivery_address.street}
onChange={this.handleAddressChange('street')}/>
<TextField id="city" label="City"
value={this.state.checkoutDetails.delivery_address.city}
onChange={this.handleAddressChange('city')}/>
<TextField id="state" label="State"
value={this.state.checkoutDetails.delivery_address.state}
onChange={this.handleAddressChange('state')}/>
<TextField id="zipcode" label="Zip Code"
value={this.state.checkoutDetails.delivery_address.zipcode}
onChange={this.handleAddressChange('zipcode')}/>
<TextField id="country" label="Country"
value={this.state.checkoutDetails.delivery_address.country}
onChange={this.handleAddressChange('country')}/>
```

When the user updates these address fields, the `handleAddressChange` method will update the relevant details in the state.

`mern-marketplace/client/cart/Checkout.js`:

```
handleAddressChange = name => event => {
    let checkoutDetails = this.state.checkoutDetails
    checkoutDetails.delivery_address[name] = event.target.value ||
    undefined
    this.setState({checkoutDetails: checkoutDetails})
}
```

The PlaceOrder component

The credit card field will be added to the checkout form using Stripe's `CardElement` component from `react-stripe-elements`.

The `CardElement` component must be part of a payment form component that is built with the `injectStripe` **higher-order component** (**HOC**) and wrapped with the `Elements` component. So we will create a component called `PlaceOrder` with `injectStripe`, and it will contain Stripe's `CardElement` and the `PlaceOrder` button.

`mern-marketplace/client/cart/PlaceOrder.js`:

```
class PlaceOrder extends Component { ... }
export default injectStripe(withStyles(styles)(PlaceOrder))
```

Then we will add this `PlaceOrder` component in the Checkout form, pass it the `checkoutDetails` object as a prop, and wrap it with the `Elements` component from `react-stripe-elements`.

`mern-marketplace/client/cart/Checkout.js`:

```
<Elements> <PlaceOrder checkoutDetails={this.state.checkoutDetails} />
</Elements>
```

The `injectStripe` HOC provides the `this.props.stripe` property that manages the `Elements` groups. This will allow us to call `this.props.stripe.createToken` within `PlaceOrder` to submit card details to Stripe and get back the card token.

Stripe CardElement component

Stripe's `CardElement` is self-contained, so we can just add it to the `PlaceOrder` component, then add styles as desired, and the card detail input is taken care of.

`mern-marketplace/client/cart/PlaceOrder.js`:

```
<CardElement className={classes.StripeElement}
      {...{style: {
      base: {
        color: '#424770',
        letterSpacing: '0.025em',
        '::placeholder': {
          color: '#aab7c4',
        },
      },
      invalid: {
        color: '#9e2146',
      },
    }}}/>
```

Placing an order

The **Place Order** button is also placed in the `PlaceOrder` component after the `CardElement`.

`mern-marketplace/client/cart/PlaceOrder.js`:

```
<Button color="secondary" variant="raised" onClick={this.placeOrder}>Place
Order</Button>
```

Clicking on the **Place Order** button will call the `placeOrder` method, which will attempt to tokenize the card details using `stripe.createToken`. If unsuccessful, the user will be informed of the error, but if successful, then the checkout details and generated card token will be sent to our server's create order API (covered in the next section).

`mern-marketplace/client/cart/PlaceOrder.js`:

```
placeOrder = ()=>{
    this.props.stripe.createToken().then(payload => {
        if(payload.error){
          this.setState({error: payload.error.message})
        }else{
          const jwt = auth.isAuthenticated()
          create({userId:jwt.user._id}, {
            t: jwt.token
          }, this.props.checkoutDetails, payload.token.id).then((data) =>
          {
            if (data.error) {
              this.setState({error: data.error})
            } else {
              cart.emptyCart(()=> {
                this.setState({'orderId':data._id,'redirect': true})
              })
            }
          })
        }
    })
  }
```

The `create` fetch method that makes a POST request to the create order API in the backend is defined in `client/order/api-order.js`. It takes the checkout details, the card token, and user credentials as parameters and sends it to the API at `/api/orders/:userId`.

mern-marketplace/client/order/api-order.js:

```
const create = (params, credentials, order, token) => {
    return fetch('/api/orders/'+params.userId, {
        method: 'POST',
        headers: {
            'Accept': 'application/json',
            'Content-Type': 'application/json',
            'Authorization': 'Bearer ' + credentials.t
        },
        body: JSON.stringify({order: order, token:token})
    })
    .then((response) => {
        return response.json()
    }).catch((err) => console.log(err))
}
```

Empty cart

If the create order API is successful, we will empty the cart using an `emptyCart` helper method in `cart-helper.js`.

mern-marketplace/client/cart/cart-helper.js:

```
emptyCart(cb) {
    if(typeof window !== "undefined"){
        localStorage.removeItem('cart')
        cb()
    }
}
```

The `emptyCart` method removes the cart object from `localStorage`, and updates the state of the view by executing the callback passed.

Redirecting to Order view

With the order placed and the cart emptied, the user is redirected to the order view that will show them the details of the order just placed.

mern-marketplace/client/cart/PlaceOrder.js:

```
if (this.state.redirect) {
    return (<Redirect to={'/order/' + this.state.orderId}/>)
}
```

This will indicate that the checkout process has been completed with a successful call to the create order API that we will set up in the server to create and store orders in the database.

Creating new order

When a user places an order, the details of the order confirmed at checkout will be used to create a new order record in the database, update or create a Stripe Customer for the user, and decrease the stock quantities of products ordered.

Order model

To store the orders, we will define a Mongoose Schema for the order model that will record the customer details along with user account reference, delivery address information, payment reference, created and updated-at timestamps, and an array of ordered products where the structure of each product will be defined in a separate subschema called `CartItemSchema`.

Ordered by and for customer

To record the details of the customer who the order is meant for, we will add `customer_name` and `customer_email` fields to the `Order` schema.

`mern-marketplace/server/models/order.model.js`:

```
customer_name: { type: String,  trim: true, required: 'Name is required' },
customer_email: { type: String, trim: true,
    match: [/.+\@.+\..+/, 'Please fill a valid email address'],
    required: 'Email is required' }
```

To reference the signed-in user who placed the order, we will add an `ordered_by` field.

`mern-marketplace/server/models/order.model.js`:

```
ordered_by: {type: mongoose.Schema.ObjectId, ref: 'User'}
```

Delivery address

The delivery address information for the order will be stored in the delivery address subdocument with `street`, `city`, `state`, `zipcode`, and `country` fields.

`mern-marketplace/server/models/order.model.js`:

```
delivery_address: {
    street: {type: String, required: 'Street is required'},
    city: {type: String, required: 'City is required'},
    state: {type: String},
    zipcode: {type: String, required: 'Zip Code is required'},
    country: {type: String, required: 'Country is required'}
},
```

Payment reference

The payment information will be relevant when the order is updated and a charge needs to be created after an ordered product is processed by the seller. We will record the Stripe Customer ID relevant to the credit card details in a `payment_id` field in the `Order` schema.

`mern-marketplace/server/models/order.model.js`:

```
payment_id: {},
```

Products ordered

The main content of the order will be the list of products ordered along with details, such as quantity of each. We will record this list in a field called `products` in the `Order` schema. The structure of each product will be defined separately in `CartItemSchema`.

`mern-marketplace/server/models/order.model.js`:

```
products: [CartItemSchema],
```

The CartItem schema

The `CartItem` schema will represent each product ordered. It will contain a reference to the product, the quantity of the product ordered by the user, a reference to the shop the product belongs to, and a status.

`mern-marketplace/server/models/order.model.js:`

```
const CartItemSchema = new mongoose.Schema({
  product: {type: mongoose.Schema.ObjectId, ref: 'Product'},
  quantity: Number,
  shop: {type: mongoose.Schema.ObjectId, ref: 'Shop'},
  status: {type: String,
    default: 'Not processed',
    enum: ['Not processed' , 'Processing', 'Shipped', 'Delivered',
  'Cancelled']}
})
const CartItem = mongoose.model('CartItem', CartItemSchema)
```

The `status` of the product can only have the values as defined in the enums, representing the current state of the product ordered as updated by the seller.

The `Order` schema defined here will record details required for the customer and seller to complete the purchase steps for the ordered products.

Create order API

The create order API route is declared in `server/routes/order.routes.js`. The order routes will be very similar to the user routes. To load the order routes in the Express app, we need to mount the routes in `express.js`, like we did for the auth and user routes.

`mern-marketplace/server/express.js:`

```
app.use('/', orderRoutes)
```

A number of actions, in the following sequence, take place when the create order API receives a POST request at `/api/orders/:userId`:

- It is ensured that the user is signed in
- A Stripe `Customer` is either created or updated using the `stripeCustomer` user controller method discussed earlier
- The stock quantities are updated for all the ordered products using the `decreaseQuanity` product controller method
- The order is created in the Order collection with the `create` order controller method

The route will be defined as follows.

mern-marketplace/server/routes/order.routes.js:

```
router.route('/api/orders/:userId')
    .post(authCtrl.requireSignin, userCtrl.stripeCustomer,
        productCtrl.decreaseQuantity, orderCtrl.create)
```

To retrieve the user associated with the :userId parameter in the route, we will use the userByID user controller method, which gets the user from the User collection and attaches it to the request object to be accessed by the next methods. We will add it with the order routes as follows.

mern-marketplace/server/routes/order.routes.js:

```
router.param('userId', userCtrl.userByID)
```

Decrease product stock quantity

We will update the product controller file to add the decreaseQuantity controller method, which will update the stock quantities of all the products purchased in the new order.

mern-marketplace/server/controllers/product.controller.js:

```
const decreaseQuantity = (req, res, next) => {
  let bulkOps = req.body.order.products.map((item) => {
    return {
        "updateOne": {
            "filter": { "_id": item.product._id } ,
            "update": { "$inc": {"quantity": -item.quantity} }
        }
    }
  })
  Product.bulkWrite(bulkOps, {}, (err, products) => {
    if(err){
      return res.status(400).json({
        error: "Could not update product"
      })
    }
    next()
  })
}
```

Since the update operation in this case involves a bulk update of multiple products in the collection after matching with an array of products ordered, we will use the `bulkWrite` method in MongoDB to send multiple `updateOne` operations to the MongoDB server with one command. The multiple `updateOne` operations required are first listed in `bulkOps` using the `map` function. This will be faster than sending multiple independent save or update operations because with `bulkWrite()` there is only one round trip to MongoDB.

Create order controller method

The `create` controller method, defined in order controllers, takes the order details, creates a new order, and saves it to the Order collection in MongoDB.

`mern-marketplace/server/controllers/order.controller.js`:

```
const create = (req, res) => {
  req.body.order.user = req.profile
  const order = new Order(req.body.order)
  order.save((err, result) => {
    if (err) {
      return res.status(400).json({
        error: errorHandler.getErrorMessage(err)
      })
    }
    res.status(200).json(result)
  })
}
```

With this implemented, orders can be created and stored in the backend by any signed-in user on the MERN Marketplace. Now we can set up APIs to fetch lists of orders by user, orders by shop, or read an individual order and display the fetched data to views in the frontend.

Orders by shop

An important feature of the marketplace is allowing sellers to see and update the status of orders they've received for products in their shops. To implement this, we will first set up APIs to list orders by shop, and then update an order as a seller changes the status of a purchased product.

List by shop API

We will implement an API to get orders for a specific shop, so authenticated sellers can view orders for each of their shops. The request for this API will be received at '/api/orders/shop/:shopId, with the route defined in order.routes.js as follows.

mern-marketplace/server/routes/order.routes.js:

```
router.route('/api/orders/shop/:shopId')
    .get(authCtrl.requireSignin, shopCtrl.isOwner, orderCtrl.listByShop)
router.param('shopId', shopCtrl.shopByID)
```

To retrieve the shop associated with the :shopId parameter in the route, we will use the shopByID shop controller method, which gets the shop from the Shop collection and attaches it to the request object to be accessed by the next methods.

The listByShop controller method will retrieve the orders that have products purchased with the matching shop ID, then populate the ID, name, and price fields for each product, with orders sorted by date from most recent to oldest.

mern-marketplace/server/controllers/order.controller.js:

```
const listByShop = (req, res) => {
  Order.find({"products.shop": req.shop._id})
  .populate({path: 'products.product', select: '_id name price'})
  .sort('-created')
  .exec((err, orders) => {
    if (err) {
      return res.status(400).json({
        error: errorHandler.getErrorMessage(err)
      })
    }
    res.json(orders)
  })
}
```

To fetch this API in the frontend, we will add a corresponding listByShop method in api-order.js, to be used in the ShopOrders component to show the orders for each shop.

mern-marketplace/client/order/api-order.js:

```
const listByShop = (params, credentials) => {
  return fetch('/api/orders/shop/'+params.shopId, {
    method: 'GET',
    headers: {
```

```
          'Accept': 'application/json',
          'Authorization': 'Bearer ' + credentials.t
      }
  }).then((response) => {
      return response.json()
  }).catch((err) => {
      console.log(err)
  })
}
```

The ShopOrders component

Sellers will view their list of orders in the ShopOrders component, with each order showing only the purchased products relevant to the shop, and allowing the seller to change the status of the product with a dropdown of possible status values:

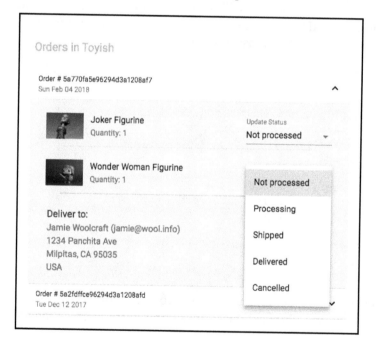

We will update MainRouter with a PrivateRoute, to load the ShopOrders component at the /seller/orders/:shop/:shopId route.

mern-marketplace/client/MainRouter.js:

```
<PrivateRoute path="/seller/orders/:shop/:shopId" component={ShopOrders}/>
```

List orders

When the `ShopOrders` component mounts, we will load the relevant orders by using the `listByShop` fetch method and set the retrieved orders to state.

`mern-marketplace/client/order/ShopOrders.js`:

```
loadOrders = () => {
    const jwt = auth.isAuthenticated()
    listByShop({
      shopId: this.match.params.shopId
    }, {t: jwt.token}).then((data) => {
      if (data.error) {
        console.log(data)
      } else {
        this.setState({orders: data})
      }
    })
  }
```

In the view, we will iterate through the list of orders and render each order in a collapsible list from `Material-UI`, which will expand on click.

`mern-marketplace/client/order/ShopOrders.js`:

```
<Typography type="title"> Orders in {this.match.params.shop} </Typography>
<List dense> {this.state.orders.map((order, index) => { return
    <span key={index}>
        <ListItem button onClick={this.handleClick(index)}>
            <ListItemText primary={'Order # '+order._id}
                secondary={(new Date(order.created)).toDateString()}/>
            {this.state.open == index ? <ExpandLess /> : <ExpandMore />}
        </ListItem>
        <Collapse component="li" in={this.state.open == index}
        timeout="auto" unmountOnExit>
            <ProductOrderEdit shopId={this.match.params.shopId}
            order={order} orderIndex={index}
            updateOrders={this.updateOrders}/>
            <Typography type="subheading"> Deliver to:</Typography>
            <Typography type="subheading" color="primary">
                {order.customer_name} ({order.customer_email})
            </Typography>
            <Typography type="subheading" color="primary">
                {order.delivery_address.street}</Typography>
            <Typography type="subheading" color="primary">
                {order.delivery_address.city},
            {order.delivery_address.state}
```

```
                    {order.delivery_address.zipcode}</Typography>
             <Typography type="subheading" color="primary">
                    {order.delivery_address.country}</Typography>
          </Collapse>
     </span>})}
  </List>
```

Each expanded order will show the order details and the `ProductOrderEdit` component. The `ProductOrderEdit` component will display the purchased products and allow the seller to edit the status of each product. The `updateOrders` method is passed as a prop to the `ProductOrderEdit` component so the status can be updated when a product status is changed.

`mern-marketplace/client/order/ShopOrders.js`:

```
updateOrders = (index, updatedOrder) => {
    let orders = this.state.orders
    orders[index] = updatedOrder
    this.setState({orders: orders})
}
```

The ProductOrderEdit component

The `ProductOrderEdit` component takes an order object as a prop, and iterates through the order's products array to display only the products purchased from the current shop, along with a dropdown to change the status value of each product.

`mern-marketplace/client/order/ProductOrderEdit.js`:

```
{this.props.order.products.map((item, index) => { return <span key={index}>
     { item.shop == this.props.shopId &&
         <ListItem button>
             <ListItemText primary={ <div>
                    <img src=
                    {'/api/product/image/'+item.product._id}/>
                    {item.product.name}
                    <p>{"Quantity: "+item.quantity}</p>
             </div>}/>
             <TextField id="select-status" select
                 label="Update Status" value={item.status}
                 onChange={this.handleStatusChange(index) }
                 SelectProps={{
                     MenuProps: { className: classes.menu },
                 }}>
                     {this.state.statusValues.map(option => (
```

```
                    <MenuItem key={option} value={option}>
                      {option}
                    </MenuItem>
              ))}
          </TextField>
        </ListItem>}
```

The possible list of status values is fetched from the server when the `ProductOrderEdit` component loads and set to state in `statusValues` to be rendered in the dropdown as a `MenuItem`.

`mern-marketplace/client/order/ProductOrderEdit.js`:

```
    loadStatusValues = () => {
        getStatusValues().then((data) => {
          if (data.error) {
            this.setState({error: "Could not get status"})
          } else {
            this.setState({statusValues: data, error: ''})
          }
        })
    }
```

When an option is selected from the possible status values, the `handleStatusChange` method is called to update the orders in state, and also to send a request to the appropriate backend API based on the value of the status selected.

`mern-marketplace/client/order/ProductOrderEdit.js`:

```
    handleStatusChange = productIndex => event => {
        let order = this.props.order
        order.products[productIndex].status = event.target.value
        let product = order.products[productIndex]
        const jwt = auth.isAuthenticated()
        if(event.target.value == "Cancelled"){
          cancelProduct({ shopId: this.props.shopId,
          productId: product.product._id },
          {t: jwt.token},
          {cartItemId: product._id, status:
          event.target.value,
          quantity: product.quantity
          }).then((data) => {
          if (data.error) {
          this.setState({error: "Status not updated,
          try again"})
          } else {
          this.props.updateOrders(this.props.orderIndex, order)
```

```
        this.setState(error: '')
         }
        })
        } else if(event.target.value == "Processing"){
        processCharge({ userId: jwt.user._id, shopId:
        this.props.shopId, orderId: order._id },
        { t: jwt.token},
        { cartItemId: product._id,
        amount: (product.quantity *
        product.product.price)
        status: event.target.value }).then((data) => { ...
        })
        } else {
        update({ shopId: this.props.shopId }, {t:
        jwt.token},
        { cartItemId: product._id,
        status: event.target.value}).then((data) => { ... })
        }
      }
```

The `cancelProduct`, `processCharge`, and `update` fetch methods are defined in `api-order.js` to call corresponding APIs in the backend to update a cancelled product's stock quantity, to create a charge on the customer's credit card when a product is processing, and to update the order with the product status change.

APIs for products ordered

Allowing sellers to update the status of a product will require the setup of four different APIs, including an API to retrieve possible status values. Then actual status updates will need APIs to handle updates to the order itself as the status is changed, to initiate related actions such as increasing stock quantity of a cancelled product, and to create a charge on the customer's credit card when a product is being processed.

Get status values

The possible status values of an ordered product are set as enums in the `CartItem` schema, and to show these values as options in the dropdown view, we will set up a GET API route at `/api/order/status_values` that retrieves these values.

`mern-marketplace/server/routes/order.routes.js`:

```
router.route('/api/order/status_values')
    .get(orderCtrl.getStatusValues)
```

The `getStatusValues` controller method will return the enum values for the `status` field from the `CartItem` schema.

`mern-marketplace/server/controllers/order.controller.js`:

```
const getStatusValues = (req, res) => {
  res.json(CartItem.schema.path('status').enumValues)
}
```

We will also set up a `fetch` method in `api-order.js`, this is used in the view to make a request to the API route.

`mern-marketplace/client/order/api-order.js`:

```
const getStatusValues = () => {
  return fetch('/api/order/status_values', {
    method: 'GET'
  }).then((response) => {
    return response.json()
  }).catch((err) => console.log(err))
}
```

Update order status

When a product's status is changed to any value other than **Processing** and **Cancelled**, a PUT request to `'/api/order/status/:shopId'` will directly update the order in the database given the current user is the verified owner of the shop with the ordered product.

`mern-marketplace/server/routes/order.routes.js`:

```
router.route('/api/order/status/:shopId')
    .put(authCtrl.requireSignin, shopCtrl.isOwner, orderCtrl.update)
```

The `update` controller method will query the Order collection and find the order with the `CartItem` object that matches the updated product, and set the `status` value of this matched `CartItem` in the `products` array of the order.

`mern-marketplace/server/controllers/order.controller.js`:

```
const update = (req, res) => {
  Order.update({'products._id':req.body.cartItemId}, {'$set': {
        'products.$.status': req.body.status
    }}, (err, order) => {
      if (err) {
        return res.status(400).send({
          error: errorHandler.getErrorMessage(err)
        })
      }
      res.json(order)
    })
}
```

In `api-order.js`, we will add an `update` fetch method to make a call to this update API with the required parameters passed from the view.

`mern-marketplace/client/order/api-order.js`:

```
const update = (params, credentials, product) => {
  return fetch('/api/order/status/' + params.shopId, {
    method: 'PUT',
    headers: {
      'Accept': 'application/json',
      'Content-Type': 'application/json',
      'Authorization': 'Bearer ' + credentials.t
    },
    body: JSON.stringify(product)
  }).then((response) => {
    return response.json()
  }).catch((err) => {
    console.log(err)
  })
}
```

Cancel product order

When a seller decides to cancel the order for a product, a PUT request will be sent to `/api/order/:shopId/cancel/:productId` so the product stock quantity can be increased, and the order updated in the database.

`mern-marketplace/server/routes/order.routes.js`:

```
router.route('/api/order/:shopId/cancel/:productId')
    .put(authCtrl.requireSignin, shopCtrl.isOwner,
  productCtrl.increaseQuantity, orderCtrl.update)
    router.param('productId', productCtrl.productByID)
```

To retrieve the product associated with the `productId` parameter in the route, we will use the `productByID` product controller method.

The `increaseQuantity` controller method is added to `product.controller.js`. It finds the product by the matching ID in the Product collection and increases the quantity value by the quantity that was ordered by the customer, now that the order for this product has been cancelled.

`mern-marketplace/server/controllers/product.controller.js`:

```
const increaseQuantity = (req, res, next) => {
  Product.findByIdAndUpdate(req.product._id, {$inc:
  {"quantity": req.body.quantity}}, {new: true})
    .exec((err, result) => {
      if (err) {
        return res.status(400).json({
          error: errorHandler.getErrorMessage(err)
        })
      }
      next()
    })
}
```

From the view, we will use a corresponding fetch method, added in `api-order.js`, to call the cancel product order API.

```
mern-marketplace/client/order/api-order.js:
```

```
const cancelProduct = (params, credentials, product) => {
  return fetch('/api/order/'+params.shopId+'/cancel/'+params.productId, {
    method: 'PUT',
    headers: {
      'Accept': 'application/json',
      'Content-Type': 'application/json',
      'Authorization': 'Bearer ' + credentials.t
    },
    body: JSON.stringify(product)
  }).then((response) => {
    return response.json()
  }).catch((err) => {
    console.log(err)
  })
}
```

Process charge for product

When a seller changes the status of a product to **Processing**, we will set up a backend API to not only update the order but to also create a charge on the customer's credit card for the price of the product multiplied by the quantity ordered.

```
mern-marketplace/server/routes/order.routes.js:
```

```
router.route('/api/order/:orderId/charge/:userId/:shopId')
      .put(authCtrl.requireSignin, shopCtrl.isOwner,
        userCtrl.createCharge, orderCtrl.update)
router.param('orderId', orderCtrl.orderByID)
```

To retrieve the order associated with the `orderId` parameter in the route, we will use the `orderByID` order controller method, which gets the order from the Order collection and attaches it to the request object to be accessed by the `next` methods, shown as follows.

```
mern-marketplace/server/controllers/order.controller.js:
```

```
const orderByID = (req, res, next, id) => {
  Order.findById(id).populate('products.product', 'name price')
    .populate('products.shop', 'name')
    .exec((err, order) => {
      if (err || !order)
        return res.status('400').json({
          error: "Order not found"
        })
      req.order = order
```

```
            next()
        })
    }
```

This process charge API will receive a PUT request at
`/api/order/:orderId/charge/:userId/:shopId`, and after successfully
authenticating the user will create the charge by calling the `createCharge` user controller
as discussed earlier in the *Using Stripe for payments* section, and then finally update the
order with the `update` method.

From the view, we will use the `processCharge` fetch method in `api-order.js`, and
provide the required route parameter values, credentials, and product details, including the
amount to charge.

`mern-marketplace/client/order/api-order.js`:

```
const processCharge = (params, credentials, product) => {
    return fetch('/api/order/'+params.orderId+'/charge/'+params.userId+'/'
    +params.shopId, {
    method: 'PUT',
    headers: {
        'Accept': 'application/json',
        'Content-Type': 'application/json',
        'Authorization': 'Bearer ' + credentials.t
    },
    body: JSON.stringify(product)
    }).then((response) => {
    return response.json()
    }).catch((err) => {
    console.log(err)
    })
}
```

Sellers can view orders received for their products in each of their shops, and they can
easily update the status of each product ordered, while the application takes care of
additional tasks, such as updating stock quantity and initiating payment. This covers the
basic order management features for the MERN Marketplace application, which can be
extended further as required.

View order details

With Order collection and the database access all set up, moving forward it is easy to add the features of listing orders for each user, and showing details of a single order in a separate view where the user can track the status of each ordered product:

Following the steps repeated throughout this book, for setting up backend APIs to retrieve data and using it in the frontend to construct frontend views, you can develop order-related views as desired, taking inspiration from the snapshots of these sample views in the MERN Marketplace application code:

The MERN Marketplace application developed in this and Chapter 6, *Exercising New MERN Skills with an Online Marketplace*, by building on the MERN skeleton application, covered the crucial features for a standard online marketplace application. This, in turn, demonstrated how the MERN stack can be extended to incorporate complex features.

Summary

In this chapter, we extended the MERN Marketplace application, and explored how to add a shopping cart for buyers, a checkout process with credit card payments, and order management for the sellers in an online marketplace application.

We discovered how the MERN stack technologies can work well with third-party integrations, as we implemented the cart checkout flow, and processed credit card charges on ordered products using the tools provided by Stripe for managing online payments.

We also unlocked more of what is possible with MERN, such as optimized bulk write operations in MongoDB for updating multiple documents in response to a single API call. This allowed us to decrease the stock quantities of multiple products in one go, such as when a user placed an order for multiple products from different stores.

The marketplace features developed in the MERN Marketplace application revealed how this stack and structure can be utilized to design and build growing applications by adding features that may be simple or more complex in nature.

In the next chapter, we will take the lessons learned so far in this book, and explore more advanced possibilities with MERN as we build a media streaming application by extending the MERN skeleton.

8

Building a Media Streaming Application

Uploading and streaming media content, specifically video content, has been a growing part of internet culture for some time now. From individuals sharing personal video content to the entertainment industry disseminating commercial content on online streaming services, we all rely on web applications that enable smooth uploading and streaming. Capabilities within the MERN stack technologies can be used to build and integrate these core streaming features into any MERN-based web application.

In this chapter, we will cover the following topics to implement basic media uploading and streaming by extending the MERN skeleton application:

- Uploading videos to MongoDB GridFS
- Storing and retrieving media details
- Streaming from GridFS to a basic media player

MERN Mediastream

We will build the MERN Mediastream application by extending the base application. It will be a simple video streaming application that allows registered users to upload videos that can be streamed by anyone browsing through the application:

The code for the complete MERN Mediastream application is available on GitHub `github.com/shamahoque/mern-mediastream`. The implementations discussed in this chapter can be accessed in the `simple-mediastream-gridfs` branch of the same repository. You can clone this code and run the application as you go through the code explanations in the rest of this chapter.

The views needed for the features related to media upload, editing, and streaming in a simple media player will be developed by extending and modifying the existing React components in the MERN skeleton application. The component-tree pictured next shows all the custom React components that make up the MERN Mediastream frontend developed in this chapter:

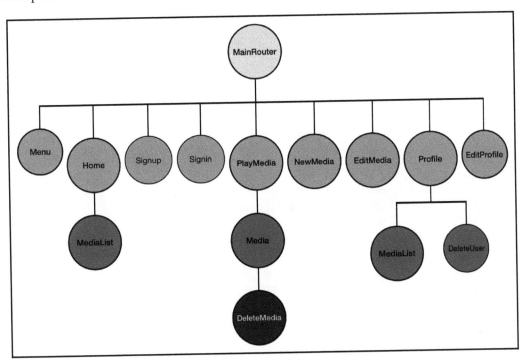

Uploading and storing media

Registered users on MERN Mediastream will be able to upload videos from their local files to store the video and related details directly on MongoDB using GridFS.

Media model

In order to store media details, we will add a Mongoose Schema for the media model in `server/models/media.model.js` with fields to record the media title, description, genre, number of views, created time, updated time, and reference to the user who posted the media.

`mern-mediastream/server/models/media.model.js`:

```
import mongoose from 'mongoose'
import crypto from 'crypto'
const MediaSchema = new mongoose.Schema({
  title: {
    type: String,
    required: 'title is required'
  },
  description: String,
  genre: String,
  views: {type: Number, default: 0},
  postedBy: {type: mongoose.Schema.ObjectId, ref: 'User'},
  created: {
    type: Date,
    default: Date.now
  },
  updated: {
    type: Date
  }
})

export default mongoose.model('Media', MediaSchema)
```

MongoDB GridFS to store large files

In previous chapters, we discussed how files uploaded by users could be stored directly in MongoDB as binary data. But this only worked for files smaller than 16 MB. In order to store larger files in MongoDB, we will need to use GridFS.

GridFS stores large files in MongoDB by dividing the file into several chunks of a maximum of 255 KB each, and then storing each chunk as a separate document. When the file has to be retrieved in response to a query to GridFS, the chunks are reassembled as needed. This opens up the option to fetch and load only parts of the file as required, rather than retrieving the whole file.

In the case of storing and retrieving video files for MERN Mediastream, we will utilize GridFS to store video files, and also to stream parts of the video depending on which part the user skips to and starts playing from.

We will use the `gridfs-stream` npm module to add GridFS features to our server-side code:

```
npm install gridfs-stream --save
```

To configure `gridfs-stream` with our database connection, we will use Mongoose to link it up as follows.

`mern-mediastream/server/controllers/media.controller.js`:

```
import mongoose from 'mongoose'
import Grid from 'gridfs-stream'
Grid.mongo = mongoose.mongo
let gridfs = null
mongoose.connection.on('connected', () => {
   gridfs = Grid(mongoose.connection.db)
})
```

The `gridfs` object will give access to the GridFS functionalities required to store the file when new media is created and to fetch the file when the media is to be streamed back to the user.

Creating a media API

We will set up a create media API on the Express server that will receive a POST request at `'/api/media/new/:userId'` with the multipart body content containing the media fields and the uploaded video file.

Route to create media

In `server/routes/media.routes.js`, we will add the create route, and utilize the `userByID` method from the user controller. The `userByID` method processes the `:userId` parameter passed in the URL and retrieves the associated user from the database.

```
mern-mediastream/server/routes/media.routes.js:
```

```
router.route('/api/media/new/:userId')
        .post(authCtrl.requireSignin, mediaCtrl.create)
router.param('userId', userCtrl.userByID)
```

A POST request to the create route will first make sure the user is signed in and then initiate the `create` method in the media controller.

Similar to the user and auth routes, we will have to mount the media routes on the Express app in `express.js` as follows.

```
mern-mediastream/server/express.js:
```

```
app.use('/', mediaRoutes)
```

Controller method to handle create request

The `create` controller method in the media controller will use the `formidable` npm module to parse the multipart request body that will contain the media details and video file uploaded by the user:

```
npm install formidable --save
```

The media fields received in the form data, and parsed with `formidable`, will be used to generate a new Media object and saved to the database.

```
mern-mediastream/server/controllers/media.controller.js:
```

```
const create = (req, res, next) => {
  let form = new formidable.IncomingForm()
    form.keepExtensions = true
    form.parse(req, (err, fields, files) => {
      if (err) {
        return res.status(400).json({
          error: "Video could not be uploaded"
        })
      }
      let media = new Media(fields)
      media.postedBy= req.profile
      if(files.video){
        let writestream = gridfs.createWriteStream({_id: media._id})
        fs.createReadStream(files.video.path).pipe(writestream)
      }
      media.save((err, result) => {
```

```
     if (err) {
       return res.status(400).json({
         error: errorHandler.getErrorMessage(err)
       })
     }
     res.json(result)
   })
 })
}
```

If there is a file in the request, `formidable` will store it temporarily in the filesystem, and we will use the media object's ID to create a `gridfs.writeStream` to read the temporary file and write it into MongoDB. This will generate the associated chunks and file information documents in MongoDB. When it is time to retrieve this file, we will identify it with the media ID.

Fetch create API in the view

In `api-media.js`, we will add a corresponding method to make a `POST` request to the create API by passing the multipart form data from the view.

`mern-mediastream/client/user/api-user.js`:

```
const create = (params, credentials, media) => {
  return fetch('/api/media/new/'+ params.userId, {
    method: 'POST',
    headers: {
      'Accept': 'application/json',
      'Authorization': 'Bearer ' + credentials.t
    },
    body: media
  }).then((response) => {
    return response.json()
  }).catch((err) => {
    console.log(err)
  })
}
```

This `create` fetch method will be used when the user submits the new media form to upload a new video.

New media form view

A registered user will see a link on the menu to add new media. This link will take them to the new media form view and allow them to upload a video file along with details of the video.

Adding media menu button

In `client/core/Menu.js`, we will update the existing code that renders the **My Profile** and **Signout** links to add the **Add Media** button link:

This will only render on the menu if the user is currently signed in.

`mern-mediastream/client/core/Menu.js`:

```
<Link to="/media/new">
    <Button style={isActive(history, "/media/new")}>
        <AddBoxIcon style={{marginRight: '8px'}}/> Add Media
    </Button>
</Link>
```

React route for NewMedia view

To take the user to the new media form view when they click the **Add Media** link, we will update the `MainRouter` file to add the `/media/new` React route, which will render the `NewMedia` component.

`mern-mediastream/client/MainRouter.js`:

```
<PrivateRoute path="/media/new" component={NewMedia}/>
```

As this new media form should only be accessed by a signed-in user, we will add it as a `PrivateRoute`.

NewMedia component

In the `NewMedia` component, we will render a form that allows a user to create media by entering the title, description, and genre, and uploading a video file from their local file system:

We will add the file upload elements using a Material-UI `Button` and an HTML5 `file` `input` element.

`mern-mediastream/client/media/NewMedia.js`:

```
<input accept="video/*"
       onChange={this.handleChange('video')}
       id="icon-button-file"
       type="file"
       style={{display: none}}/>
<label htmlFor="icon-button-file">
    <Button color="secondary" variant="raised" component="span">
        Upload <FileUpload/>
    </Button>
</label>
<span>{this.state.video ? this.state.video.name : ''}</span>
```

The `Title`, `Description`, and `Genre` form fields will be added with `TextField` components.

`mern-mediastream/client/media/NewMedia.js`:

```
<TextField id="title" label="Title" value={this.state.title}
        onChange={this.handleChange('title')} margin="normal"/><br/>
<TextField id="multiline-flexible" label="Description"
        multiline rows="2"
        value={this.state.description}
        onChange={this.handleChange('description')}/><br/>
<TextField id="genre" label="Genre" value={this.state.genre}
        onChange={this.handleChange('genre')}/><br/>
```

These form field changes will be tracked with the `handleChange` method.

`mern-mediastream/client/media/NewMedia.js`:

```
handleChange = name => event => {
    const value = name === 'video'
      ? event.target.files[0]
      : event.target.value
    this.mediaData.set(name, value)
    this.setState({ [name]: value })
}
```

The `handleChange` method updates the state with the new values and populates `mediaData`, which is a `FormData` object. The `FormData` API ensures that the data to be sent to the server is stored in the correct format needed for the encoding-type `multipart/form-data`. This `mediaData` object is initialized in `componentDidMount`.

`mern-mediastream/client/media/NewMedia.js`:

```
componentDidMount = () => {
    this.mediaData = new FormData()
}
```

Upon form submit, the `create` fetch method is called with the necessary credentials and the form data passed as parameters:

```
clickSubmit = () => {
    const jwt = auth.isAuthenticated()
    create({
      userId: jwt.user._id
    }, {
      t: jwt.token
    }, this.mediaData).then((data) => {
      if (data.error) {
        this.setState({error: data.error})
      } else {
```

```
                this.setState({redirect: true, mediaId: data._id})
            }
        })
    }
```

On successful media creation, the user may be redirected to a different view as desired, for example, to a Media view with the new media details.

`mern-mediastream/client/media/NewMedia.js`:

```
    if (this.state.redirect) {
            return (<Redirect to={'/media/' + this.state.mediaId}/>)
    }
```

In order to allow users to stream and view this video file stored in MongoDB, next we will implement how to retrieve and render the video in the view.

Retrieve and stream media

On the server, we will set up a route to retrieve a single video file, which we will then use as a source in a React media player to render the streaming video.

Get video API

We will add a route in the media routes to fetch a video when a GET request is received at `'/api/medias/video/:mediaId'`.

`mern-mediastream/server/routes/media.routes.js`:

```
    router.route('/api/medias/video/:mediaId')
            .get(mediaCtrl.video)
    router.param('mediaId', mediaCtrl.mediaByID)
```

The `:mediaId` parameter in the route URL will be processed in the `mediaByID` controller to fetch the associated document from the Media collection and attached to the request object, so it may be used in the `video` controller method as required.

mern-mediastream/server/controllers/media.controller.js:

```
const mediaByID = (req, res, next, id) => {
  Media.findById(id).populate('postedBy', '_id name').exec((err, media) =>
{
    if (err || !media)
      return res.status('400').json({
        error: "Media not found"
      })
    req.media = media
    next()
  })
}
```

The `video` controller method in `media.controller.js` will use `gridfs` to find the video associated with the `mediaId` in MongoDB. Then, if the matching video is found and depending on whether the request contains range headers, the response will send back the correct chunks of video with the related content information set as response headers.

mern-mediastream/server/controllers/media.controller.js:

```
const video = (req, res) => {
  gridfs.findOne({
      _id: req.media._id
  }, (err, file) => {
      if (err) {
          return res.status(400).send({
              error: errorHandler.getErrorMessage(err)
          })
      }
      if (!file) {
          return res.status(404).send({
              error: 'No video found'
          })
      }

      if (req.headers['range']) {
          ...
          ... consider range headers and send only relevant chunks in
          response ...
          ...
      } else {
          res.header('Content-Length', file.length)
          res.header('Content-Type', file.contentType)

          gridfs.createReadStream({
              _id: file._id
```

```
            }).pipe(res)
        }
    })
}
```

4If the request contains range headers, for example when the user drags to the middle of the video and starts playing from that point, we need to convert the range headers to start and end positions that will correspond with the correct chunks stored using GridFS. Then we will pass these start and end values as a range to the gridfs-stream's `createReadStream` method, and also set the response headers with additional file details including content length, range, and type.

`mern-mediastream/server/controllers/media.controller.js`:

```
let parts = req.headers['range'].replace(/bytes=/, "").split("-")
let partialstart = parts[0]
let partialend = parts[1]

let start = parseInt(partialstart, 10)
let end = partialend ? parseInt(partialend, 10) : file.length - 1
let chunksize = (end - start) + 1

res.writeHead(206, {
    'Accept-Ranges': 'bytes',
    'Content-Length': chunksize,
    'Content-Range': 'bytes ' + start + '-' + end + '/' + file.length,
    'Content-Type': file.contentType
})

gridfs.createReadStream({
        _id: file._id,
        range: {
                startPos: start,
                endPos: end
              }
}).pipe(res)
```

The final `readStream` piped to the response can be rendered directly in a basic HTML5 media player or a React-flavored media player in the frontend view.

React media player to render the video

A good option for a React-flavored media player is the `ReactPlayer` component available as an npm, which can be customized as required:

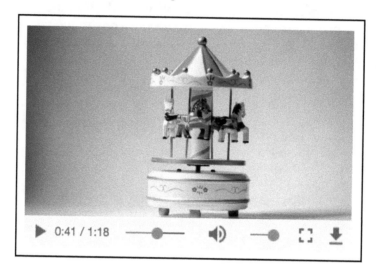

It can be used in the application by installing the corresponding npm module:

```
npm install react-player --save
```

For basic usage with default controls provided by the browser, we can add it to any React view in the application that has access to the ID of the media to be rendered:

```
<ReactPlayer url={'/api/media/video/'+media._id} controls/>
```

In the next chapter, we will look into advanced options for customizing this `ReactPlayer` with our own controls.

To learn more about what is possible with `ReactPlayer`, visit `cookpete.com/react-player`.

Media list

In MERN Mediastream, we will add list views of relevant media with a snapshot of each video to give visitors easier access and an overview of the videos on the application. We will set up list APIs in the backend to retrieve different lists, such as videos uploaded by a single user and the most popular videos with the highest views in the application. Then, these retrieved lists can be rendered in the MediaList component, which will receive a list as a prop from a parent component that fetches the specific API:

In the preceding screenshot, the Profile component uses the list by user API to fetch the list of media posted by the user seen in the preceding profile, and passes the received list to the MediaList component to render each video and media details.

MediaList component

The MediaList component is a reusable component that will take a list of media and iterate through it to render each item in the view. In MERN Mediastream, we use it to render a list of the most popular media in the home view and a list of media uploaded by a specific user in their profile.

`mern-mediastream/client/media/MediaList.js`:

```
<GridList cols={3}>
    {this.props.media.map((tile, i) => (
        <GridListTile key={i}>
          <Link to={"/media/"+tile._id}>
            <ReactPlayer url={'/api/media/video/'+tile._id}
                        width='100%' height='inherit'/>
          </Link>
          <GridListTileBar
            title={<Link to={"/media/"+tile._id}>{tile.title}</Link>}
            subtitle={<span>{tile.views} views
                  <span style={{float: 'right'}}>{tile.genre}</span>}/>
        </GridListTile>
    ))}
</GridList>
```

The `MediaList` component uses the Material-UI `GridList` components as it iterates through the list sent in the props, and renders media details for each item in the list, along with a `ReactPlayer` component that renders the video URL without showing any controls. In the view, this gives the visitor a brief overview of the media and also a glimpse of the video content.

List popular media

In order to retrieve specific lists of media from the database, we need to set up relevant APIs on the server. For popular media, we will set up a route that receives a GET request at `/api/media/popular`.

`mern-mediastream/server/routes/media.routes.js`:

```
router.route('/api/media/popular')
        .get(mediaCtrl.listPopular)
```

The `listPopular` controller method will query the Media collection to retrieve ten media documents that have the highest `views` in the whole collection.

`mern-mediastream/server/controllers/media.controller.js`:

```
const listPopular = (req, res) => {
  Media.find({}).limit(10)
  .populate('postedBy', '_id name')
  .sort('-views')
  .exec((err, posts) => {
```

```
    if (err) {
      return res.status(400).json({
        error: errorHandler.getErrorMessage(err)
      })
    }
    res.json(posts)
  })
}
```

To use this API in the view, we will set up a corresponding fetch method in api-media.js.

mern-mediastream/client/media/api-media.js:

```
const listPopular = (params) => {
  return fetch('/api/media/popular', {
    method: 'GET',
    headers: {
      'Accept': 'application/json',
      'Content-Type': 'application/json'
    }
  }).then(response => {
    return response.json()
  }).catch((err) => console.log(err))
}
```

This fetch method will be called when the Home component mounts so the list can be set to state and passed to the MediaList component in the view.

mern-mediastream/client/core/Home.js:

```
componentDidMount = () => {
    listPopular().then((data) => {
      if (data.error) {
        console.log(data.error)
      } else {
        this.setState({media: data})
      }
    })
  }
```

In the Home view, we will add the MediaList as follows, with the list provided as a prop:

```
<MediaList media={this.state.media}/>
```

List media by users

To retrieve a list of media uploaded by a specific user, we will set up an API with a route that accepts a GET request at `'/api/media/by/:userId'`.

`mern-mediastream/server/routes/media.routes.js`:

```
router.route('/api/media/by/:userId')
        .get(mediaCtrl.listByUser)
```

The `listByUser` controller method will query the Media collection to find media documents that have `postedBy` values matching the `userId`.

`mern-mediastream/server/controllers/media.controller.js`:

```
const listByUser = (req, res) => {
  Media.find({postedBy: req.profile._id})
  .populate('postedBy', '_id name')
  .sort('-created')
  .exec((err, posts) => {
    if (err) {
      return res.status(400).json({
        error: errorHandler.getErrorMessage(err)
      })
    }
    res.json(posts)
  })
}
```

To use this list by user API in the frontend view, we will set up a corresponding `fetch` method in `api-media.js`.

`mern-mediastream/client/user/api-user.js`:

```
const listByUser = (params) => {
  return fetch('/api/media/by/'+ params.userId, {
    method: 'GET',
    headers: {
      'Accept': 'application/json',
      'Content-Type': 'application/json'
    }
  }).then(response => {
    return response.json()
  }).catch((err) => console.log(err))
}
```

This fetch method can be used in the `Profile` component, similar to the `listPopular` fetch method used in the home view, to retrieve the list data, set to state, and then pass to the `MediaList` component.

Display, update, and delete media

Any visitor to MERN Mediastream will be able to view media details and stream the video, while only registered users will be able to edit the details and delete the media any time after they post it on the application.

Display media

Any visitor to the MERN Mediastream will be able to browse to a single media view to play the video and read the details associated with the media. Every time a specific video is loaded on the application, we will also increment the number of views associated with the media.

Read media API

To fetch media information for a specific media record, we will set up a route that accepts a GET request at `'/api/media/:mediaId'`.

mern-mediastream/server/routes/media.routes.js:

```
router.route('/api/media/:mediaId')
    .get( mediaCtrl.incrementViews, mediaCtrl.read)
```

The `mediaId` in the request URL will cause the `mediaByID` controller method to execute and attach the retrieved media document to the request object. Then this media data will be returned in the response by the `read` controller method.

mern-mediastream/server/controllers/media.controller.js:

```
const read = (req, res) => {
  return res.json(req.media)
}
```

A GET request to this API will also execute the `incrementViews` controller method, which will find the matching media record and increment the `views` value by 1 before saving the updated record to the database.

`mern-mediastream/server/controllers/media.controller.js`:

```
const incrementViews = (req, res, next) => {
  Media.findByIdAndUpdate(req.media._id, {$inc: {"views": 1}}, {new: true})
    .exec((err, result) => {
      if (err) {
        return res.status(400).json({
          error: errorHandler.getErrorMessage(err)
        })
      }
      next()
    })
}
```

In order to use this read API in the frontend, we will set up a corresponding fetch method in `api-media.js`.

`mern-mediastream/client/user/api-user.js`:

```
const read = (params) => {
  return fetch(config.serverUrl+'/api/media/' + params.mediaId, {
    method: 'GET'
  }).then((response) => {
    return response.json()
  }).catch((err) => console.log(err))
}
```

The read API can be used to render individual media details in a view or to pre-populate a media edit form.

Media component

The `Media` component will render details of an individual media record and stream the video in a basic `ReactPlayer` with default browser controls:

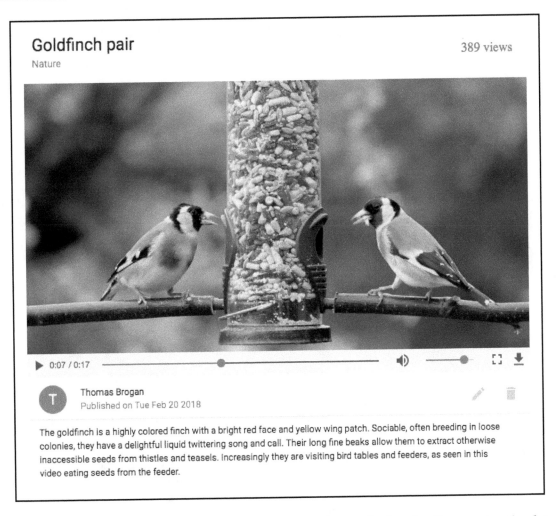

The Media component can call the read API to fetch the media data itself or receive the data as props from a parent component that makes the call to the read API. In the latter case, the parent component will add the Media component, as follows.

`mern-mediastream/client/media/PlayMedia.js`:

```
<Media media={this.state.media}/>
```

In MERN Mediastream, we add the Media component in a PlayMedia component that fetches the media content from the server using the read API, and passes it to Media as a prop. The Media component will take this data and render it in the view to display the details and load the video in a ReactPlayer component.

The title, genre, and view count can be rendered in a Material-UI `CardHeader` component.

mern-mediastream/client/media/Media.js:

```
<CardHeader
    title={this.props.media.title}
    action={<span>
                 {this.props.media.views + ' views'}
            </span>}
    subheader={this.props.media.genre}
/>
```

The video URL, which is basically the GET API route we set up in the backend, is loaded in a `ReactPlayer` with default browser controls.

mern-mediastream/client/media/Media.js:

```
const mediaUrl = this.props.media._id
           ? `/api/media/video/${this.props.media._id}`
           : null
               ...
<ReactPlayer url={mediaUrl}
             controls
             width={'inherit'}
             height={'inherit'}
             style={{maxHeight: '500px'}}
             config={{ attributes:
                          { style: { height: '100%', width: '100%'} }
}}/>
```

The `Media` component renders additional details about the user who posted the video, and the media description, along with the date the media was created.

mern-mediastream/client/media/Media.js:

```
<ListItem>
    <ListItemAvatar>
      <Avatar>
        {this.props.media.postedBy.name &&
                      this.props.media.postedBy.name[0]}
      </Avatar>
    </ListItemAvatar>
    <ListItemText primary={this.props.media.postedBy.name}
             secondary={"Published on " +
                      (new Date(this.props.media.created))
                      .toDateString()}/>
</ListItem>
```

```
<ListItem>
    <ListItemText primary={this.props.media.description}/>
</ListItem>
```

The Media component also conditionally shows an edit and a delete option if the currently-signed-in user is also the one who posted the media being displayed.

mern-mediastream/client/media/Media.js:

```
{(auth.isAuthenticated().user && auth.isAuthenticated().user._id)
    == this.props.media.postedBy._id && (<ListItemSecondaryAction>
        <Link to={"/media/edit/" + this.props.media._id}>
          <IconButton aria-label="Edit" color="secondary">
            <Edit/>
          </IconButton>
        </Link>
        <DeleteMedia mediaId={this.props.media._id} mediaTitle=
      {this.props.media.title}/>
      </ListItemSecondaryAction>)}
```

The edit option links to the media edit form, and the delete option opens a dialog box that can initiate the deletion of this particular media document from the database.

Update media details

Registered users will have access to an edit form for each of their media uploads, updating and submitting this form will save the changes to the document in the Media collection.

Media update API

To allow users to update media details, we will set up a media update API that accepts a PUT request at '/api/media/:mediaId' with the updated details in the request body.

mern-mediastream/server/routes/media.routes.js:

```
router.route('/api/media/:mediaId')
      .put(authCtrl.requireSignin,
            mediaCtrl.isPoster,
                mediaCtrl.update)
```

When this request is received, the server will first ensure the signed-in user is the original poster of the media content by calling the isPoster controller method.

`mern-mediastream/server/controllers/media.controller.js:`

```
const isPoster = (req, res, next) => {
  let isPoster = req.media && req.auth
  && req.media.postedBy._id == req.auth._id
  if(!isPoster){
    return res.status('403').json({
      error: "User is not authorized"
    })
  }
  next()
}
```

If the user is authorized, the `update` controller method will be called `next`, to update the existing media document with the changes and then save it to the database.

`mern-mediastream/server/controllers/media.controller.js:`

```
const update = (req, res, next) => {
  let media = req.media
  media = _.extend(media, req.body)
  media.updated = Date.now()
  media.save((err) => {
    if (err) {
      return res.status(400).send({
        error: errorHandler.getErrorMessage(err)
      })
    }
    res.json(media)
  })
}
```

To access the update API in the frontend, we will add a corresponding fetch method in `api-media.js` that takes the necessary credentials and media details as parameters.

`mern-mediastream/client/user/api-user.js:`

```
const update = (params, credentials, media) => {
  return fetch('/api/media/' + params.mediaId, {
    method: 'PUT',
    headers: {
      'Accept': 'application/json',
      'Content-Type': 'application/json',
      'Authorization': 'Bearer ' + credentials.t
    },
    body: JSON.stringify(media)
  }).then((response) => {
```

```
      return response.json()
   }).catch((err) => {
      console.log(err)
   })
}
```

This fetch method will be used in the media edit form when the user makes updates and submits the form.

Media edit form

The media edit form will be similar to the new media form, but without the upload option, and the fields will be pre-populated with the existing details:

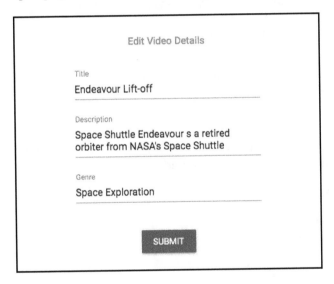

The `EditMedia` component containing this form, which can only be accessed by signed-in users, will be rendered at `'/media/edit/:mediaId'`. This private route will be declared in `MainRouter` with the other frontend routes.

`mern-mediastream/client/MainRouter.js`:

```
<PrivateRoute path="/media/edit/:mediaId" component={EditMedia}/>
```

Once the `EditMedia` component mounts on the view, a fetch call will be made to the read media API to retrieve the media details and set to state so the values are rendered in the text fields.

`mern-mediastream/client/media/EditMedia.js:`

```
componentDidMount = () => {
  read({mediaId: this.match.params.mediaId}).then((data) => {
    if (data.error) {
      this.setState({error: data.error})
    } else {
      this.setState({media: data})
    }
  })
}
```

The form field elements will be the same as in the NewMedia component. When a user updates any of the values in the form, the changes will be registered in the media object in state with a call to the handleChange method.

`mediastream/client/media/EditMedia.js:`

```
handleChange = name => event => {
    let updatedMedia = this.state.media
    updatedMedia[name] = event.target.value
    this.setState({media: updatedMedia})
}
```

When the user is done editing and clicks submit, a call will be made to the update API with the required credentials and the changed media values.

`mediastream/client/media/EditMedia.js:`

```
clickSubmit = () => {
  const jwt = auth.isAuthenticated()
  update({
    mediaId: this.state.media._id
  }, {
    t: jwt.token
  }, this.state.media).then((data) => {
    if (data.error) {
      this.setState({error: data.error})
    } else {
      this.setState({error: '', redirect: true, media: data})
    }
  })
}
```

This will update the media details, and the video file associated with the media will remain as it is in the database.

Deleting media

An authenticated user can delete the media they uploaded to the application completely, including the media document in the Media collection, and the file chunks stored in MongoDB using GridFS.

The Delete media API

In the backend, we will add a DELETE route that allows an authorized user to delete their uploaded media records.

`mern-mediastream/server/routes/media.routes.js`:

```
router.route('/api/media/:mediaId')
    .delete(authCtrl.requireSignin,
                mediaCtrl.isPoster,
                    mediaCtrl.remove)
```

When the server receives a DELETE request at `'/api/media/:mediaId'`, it will first make sure the signed-in user is the original poster of the media that needs to be deleted. Then the `remove` controller method will delete the specified media details from the database.

`mern-mediastream/server/controllers/media.controller.js`:

```
const remove = (req, res, next) => {
  let media = req.media
    media.remove((err, deletedMedia) => {
      if (err) {
        return res.status(400).json({
          error: errorHandler.getErrorMessage(err)
        })
      }
      gridfs.remove({ _id: req.media._id })
      res.json(deletedMedia)
    })
}
```

Besides deleting the media record from the Media collection, we also use `gridfs` to remove the associated file details and chunks stored in the database.

We will also add a corresponding method in `api-media.js` to fetch the `delete` API from the view.

```
mern-mediastream/client/user/api-user.js:
```

```
const remove = (params, credentials) => {
  return fetch('/api/media/' + params.mediaId, {
    method: 'DELETE',
    headers: {
      'Accept': 'application/json',
      'Content-Type': 'application/json',
      'Authorization': 'Bearer ' + credentials.t
    }
  }).then((response) => {
    return response.json()
  }).catch((err) => {
    console.log(err)
  })
}
```

The DeleteMedia component

The DeleteMedia component is added to the Media component and is only visible to the signed-in user who added this specific media. This component takes the media ID and title as props:

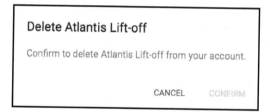

This DeleteMedia component is basically an icon button that on click opens a confirm dialog to ask the user whether they are sure they want to delete their video.

```
mern-mediastream/client/media/DeleteMedia.js:
```

```
<IconButton aria-label="Delete" onClick={this.clickButton}
color="secondary">
    <DeleteIcon/>
</IconButton>
<Dialog open={this.state.open} onClose={this.handleRequestClose}>
  <DialogTitle>{"Delete "+this.props.mediaTitle}</DialogTitle>
  <DialogContent>
      <DialogContentText>
```

```
              Confirm to delete {this.props.mediaTitle} from your account.
          </DialogContentText>
       </DialogContent>
       <DialogActions>
          <Button onClick={this.handleRequestClose} color="primary">
             Cancel
          </Button>
          <Button onClick={this.deleteMedia}
                    color="secondary"
                    autoFocus="autoFocus"
                    variant="raised">
             Confirm
          </Button>
       </DialogActions>
   </Dialog>
```

When the user confirms the delete intent, the `delete` fetch method is called.

`mern-mediastream/client/media/DeleteMedia.js`:

```
   deleteMedia = () => {
       const jwt = auth.isAuthenticated()
       remove({
          mediaId: this.props.mediaId
       }, {t: jwt.token}).then((data) => {
          if (data.error) {
             console.log(data.error)
          } else {
             this.setState({redirect: true})
          }
       })
   }
```

Then on successful deletion, the user is redirected to the home page.

`mern-mediastream/client/media/DeleteMedia.js`:

```
   if (this.state.redirect) {
       return <Redirect to='/'/>
   }
```

The MERN Mediastream application developed in this chapter is a complete media streaming application with capabilities of uploading video files to the database, streaming stored videos back to the viewers, support for CRUD operations such as media create, update, read, and delete, along with options to list media by uploader or popularity.

Summary

In this chapter, we developed a media streaming application by extending the MERN Skeleton application and leveraging MongoDB GridFS.

Besides adding basic add, update, delete, and listing features for media, we looked into how MERN-based applications can allow users to upload video files, store these files into MongoDB GridFS as chunks, and stream the video back to the viewer partially or fully as required. We also covered a basic use of `ReactPlayer` with default browser controls to stream the video file.

In the next chapter, we will see how we can customize `ReactPlayer` with our own controls and functionality so users have more options, such as playing the next video in a list. In addition, we will discuss how to improve the SEO of the media details by implementing server-side rendering with data for the media view.

9
Customizing the Media Player and Improving SEO

Users visit a media-streaming application mainly to play the media and explore other related media. This makes the media player, and the view that renders the related media details, crucial to a streaming application.

In this chapter, we will focus on developing the play media page for the MERN Mediastream application that we started building in the previous chapter. We will address the following topics to bolster the media-playing functionalities, and to help boost the presence of the media content across the web so that it reaches more users:

- Customize controls on `ReactPlayer`
- Play next from a list of related videos
- Autoplay a list of related media
- Server-side render the Media view with data to improve SEO

MERN Mediastream with a custom media player

The MERN Mediastream application developed in the previous chapter implemented a simple media player with default browser controls that played one video at a time. In this chapter, we will update the view that plays the media with a customized `ReactPlayer` and a related media list that can be set to play automatically when the current video ends. The updated view with the custom player and related playlist will look as pictured in this screenshot:

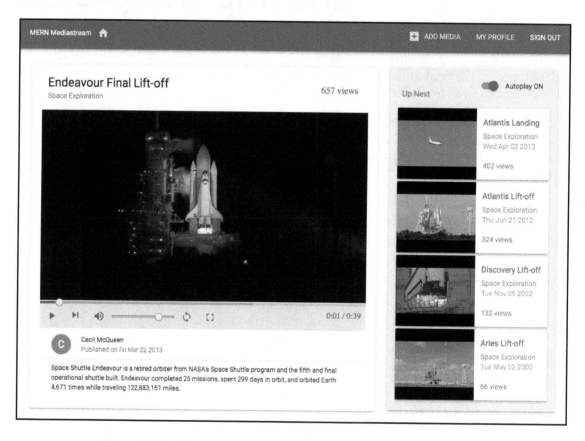

The code for the complete MERN Mediastream application is available on GitHub at `github.com/shamahoque/mern-mediastream`. You can clone this code and run the application as you go through the code explanations in the rest of this chapter.

The following component tree diagram shows all the custom components that make up the MERN Mediastream frontend, highlighting the components that will be improved or added in this chapter:

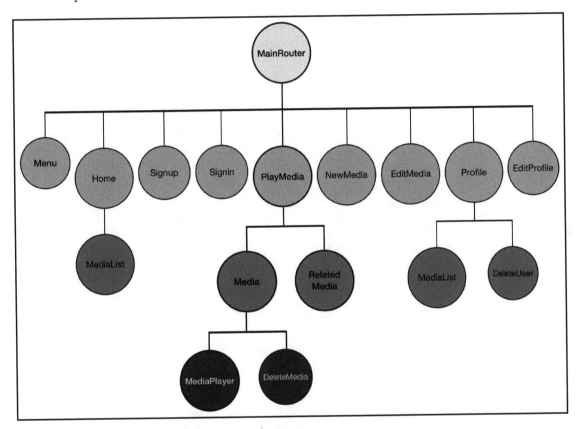

New components added in this chapter include the `MediaPlayer` component, which adds a `ReactPlayer` with custom controls, and a `RelatedMedia` component, which contains a list of related videos.

The play media page

When visitors want to view specific media on MERN Mediastream, they will be taken to the play media page, which will contain the media details, a media player to stream the video, and a list of related media that can be played next.

Component structure

We will compose the component structure in the play media page in a way that allows the media data to trickle down to the inner components from the parent component. In this case, the PlayMedia component will be the parent component, containing the RelatedMedia component, and the Media component with a nested MediaPlayer component:

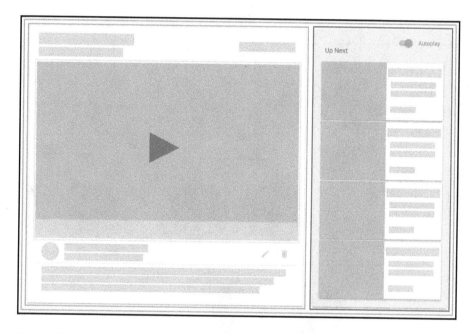

When individual media links are accessed, the PlayMedia component will mount and retrieve the media data and related media list from the server. Then, the relevant data will be passed as props to the Media and RelatedMedia child components.

The RelatedMedia component will link to a list of other related media, and clicking each will re-render the PlayMedia component and inner components with the new data.

We will update the Media component we developed in Chapter 8, *Building a Media-Streaming Application*, to add a customized media player as a child component. This customized MediaPlayer component will also utilize the data passed from PlayMedia to stream the current video and link to the next video in the related media list.

In the `PlayMedia` component, we will add an autoplay toggle that will let users choose to autoplay the videos in the related media list, one after the other. The autoplay state will be managed from the `PlayMedia` component but this feature will require the data in state to re-render when a video ends in the `MediaPlayer`, which is a nested child component, so the next video can start playing automatically while keeping track of the related list.

To achieve this, the `PlayMedia` component will need to provide a state updating method as a prop, which will be used in the `MediaPlayer` component to update the shared and interdependent state values across these components.

Taking this component structure into consideration, we will extend and update the MERN Mediastream application to implement a functional play media page.

Related media list

The related media list will consist of other media records that belong to the same genre as the given video and is sorted by the highest number of views.

Related list API

In order to retrieve the list of related media from the database, we will set up an API on the server that will receive a GET request at `'/api/media/related/:mediaId'`.

mern-mediastream/server/routes/media.routes.js:

```
router.route('/api/media/related/:mediaId')
        .get(mediaCtrl.listRelated)
```

The `listRelated` controller method will query the Media collection to find records with the same genre as the media provided, and also exclude this media record from the results returned. The results returned will be sorted by the highest number of views and limited to the top four media records. Each `media` object in the returned results will also contain the name and ID of the user who posted the media.

mern-mediastream/server/controllers/media.controller.js:

```
const listRelated = (req, res) => {
  Media.find({ "_id": { "$ne": req.media },
  "genre": req.media.genre}).limit(4)
  .sort('-views')
  .populate('postedBy', '_id name')
```

```
    .exec((err, posts) => {
      if (err) {
        return res.status(400).json({
          error: errorHandler.getErrorMessage(err)
        })
      }
      res.json(posts)
    })
  }
```

On the client side, we will set up a corresponding `fetch` method that will be used in the `PlayMedia` component to retrieve the related list of media using this API.

`mern-mediastream/client/media/api-media.js`:

```
  const listRelated = (params) => {
    return fetch('/api/media/related/'+ params.mediaId, {
      method: 'GET',
      headers: {
        'Accept': 'application/json',
        'Content-Type': 'application/json'
      }
    }).then(response => {
      return response.json()
    }).catch((err) => console.log(err))
  }
```

The RelatedMedia component

The `RelatedMedia` component takes the list of related media as a prop from the `PlayMedia` component, and renders the details along with a video snapshot of each video in the list.

We iterate through the media list using the `map` function to render each media item.

`mern-mediastream/client/media/RelatedMedia.js`:

```
  {this.props.media.map((item, i) => {
    return
      <span key={i}>... video snapshot ... | ... media details ...</span>
  })
  }
```

To show the video snapshot, we will use a basic `ReactPlayer` without the controls.

`mern-mediastream/client/media/RelatedMedia.js`:

```
<Link to={"/media/"+item._id}>
  <ReactPlayer url={'/api/media/video/'+item._id} width='160px'
  height='140px'/>
</Link>
```

Clicking on the snapshot will re-render the PlayMedia view to load the linked media details:

Beside the snapshot, we will display the details of each video including title, genre, created date, and number of views.

`mern-mediastream/client/media/RelatedMedia.js`:

```
<Typography type="title" color="primary">{item.title}</Typography>
<Typography type="subheading"> {item.genre} </Typography>
<Typography component="p">
        {(new Date(item.created)).toDateString()}
</Typography>
<Typography type="subheading">{item.views} views</Typography>
```

To use this `RelatedMedia` component in the view, we will add it in the `PlayMedia` component.

The PlayMedia component

The `PlayMedia` component consists of the `Media` and `RelatedMedia` child components along with an autoplay toggle, and it provides data to these components when it loads in the view. To render the `PlayMedia` component when individual media links are accessed by the user, we will add a `Route` in `MainRouter` to mount `PlayMedia` at `'/media/:mediaId'`.

`mern-mediastream/client/MainRouter.js`:

```
<Route path="/media/:mediaId" component={PlayMedia}/>
```

When the `PlayMedia` component mounts, it will fetch the media data and the related media list from the server using the `loadMedia` function based on the `media ID` parameter in the route link.

`mern-mediastream/client/media/PlayMedia.js`:

```
loadMedia = (mediaId) => {
    read({mediaId: mediaId}).then((data) => {
      if (data.error) {
        this.setState({error: data.error})
      } else {
        this.setState({media: data})
          listRelated({
            mediaId: data._id}).then((data) => {
            if (data.error) {
              console.log(data.error)
            } else {
```

```
                    this.setState({relatedMedia: data})
                }
            })
        }
    })
}
```

The `loadMedia` function uses the media ID and the `read` API `fetch` method to retrieve the media details from the server. Then, it uses the `listRelated` API fetch method to retrieve the related media list from the server and sets the values to state.

The `loadMedia` function is called with the `mediaId` value when the component mounts and also when it will receive props.

`mern-mediastream/client/media/PlayMedia.js`:

```
componentDidMount = () => {
    this.loadMedia(this.match.params.mediaId)
}
componentWillReceiveProps = (props) => {
    this.loadMedia(props.match.params.mediaId)
}
```

To access the `mediaId` parameter in the route URL when the component mounts, we need to access the react-router `match` object in the component's constructor.

`mern-mediastream/client/media/PlayMedia.js`:

```
constructor({match}) {
    super()
    this.state = {
        media: {postedBy: {}},
        relatedMedia: [],
        autoPlay: false,
    }
    this.match = match
}
```

The media and related media list values stored in the component's state are used to pass relevant props to the child components that are added in the view. For example, the RelatedMedia component is only rendered if the list of related media contains any items, and passed to the list as a prop.

mern-mediastream/client/media/PlayMedia.js:

```
{this.state.relatedMedia.length > 0 &&
    (<RelatedMedia media={this.state.relatedMedia}/>) }
```

Later in the chapter, in the *Autoplaying related media* section, we will add the autoplay toggle component above the RelatedMedia component only if the length of the related media list is greater than zero. We will also discuss the implementation of the handleAutoPlay method that will be passed as a prop to the Media component, along with the media detail object, and the video URL for the first media in the related media list as the next URL to play.

mern-mediastream/client/media/PlayMedia.js:

```
const nextUrl = this.state.relatedMedia.length > 0
        ? `/media/${this.state.relatedMedia[0]._id}` : ''
<Media media={this.state.media}
      nextUrl={nextUrl}
      handleAutoplay={this.handleAutoplay}/>
```

The Media component renders the media details, and also a media player that allows viewers to control the streaming of the video.

Media player

We will customize the player controls on ReactPlayer to replace the default browser controls with a custom look and functionality, as seen in this screenshot:

The controls will be added below the video and will include the progress seekbar, the play, pause, next, volume, loop, and fullscreen options, and also display the played-duration time.

Updating the Media component

We will create a new `MediaPlayer` component that will contain the customized `ReactPlayer`. In the `Media` component, we will replace the previously used `ReactPlayer` with the new `MediaPlayer` component, and pass on the video source URL, the next video's URL and the `handleAutoPlay` method, which are received as `props` from the `PlayMedia` component.

```
mern-mediastream/client/media/Media.js:

    const mediaUrl = this.props.media._id
                ? `/api/media/video/${this.props.media._id}`
                : null
    ...
    <MediaPlayer srcUrl={mediaUrl}
                nextUrl={this.props.nextUrl}
                handleAutoplay={this.props.handleAutoplay}/>
```

Initializing the media player

The `MediaPlayer` component will contain the `ReactPlayer` component, starting with the initial control values before we add the custom controls and handling code.

First, we will set the initial control values to `state`.

```
mern-mediastream/client/media/MediaPlayer.js:

    state = {
        playing: true,
        volume: 0.8,
        muted: false,
        played: 0,
        loaded: 0,
        duration: 0,
        ended:false,
        playbackRate: 1.0,
        loop: false,
        fullscreen: false,
        videoError: false
    }
```

In the view, we will add `ReactPlayer` with the control values and source URL, using the prop sent from the `Media` component.

```
mern-mediastream/client/media/MediaPlayer.js:

    const { playing, ended, volume, muted, loop, played, loaded, duration,
    playbackRate, fullscreen, videoError } = this.state
    ...
      <ReactPlayer
         ref={this.ref}
         width={fullscreen ? '100%':'inherit'}
         height={fullscreen ? '100%':'inherit'}
```

```
style={fullscreen ? {position:'relative'} : {maxHeight: '500px'}}
config={{ attributes: { style: { height: '100%', width: '100%' } } }}
url={this.props.srcUrl}
playing={playing}
loop={loop}
playbackRate={playbackRate}
volume={volume}
muted={muted}
onEnded={this.onEnded}
onError={this.videoError}
onProgress={this.onProgress}
onDuration={this.onDuration}/>
```

We will get a reference to this player, so it can be used in the change-handling code for the custom controls.

mern-mediastream/client/media/MediaPlayer.js:

```
ref = player => {
    this.player = player
}
```

If the source video cannot be loaded, we will catch the error.

mern-mediastream/client/media/MediaPlayer.js:

```
videoError = e => {
  this.setState({videoError: true})
}
```

Then we will conditionally show an error message in the view.

mern-mediastream/client/media/MediaPlayer.js:

```
{videoError && <p className={classes.videoError}>Video Error. Try again
later.</p>}
```

Custom media controls

We will add custom player control elements below the video and manipulate their functionality using the options and events provided by the ReactPlayer API.

Play, pause, and replay

Users will be able to play, pause, and replay the current video, and we will implement these three options using `Material-UI` components bound to `ReactPlayer` attributes and events:

To implement the play, pause, and replay functionality, we will add a play, pause, or replay icon button conditionally depending on whether the video is playing, paused, or has ended.

`mern-mediastream/client/media/MediaPlayer.js`:

```
<IconButton color="primary" onClick={this.playPause}>
    <Icon>{playing ? 'pause': (ended ? 'replay' : 'play_arrow')}</Icon>
</IconButton>
```

When the user clicks the button, we will update the playing value in state, so that `ReactPlayer` is updated.

`mern-mediastream/client/media/MediaPlayer.js`:

```
playPause = () => {
    this.setState({ playing: !this.state.playing })
}
```

Play next

Users will be able to play the next video in the related media list using the next button:

The next button will be disabled if the related list does not contain any media. The play next icon will basically link to the next URL value passed in as a prop from `PlayMedia`.

```
mern-mediastream/client/media/MediaPlayer.js:
```

```
    <IconButton disabled={!this.props.nextUrl} color="primary">
        <Link to={this.props.nextUrl}>
            <Icon>skip_next</Icon>
        </Link>
    </IconButton>
```

Clicking on this `next` button will reload the `PlayMedia` component with the new media details and start playing the video.

Loop on ended

Users will also be able to set the current video to keep playing in a loop using the loop button:

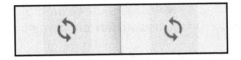

We will set up a loop icon button that will render in a different color to indicate whether it is set or unset.

```
mern-mediastream/client/media/MediaPlayer.js:
```

```
    <IconButton color={loop? 'primary' : 'default'}
                onClick={this.onLoop}>
        <Icon>loop</Icon>
    </IconButton>
```

When the loop icon button is clicked, it updates the `loop` value in state.

```
mern-mediastream/client/media/MediaPlayer.js:
```

```
    onLoop = () => {
        this.setState({ loop: !this.state.loop })
    }
```

We will need to catch the `onEnded` event, to check whether `loop` has been set to true, so the `playing` value can be updated accordingly.

`mern-mediastream/client/media/MediaPlayer.js`:

```
onEnded = () => {
    if(this.state.loop){
      this.setState({ playing: true})
    }else{
      this.setState({ ended: true, playing: false })
    }
}
```

So if the `loop` is set to true, when the video ends, it will start playing again, otherwise it will stop playing and render the replay button.

Volume control

In order to control the volume on the video being played, users will have the option to increase or decrease the volume, as well as to mute or un-mute. The rendered volume controls will be updated based on the user action and current value of the volume:

- A volume up icon will be rendered if the volume is raised:

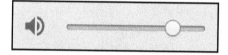

- A volume off icon will be rendered if the user decreases the volume to zero:

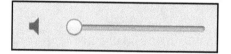

- A volume mute icon button will be shown if the user clicks the icon to mute the volume:

To implement this, we will conditionally render the different icons in an `IconButton`, based on the `volume`, `muted`, `volume_up`, and `volume_off` values:

```
<IconButton color="primary" onClick={this.toggleMuted}>
    <Icon> {volume > 0 && !muted && 'volume_up' ||
            muted && 'volume_off' ||
            volume==0 && 'volume_mute'} </Icon>
</IconButton>
```

When this volume button is clicked, it will either mute or unmute the volume.

`mern-mediastream/client/media/MediaPlayer.js`:

```
toggleMuted = () => {
    this.setState({ muted: !this.state.muted })
}
```

To allow users to increase or decrease the volume, we will add an `input` range that will allow users to set a volume value between 0 and 1.

`mern-mediastream/client/media/MediaPlayer.js`:

```
<input type="range"
        min={0}
        max={1}
        step='any'
        value={muted? 0 : volume}
        onChange={this.setVolume}/>
```

Changing the `value` on the input range will set the `volume` value accordingly.

`mern-mediastream/client/media/MediaPlayer.js`:

```
setVolume = e => {
    this.setState({ volume: parseFloat(e.target.value) })
}
```

Progress control

We will use a Material-UI `LinearProgress` component to indicate how much of the video has been buffered, and how much has been played. Then we'll combine this component with a `range input` to give users the ability to move the time slider to a different part of the video and play from there:

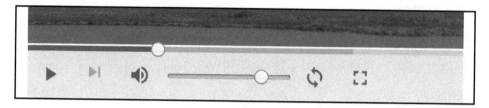

The `LinearProgress` component will take the `played` and `loaded` values to show each in a different color:

```
<LinearProgress color="primary" variant="buffer"
                value={played*100} valueBuffer={loaded*100}
                style={{width: '100%'}}
                classes={{ colorPrimary: classes.primaryColor,
                        dashedColorPrimary: classes.primaryDashed,
                        dashed: {animation: 'none'} }}
/>
```

To update the `LinearProgress` component when the video is playing or loading, we will use the `onProgress` event listener to set the current values for `played` and `loaded`.

`mern-mediastream/client/media/MediaPlayer.js`:

```
onProgress = progress => {
    if (!this.state.seeking) {
      this.setState({played: progress.played, loaded: progress.loaded})
    }
}
```

For time-sliding control, we will add the `range input` element and use CSS styles to place it over the `LinearProgress` component. The current value of the range will update as the `played` value changes, so the range value seems to be moving with the progression of the video.

mern-mediastream/client/media/MediaPlayer.js:

```
<input type="range" min={0} max={1}
       value={played} step='any'
       onMouseDown={this.onSeekMouseDown}
       onChange={this.onSeekChange}
       onMouseUp={this.onSeekMouseUp}
       style={{ position: 'absolute',
                width: '100%',
                top: '-7px',
                zIndex: '999',
                '-webkit-appearance': 'none',
                backgroundColor: 'rgba(0,0,0,0)' }}
/>
```

In the case where the user drags and sets the range picker on their own, we will add code to handle the onMouseDown, onMouseUp, and onChange events to start the video from the desired position.

When the user starts dragging by holding the mouse down, we will set seeking to true, so that the progress values are not set to played and loaded.

mern-mediastream/client/media/MediaPlayer.js:

```
onSeekMouseDown = e => {
    this.setState({ seeking: true })
}
```

As the range value change occurs, we will set the played value and also the ended value, after checking whether the user dragged the time slider to the end of the video.

mern-mediastream/client/media/MediaPlayer.js:

```
onSeekChange = e => {
    this.setState({ played: parseFloat(e.target.value),
                    ended: parseFloat(e.target.value) >= 1 })
}
```

When the user is done dragging and lifts their click on the mouse, we will set seeking to false, and set the seekTo value for the player to the current value in the range input.

mern-mediastream/client/media/MediaPlayer.js:

```
onSeekMouseUp = e => {
    this.setState({ seeking: false })
    this.player.seekTo(parseFloat(e.target.value))
}
```

This way, the user will be able to select any part of the video and also get visual information of the time progress of the video being streamed.

Fullscreen

Users will be able to view the video in fullscreen by clicking the fullscreen button in the controls:

In order to implement a fullscreen option for the video, we will use the `screenfull` npm module to track when the view is in fullscreen, and `findDOMNode` from `react-dom` to specify which DOM element will be made fullscreen with `screenfull`.

To set up the `fullscreen` code, we first install `screenfull`:

```
npm install screenfull --save
```

Then import `screenfull` and `findDOMNode` into the `MediaPlayer` component.

mern-mediastream/client/media/MediaPlayer.js:

```
import screenfull from 'screenfull'
import { findDOMNode } from 'react-dom'
```

When the `MediaPlayer` component mounts, we will add a `screenfull` change event listener that will update the `fullscreen` value in state to indicate whether the screen is in fullscreen or not.

mern-mediastream/client/media/MediaPlayer.js:

```
componentDidMount = () => {
  if (screenfull.enabled) {
    screenfull.on('change', () => {
        let fullscreen = screenfull.isFullscreen ? true : false
        this.setState({fullscreen: fullscreen})
    })
  }
}
```

In the view, we will add an `icon` button for `fullscreen` with the other control buttons.

`mern-mediastream/client/media/MediaPlayer.js`:

```
<IconButton color="primary" onClick={this.onClickFullscreen}>
  <Icon>fullscreen</Icon>
</IconButton>
```

When the user clicks this button, we will use `screenfull` and `findDOMNode` to make the video player fullscreen.

`mern-mediastream/client/media/MediaPlayer.js`:

```
onClickFullscreen = () => {
    screenfull.request(findDOMNode(this.player))
}
```

The user can then watch the video in fullscreen, where they can press *Esc* at any time to exit fullscreen and get back to the PlayMedia view.

Played duration

In the custom media controls section of the media player, we want to show the time that has already passed, and the total duration of the video in a readable time format:

```
0:25 / 1:18
```

To show the time, we can utilize the HTML `time` element.

`mern-mediastream/client/media/MediaPlayer.js`:

```
<time dateTime={`P${Math.round(duration * played)}S`}>
      {this.format(duration * played)}
</time> /
<time dateTime={`P${Math.round(duration)}S`}>
    {this.format(duration)}
</time>
```

We will get the `duration` value for a video by using the `onDuration` event and then set it to state, so it can be rendered in the time element.

`mern-mediastream/client/media/MediaPlayer.js`:

```
onDuration = (duration) => {
    this.setState({ duration })
}
```

To make the duration value readable, we will use the following `format` function.

`mern-mediastream/client/media/MediaPlayer.js`:

```
format = (seconds) => {
  const date = new Date(seconds * 1000)
  const hh = date.getUTCHours()
  let mm = date.getUTCMinutes()
  const ss = ('0' + date.getUTCSeconds()).slice(-2)
  if (hh) {
    mm = ('0' + date.getUTCMinutes()).slice(-2)
    return `${hh}:${mm}:${ss}`
  }
  return `${mm}:${ss}`
}
```

The `format` function takes the duration value in seconds, and converts it to the `hh/mm/ss` format.

The controls added to the custom media player are all mostly based on some of the available functionality in the `ReactPlayer` module, and its examples provided as documentation. There are more options available for further customizations and extensions, which may be explored more depending on specific feature requirements.

Autoplaying related media

We will complete the autoplay functionality discussed earlier by adding a toggle in `PlayMedia`, and implementing the `handleAutoplay` method, which needs to be called when a video ends, in the `MediaPlayer` component.

Toggling autoplay

Besides letting the user set autoplay, the toggle will also indicate whether it is currently set or not:

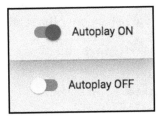

For the autoplay toggle, we will use a `Material-UI Switch` component along with a `FormControlLabel`, and add it to the `PlayMedia` component over the `RelatedMedia` component to be rendered only when there are media in the related media list.

mern-mediastream/client/media/PlayMedia.js:

```
<FormControlLabel
    control={
            <Switch
              checked={this.state.autoPlay}
              onChange={this.handleChange}
              color="primary"
            />
          }
      label={this.state.autoPlay? 'Autoplay ON':'Autoplay OFF'}
/>
```

To handle the change to the toggle and reflect it in the state's `autoplay` value, we will use the following `onChange` handler function.

mern-mediastream/client/media/PlayMedia.js:

```
handleChange = (event) => {
    this.setState({ autoPlay: event.target.checked })
}
```

Handle autoplay across components

`PlayMedia` passes the `handleAutoPlay` method to the `Media` component as a prop to be used by the `MediaPlayer` component when a video ends.

The functionality desired here is that when a video ends, if autoplay is set to true and the current related list of media is not empty, PlayMedia should load the media details of the first video in the related list. In turn, the Media and MediaPlayer components should update with the new media details, start playing the new video and render the controls on the player appropriately. The list in the RelatedMedia component should also update with the current media removed from the list, so only the remaining playlist items are visible.

mern-mediastream/client/media/PlayMedia.js:

```
handleAutoplay = (updateMediaControls) => {
    let playList = this.state.relatedMedia
    let playMedia = playList[0]

    if(!this.state.autoPlay || playList.length == 0 )
      return updateMediaControls()
    if(playList.length > 1){
      playList.shift()
      this.setState({media: playMedia, relatedMedia:playList})
    }else{
      listRelated({
          mediaId: playMedia._id}).then((data) => {
            if (data.error) {
              console.log(data.error)
            } else {
              this.setState({media: playMedia, relatedMedia: data})
            }
        })
    }
  }
```

The handleAutoplay method takes care of the following when a video ends in the MediaPlayer component:

- It takes a callback function from the onEnded event listener in the MediaPlayer component. This callback will be executed if autoplay is not set or the related media list is empty, so that the controls on the MediaPlayer are rendered to show that the video has ended.
- If autoplay is set and there is more than one related media in the list, then:
  - The first item in the related media list is set as the current media object in state so it can be rendered
  - The related media list is updated by removing this first item that will now start playing in the view

- If autoplay is set and there is only one item in the related media list, this last item is set to media so it can start playing, and the `listRelated` fetch method is called to repopulate the RelatedMedia view with the related media of this last item.

Update state when video ends in MediaPlayer

The `MediaPlayer` receives the `handleAutoplay` method as a prop from `PlayMedia`. We will update the listener code for the `onEnded` event to execute this method only when the `loop` is set to `false` for the current video.

mern-mediastream/client/media/MediaPlayer.js:

```
onEnded = () => {
  if(this.state.loop){
    this.setState({ playing: true})
  }else{
    this.props.handleAutoplay(() => {
                              this.setState({ ended: true,
                                              playing: false })
                              })
  }
}
```

A callback function is passed to the `handleAutoplay` method, in order to set playing to false and render the replay icon button instead of the play or pause icon button, after it is determined in `PlayMedia` that the autoplay has not been set or that the related media list is empty.

The autoplay functionality will continue playing the related videos one after the other with this implementation. This implementation demonstrates another way to update state across the components when the values are interdependent.

Server-side rendering with data

Search engine optimization is important for any web application that delivers content to its users, and wants to make the content easy to find. Generally, content on any webpage will have a better chance of getting more viewers if the content is easily readable to search engines. When a search engine bot accesses a web URL, it will get the server-side rendered output. Hence to make the content discoverable, the content should be part of the server-side rendered output.

In MERN Mediastream, we will use the case of making media details popular across search engine results, to demonstrate how to inject data into a server-side rendered view in a MERN application. We will focus on implementing server-side rendering with data injected for the `PlayMedia` component that is returned at the `'/media/:mediaId'` path. The general steps outlined here can be used to implement SSR with data for other views.

Route config

In order to load data for the React views when these are rendered on the server, we will use the React Router Config npm module, which provides static route configuration helpers for React Router:

```
npm install react-router-config --save
```

We will create a route configuration file that will be used to match routes with incoming request URLs on the server to check whether data must be injected before the server returns the rendered markup.

For the route configuration in MERN Mediastream, we will only list the route that renders the `PlayMedia` component.

`mern-mediastream/client/routeConfig.js`:

```
import PlayMedia from './media/PlayMedia'
import { read } from './media/api-media.js'
const routes = [
  {
    path: '/media/:mediaId',
    component: PlayMedia,
    loadData: (params) => read(params)
  }
]
export default routes
```

For this route and component, we will specify the `read` fetch method from `api-media.js` as the load data method. Then it will be used to retrieve and inject the data into the PlayMedia view when the server generates the markup.

Updating SSR code for the Express server

We will update the existing basic server-side rendering code in server/express.js to add the data-loading functionality for the React views that will get rendered server side.

Using route config to load data

We will define loadBranchData to use matchRoutes from react-router-config, and the routes defined in the route configuration file to look for a route matching the incoming request URL.

mern-mediastream/server/express.js:

```
import { matchRoutes } from 'react-router-config'
import routes from './../client/routeConfig'
const loadBranchData = (location) => {
  const branch = matchRoutes(routes, location)
  const promises = branch.map(({ route, match }) => {
    return route.loadData
      ? route.loadData(branch[0].match.params)
      : Promise.resolve(null)
  })
  return Promise.all(promises)
}
```

If a matching route is found, then any associated loadData method will be executed to return a Promise containing the fetched data or null if there were no loadData methods.

The loadBranchData defined here will need to be called whenever the server receives a request, so if any matching route is found, we can fetch the relevant data and inject it into the React components while rendering server side.

Isomorphic-fetch

We will also import isomorphic-fetch in express.js so that the read fetch method, or any other fetch that we defined for the client, can now be used on the server.

```
mern-mediastream/server/express.js:
```

```
import 'isomorphic-fetch'
```

Absolute URL

One issue with using `isomorphic-fetch` is that it currently requires the fetch URLs to be absolute. So we need to update the URL used in the `read` fetch method, defined in `api-media.js`, into an absolute URL.

Instead of hardcoding a server address in the code, we will set a `config` variable in `config.js`.

```
mern-mediastream/config/config.js:
```

```
serverUrl: process.env.serverUrl || 'http://localhost:3000'
```

Then we will update the `read` method in `api-media.js` to make it use an absolute URL to call the read API on the server.

```
mern-mediastream/client/media/api-media.js:
```

```
import config from '../../config/config'
const read = (params) => {
  return fetch(config.serverUrl +'/api/media/' + params.mediaId, {
    method: 'GET'
  }).then((response) => { ... })
```

This will make the `read` fetch call compatible with `isomorphic-fetch` so it can be used without a problem on the server.

Injecting data into React app

In the existing server-side render code in the backend, we use `ReactDOMServer` to convert the React app to markup. We will update this code in `express.js` to inject data as a prop into `MainRouter` after it is fetched using the `loadBranchData` method.

`mern-mediastream/server/express.js`:

```
...
loadBranchData(req.url).then(data => {
    const markup = ReactDOMServer.renderToString(
      <StaticRouter location={req.url} context={context}>
        <JssProvider registry={sheetsRegistry}
      generateClassName={generateClassName}>
      <MuiThemeProvider theme={theme} sheetsManager={new Map()}>
        < MainRouter data={data}/>
      </MuiThemeProvider>
    </JssProvider>
      </StaticRouter>
    )
...
}).catch(err => {
   res.status(500).send("Data could not load")
  })
...
```

For this data to be added in the rendered `PlayMedia` component when the server generates the markup, we need to update the client-side code to consider server injected data.

Applying server-injected data in client code

On the client side, we will access the data passed from the server and add it to the PlayMedia view.

Passing data props to PlayMedia from MainRouter

While generating markup with `ReactDOMServer.renderToString`, we pass the preloaded data to `MainRouter` as a prop. We can access that data prop in the constructor for `MainRouter`.

`mern-mediastream/client/MainRouter.js`:

```
constructor({data}) {
  super()
    this.data = data
}
```

To give `PlayMedia` access to this data, we will change the `Route` component for `PlayMedia` to pass this data as a prop.

`mern-mediastream/client/MainRouter.js`:

```
<Route path="/media/:mediaId"
       render={ (props) => (
           <PlayMedia {...props} data={this.data} />
       )} />
```

Rendering received data in PlayMedia

In the `PlayMedia` component, we will check for data passed from the server and set the values to state so the media details are rendered in the view.

`mern-mediastream/client/media/PlayMedia.js`:

```
...
render() {
    if (this.props.data && this.props.data[0] != null) {
      this.state.media = this.props.data[0]
      this.state.relatedMedia = []
    }
...
}
```

This will produce server-generated markup with media data injected in the PlayMedia view.

Checking the implementation of SSR with data

For MERN Mediastream, any of the links that render PlayMedia should now generate markup on the server side with media details preloaded. We can verify that the implementation for server-side rendering with data is working properly by opening the app URL in a browser with JavaScript turned off. We will look into how to achieve this in the Chrome browser and what the resulting view should show to the user and to the search engine.

Test in Chrome

Testing this implementation in Chrome just requires updating the Chrome settings and loading the application in a tab with JS blocked.

Loading a page with JS enabled

First, open the application in Chrome, then browse to any media link and let it render normally with JavaScript enabled. This should show the implemented PlayMedia view with the functioning media player and the related media list.

Disabling JS from settings

Next, disable JavaScript on Chrome. For this you can go to advanced settings at `chrome://settings/content/javascript`, and use the toggle to block JavaScript:

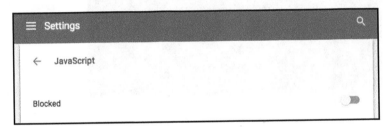

Now, refresh the media link in the MERN Mediastream tab, and there will be an icon next to the address URL showing that JavaScript is indeed disabled:

PlayMedia view with JS blocked

The PlayMedia view should render similar to the following picture, with only the media details populated. But the user interface is no longer interactive as JavaScript is blocked and only the default browser controls are operational:

This is what a search engine bot will read for media content and what a user will see when no JavaScript loads on the browser.

MERN Mediastream now has fully operational media-playing tools that will allow users to browse and play videos with ease. In addition, the media views that display individual media content are now search-engine optimized because of server-side rendering with preloaded data.

Summary

In this chapter, we completely upgraded the play media page on MERN Mediastream by adding custom media player controls using options available with `ReactPlayer` enabling the autoplay functionality for a related media playlist after retrieving the related media from the database and making the media details search engine readable by injecting data from the server when the view is rendered on the server.

Now that we have explored advanced capabilities, such as streaming and SEO, with the MERN stack technologies, in the upcoming chapters, we will test the potential of this stack further by incorporating virtual reality elements into a web application.

10
Developing a Web-Based VR Game

The advent of **virtual reality** (**VR**) and **augmented reality** (**AR**) technologies are transforming how users interact with software and, in turn, the world around them. The possible applications of VR and AR are innumerable, and though the game industry has been an early adopter, these rapidly developing technologies have the potential to shift paradigms across multiple disciplines and industries.

In order to demonstrate how the MERN stack paired with React 360 can easily add VR capabilities to any web application, we will discuss and develop a dynamic, web-based VR game in this and the next chapter.

By covering the following topics, this chapter will focus on defining the features of the VR game and developing the game view using React 360:

- VR game specifications
- Key concepts for developing 3D VR applications
- Getting started with React 360
- Defining game data
- Implementing the game view
- Bundling the React 360 code for integration with the MERN skeleton

MERN VR Game

The MERN VR Game web application will be developed by extending the MERN skeleton and integrating VR capabilities using React 360. It will be a dynamic, web-based VR game application, in which registered users can make their own games, and any visitor to the application can play these games:

The features of the game itself will be simple enough to expose the capabilities of introducing VR into a MERN-based application, without delving too deeply into advanced concepts of React 360 that may be used to implement more complex VR features.

The code to implement features of the VR game using React 360 is available on GitHub at `github.com/shamahoque/MERNVR`. You can clone this code and run the application as you go through the code explanations in the rest of this chapter.

Game features

Each game in MERN VR Game will basically be a different VR world, where users can interact with 3D objects placed at different locations in the 360 degree panoramic world.

The gameplay will be similar to that of a scavenger hunt, and to complete each game, users will have to find and collect the 3D objects that are relevant to the clue or description for each game. This means the game world will contain some VR objects that can be collected by the player, and some VR objects that cannot be collected, but that may be placed by makers of the game as props or hints.

Focus of this chapter

In this chapter, we will build out the game features using React 360, focusing primarily on concepts that will be relevant to implement the features defined earlier. Once the game features are ready, we will discuss how the React 360 code can be bundled and prepared to be integrated with the MERN application code developed in Chapter 11, *Making the VR Game Dynamic Using MERN*.

React 360

React 360 makes it possible to build VR experiences using the same declarative and component-based approach in React. The underlying technology of React 360 makes use of the Three.js JavaScript 3D engine to render 3D graphics with WebGL within any compatible web browser, and also provides access to VR headsets with the Web VR API.

Though React 360 builds on top of React and the apps run in the browser, React 360 has a lot in common with React Native, thus making React 360 apps cross-platform. This also means concepts from React Native are also applicable for React 360. Covering all the React 360 concepts is outside the scope of this book, hence we will focus on concepts required to build the game and integrate it with the MERN stack web application.

Getting started with React 360

React 360 provides developer tools that make it easy to start developing a new React 360 project. The steps to get started are detailed in the React 360 docs, so we will only summarize the steps, and point out the files relevant to developing the game.

Since we already have Node installed for the MERN applications, we can start by installing the React 360 CLI tool:

```
npm install -g react-360-cli
```

Use this React 360 CLI tool to create a new application and install the required dependencies:

```
react-360 init MERNVR
```

This will add the application with all the necessary files in a folder named MERNVR in the current directory. Finally, we can go into this folder from the command line, and run the application:

```
npm start
```

The start command will initialize the local development server, and the default React 360 application can be viewed in the browser at http://localhost:8081/index.html.

To update the starter application and implement our game features, we will modify code mainly in the index.js file with some minor updates in the client.js file found in the MERNVR project folder.

The default code in index.js for the starter application should be as follows, and it renders a **Welcome to React 360** text in a 360 world in the browser:

```
import React from 'react'
import { AppRegistry, StyleSheet, Text, View } from 'react-360'

export default class MERNVR extends React.Component {
  render() {
    return (
      <View style={styles.panel}>
        <View style={styles.greetingBox}>
          <Text style={styles.greeting}>
            Welcome to React 360
          </Text>
        </View>
      </View>
    )
  }
}

const styles = StyleSheet.create({
  panel: {
    // Fill the entire surface
    width: 1000,
    height: 600,
    backgroundColor: 'rgba(255, 255, 255, 0.4)',
    justifyContent: 'center',
    alignItems: 'center',
  },
  greetingBox: {
    padding: 20,
    backgroundColor: '#000000',
    borderColor: '#639dda',
```

```
    borderWidth: 2,
  },
  greeting: {
    fontSize: 30,
  }
})

AppRegistry.registerComponent('MERNVR', () => MERNVR)
```

This `index.js` file contains the application's content and the main code. The code in `client.js` contains the boilerplate that connects the browser to the React application in `index.js`. The default `client.js` in the starter project folder should look as follows:

```
import {ReactInstance} from 'react-360-web'

function init(bundle, parent, options = {}) {
  const r360 = new ReactInstance(bundle, parent, {
    // Add custom options here
    fullScreen: true,
    ...options,
  })

  // Render your app content to the default cylinder surface
  r360.renderToSurface(
    r360.createRoot('MERNVR', { /* initial props */ }),
    r360.getDefaultSurface()
  )

  // Load the initial environment
  r360.compositor.setBackground(r360.getAssetURL('360_world.jpg'))
}

window.React360 = {init}
```

This code basically executes the React code defined in `index.js`, essentially creating a new instance of React 360 and loading the React code by attaching it to the DOM.

With the default React 360 project set up, and before modifying the code to implement the game, we will first look at some of the key concepts related to developing 3D VR experiences in the context of how these concepts are applied with React 360.

Key concepts for developing the VR game

Before creating VR content and an interactive 360 degree experience for the game, it is important to first understand some key aspects of the virtual world and how React 360 components can be used to work with these VR concepts.

Equirectangular panoramic images

The VR world for the game will be composed of a panoramic image which is added to the React 360 Environment as a background image.

Panorama images are generally 360 degree images or spherical panoramas projected onto a sphere that completely surrounds the viewer. A common and popular format for 360 degree panorama images is the equirectangular format. React 360 degree currently supports mono and stereo formats for equirectangular images.

To learn more about the 360 image and video support in React 360, refer to the React 360 docs

at `facebook.github.io/react-360/docs/setup.html`.

The image shown here is an example of an equirectangular, 360 degree panoramic image. To set the world background for a game in MERN VR Game, we will use this kind of image:

An equirectangular panoramic image consists of a single image with an aspect ratio of 2:1, where the width is twice the height. These images are created with a special 360 degree camera. An excellent source of equirectangular images is Flickr, you just need to search for the `equirectangular` tag.

Creating the game world by setting the background scene using a equirectangular image in a React 360 Environment will make the VR experience immersive and transport the user to a virtual location. To enhance this experience and add 3D objects in this VR world effectively, we need to learn more about the layout and coordinate system relevant to the 3D space.

3D position – coordinates and transforms

We need to understand positions and orientation in the VR world space, in order to place 3D objects at desired locations, and to make the VR experience feel more real.

3D coordinate system

For mapping in a 3D space, React 360 uses a three-dimensional meter based coordinate system similar to the OpenGL® 3D Coordinate System, allowing individual components to be transformed, moved, or rotated in 3D relative to the layout in their parent component.

The 3D coordinate system used in React 360 is a right-handed system. This means the positive x-axis is to the right, the positive y-axis is up, and the positive z-axis is backwards. This provides a better mapping with common coordinate systems of the world space in assets and 3D world modeling.

If we try to visualize the 3D space, the user starts out at the center of the **X-Y-Z** axes pictured in the next image. The **Z**-axis points forward toward the user and the user is looking out at the **-Z**-axis direction. The **Y**-axis runs up and down, whereas the **X**-axis runs from side to side.

The curved arrow in the image shows the direction of positive rotation values:

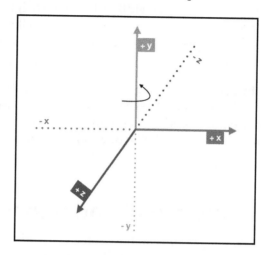

Transform

In the following two images, the 3D book object is placed in two different positions and orientations by changing the `transform` properties in the style attribute of the React 360 `Entity` component that is rendering the 3D object. The transform here is based on the transform style of React, which React 360 extends to be fully 3D, considering the X-Y-Z axes:

The `transform` properties are added to components in the `style` attribute as an array of keys and values in the following form:

```
style={{ ...
        transform: [
          {TRANSFORM_COMMAND: TRANSFORM_VALUE},
          ...
        ]
... }}
```

The transform commands and values relevant to the 3D objects to be placed in our games are `translate [x, y, z]`, with values in meters, `rotate [x, y, z]`, with values in degrees, and `scale`, to determine the size of the object across all axes. We will also utilize the matrix command, which accepts a value as an array of 16 numbers representing the translation, rotation, and scale values.

> To learn more about the React 360 3D coordinates and transforms, take a look at the React 360 docs
> at `facebook.github.io/react-360/docs/setup.html`.

React 360 components

React 360 provides a range of components that can be used out of the box to create the VR user interface for the game. Next, we will summarize the specific components that will be used to build out the game features.

Core components

The core components in React 360 include React Native's built-in components: `Text` and `View`. In the game, we will use these two components to add content in the game world.

View

The `View` component is the most fundamental component for building a user interface in React Native, and it maps directly to the native view equivalent on whatever platform React Native is running on. In our case, it will be `<div>` on the browser:

```
<View>
  <Text>Hello</Text>
</View>
```

The `View` component is typically used as a container for other components, it can be nested inside other views and can have zero to many children of any type.

We will use `View` components to hold the game world view, and to add 3D object entities and text to the game.

Text

The `Text` component is a React Native component for displaying text and we will use it to render strings in a 3D space, by placing `Text` components in `View` components:

```
<View>
        <Text>Welcome to the MERN VR Game</Text>
</View>
```

Components for 3D VR experience

React 360 provides a set of its own components to create the VR experience. Specifically, we will use the `Entity` component to add 3D objects and a `VrButton` component to capture clicks from the user.

Entity

In order to add 3D objects to the game world, we will use the `Entity` component, which allows us to render 3D objects in React 360:

```
<Entity
  source={{
        obj: {uri: "http://linktoOBJfile.obj "},
        mtl: {uri: "http://linktoMTLfile.obj "}
      }}
/>
```

Files containing the specific 3D object's information are added to the `Entity` component using a `source` attribute. The source attribute takes an object of key-value pairs to map resource file types to their locations. React 360 supports the Wavefront OBJ file format, a common representation for 3D models. So in the source attribute, the `Entity` component supports the following keys:

- `obj`: Location of an OBJ-formatted model
- `mtl`: Location of an MTL-formatted material (the companion to OBJ)

The values for the `obj` and `mtl` properties point to the location of these files and can be static strings, `asset()` calls, `require()` statements, or URI strings.

OBJ (or .OBJ) is a geometry definition file format first developed by Wavefront Technologies. It is a simple data format that represents 3D geometry as a list of vertices and texture vertices. OBJ coordinates have no units, but OBJ files can contain scale information in a human-readable comment line. Learn more about this format at `paulbourke.net/dataformats/obj/`.

MTL (or .MTL) are material library files that contain one or more material definitions, each of which includes the color, texture, and reflection map of individual materials. These are applied to the surfaces and vertices of objects. Learn more about this format at `paulbourke.net/dataformats/mtl/`.

The `Entity` component also takes `transform` property values in the `style` attribute, so the objects can be placed at the desired positions and orientations in the 3D world space. In our MERN VR Game application, makers will add URLs pointing to the VR object files (both `.obj` and `.mtl`) for each of their `Entity` objects in a game, and also specify the `transform` property values to indicate where and how the 3D objects should be placed in the game world.

A good source of 3D objects is `https://clara.io/`, with multiple file formats available for download and use.

VrButton

The `VrButton` component in React 360 will help to implement a simple, button-style, `onClick` behavior for the objects and `Text` buttons that will be added to the game. A `VrButton` is not visible in the view by default and will only act as a wrapper to capture events, but it can be styled in the same ways as a `View` component:

```
<VrButton onClick={this.clickHandler}>
    <View>
        <Text>Click me to make something happen!</Text>
    </View>
</VrButton>
```

This component is a helper for managing click-type interactions from the user across different input devices. Input events that will trigger the click event include a space button press on the keyboard, a left-click on the mouse, and a touch on the screen.

React 360 API

Besides the React 360 components discussed previously, we will utilize the APIs provided by React 360 to implement functionality such as setting the background scene, playing audio, dealing with external links, adding styles, capturing the current orientation of the user's view, and using static asset files.

Environment

We will use the `Environment` API to change the background scene from the React code using its `setBackgroundImage` method:

```
Environment.setBackgroundImage( {uri: 'http://linktopanoramaimage.jpg' } )
```

This method sets the current background image with the resource at the specified URL. When we integrate the React 360 game code with the MERN stack containing the game application backend, we can use this to set the game world image dynamically using image links provided by the user.

Native Modules

Native Modules in React 360 give the ability to access functionality only available in the main browser environment. In the game, we will use the `AudioModule` in Native Modules to play sounds in response to user activity, and the `Location` module that gives access to `window.location` in the browser to handle external links. These modules can be accessed in `index.js` as follows:

```
import {
    ...
  NativeModules
} from 'react-360'

const { AudioModule, Location } = NativeModules
```

AudioModule

When the user interacts with the 3D objects, we will play sounds based on whether the object can be collected or not, and also whether the game has been completed. The `AudioModule` in Native Modules allows adding sound to the VR world as background environmental audio, one-off sound effects, and spatialized audio. In our game, we will use environmental audio and one-off sound effects.

- **Environmental audio**: To play an audio on loop and set the mood when the game is successfully completed, we will use the `playEnvironmental` method that takes an audio file path as the `source` and `loop` option as a `playback` parameter:

```
AudioModule.playEnvironmental({
    source: asset('happy-bot.mp3'),
    loop: true
})
```

- **Sound effects**: To play a single sound once when the user clicks on 3D objects, we will use the `playOneShot` method that takes an audio file path as the `source`:

```
AudioModule.playOneShot({
    source: asset('clog-up.mp3'),
})
```

The `source` attribute in the options passed to `playEnvironmental` and `playOneShot` takes a resource file location to load the audio. It can be an `asset()` statement, or a resource URL declaration in the form of `{uri: 'PATH'}`.

Location

After we integrate the React 360 code with the MERN stack containing the game application backend, the VR game will be launched from the MERN server at a declared route containing the specific game's ID. Then, once a user completes a game, they will also have the option to leave the VR space, and go to a URL containing a list of other games. To handle these incoming and outgoing app links in the React 360 code, we will utilize the `Location` module in Native Modules.

The Location module is essentially the Location object returned by the read-only window.location property in the browser. We will use the replace method and search property in the Location object to implement features related to external links.

- **Handling outgoing links**: When we want to direct the user out of the VR application to another link, we can use the replace method in Location:

  Location.replace(url)

- **Handling incoming links**: When the React 360 app is launched from an external URL and after the registered component mounts, we can access the URL and retrieve its query string part using the search property in Location:

  ```
  componentDidMount = () => {
      let queryString = Location.search
      let gameId = queryString.split('?id=')[1]
  }
  ```

For the purpose of integrating this React 360 component with MERN VR Game, and dynamically loading game details, we will capture this initial URL to parse the game ID from a query parameter and then use it to make a read API call to the MERN application server. This implementation is elaborated upon in Chapter 11, *Making the VR Game Dynamic Using MERN*.

StyleSheet

The StyleSheet API from React Native can also be used in React 360 to define several styles in one place rather than adding styles to individual components:

```
const styles = StyleSheet.create({
  subView: {
    width: 10,
    borderColor: '#d6d7da',
  },
  text: {
    fontSize: '1em',
    fontWeight: 'bold',
  }
})
```

The defined styles can be added to components as required:

```
<View style={styles.subView}>
  <Text style={styles.text}>hello</Text>
</View>
```

 The default distance units for CSS properties, such as width and height, are in meters when mapping to 3D space in React 360, whereas the default distance units are in pixels for 2D interfaces, as in React Native.

VrHeadModel

VrHeadModel is a utility module in React 360 that simplifies obtaining the current orientation of the headset. Since the user is moving around in a VR space, when a desired feature requires that an object or text should be placed in front of or with respect to the user's current orientation, it becomes necessary to know where exactly the user is currently gazing.

In MERN VR Game, we will use this to show the game **completed message** to the user in front of their view, no matter where they end up turning to from the initial position.

For example, the user may be looking up or down when collecting the final object, and the completed message should pop up wherever the user is gazing. To implement this, we will retrieve the current head matrix as an array of numbers using getHeadMatrix() from VrHeadModel, and set it as a value for the transform property in the style attribute of the View containing the game completed message.

Assets

The asset() functionality in React 360 allows us to retrieve external resource files, such as audio and image files. We will place the sound audio files for the game in the static_assets folder, to be retrieved using asset() for each audio added to the game:

```
AudioModule.playOneShot({
    source: asset('collect.mp3'),
})
```

React 360 input events

In order to make the game interface interactive, we will utilize some of the input event handlers exposed in React 360. Input events are collected from mouse, keyboard, touch, and gamepad interactions, and also with the gaze button click on a VR headset. The specific input events we will work with are the onEnter, onExit, and onClick events.

- **onEnter**: This event is fired whenever the platform cursor begins intersecting with a component. We will capture this event for the VR objects in the game, so the objects can start rotating around the Y-axis when the platform cursor enters the specific object.
- **onExit**: This event is fired whenever the platform cursor stops intersecting with a component. It has the same properties as the onEnter event and we will use it to stop rotating the VR object just exited.
- **onClick**: The onClick event is used with the VrButton component, and is fired when there is click interaction with VrButton. We will use this to set click event handlers on the VR objects, and also on the game complete message to redirect the user out of the VR application to a link containing a list of games.

With the VR-related concepts and React 360 components discussed in this section, we are ready to define the game data details and start implementing the complete VR game.

Game details

Each game in MERN VR Game will be defined in a common data structure that the React 360 application will also adhere to when rendering the individual game details.

Game data structure

The game data structure will hold details such as the game's name, a URL pointing to the location of the equirectangular image for the game world, and two arrays containing details for each VR object to be added to the game world:

- **name**: A string representing the name of the game
- **world**: A string with the URL pointing to the equirectangular image either hosted on cloud storage, CDNS, or stored on MongoDB
- **answerObjects**: An array of objects containing details of the VR objects that can be collected by the player

- **wrongObjects**: An array of objects containing details of the other VR objects to be placed in the VR world that cannot be collected by the player

Details of VR objects

The `answerObjects` array will contain details of the 3D objects that can be collected, and the `wrongObjects` array will contain details of 3D objects that cannot be collected. Each object will contain links to the 3D data resource files and `transform` style property values.

OBJ and MTL links

The 3D data information resources for the VR objects will be added in the `objUrl` and `mtlUrl` keys:

- **objUrl**: Link to the `.obj` file for the 3D object
- **mtlUrl**: Link to the accompanying `.mtl` file

The `objUrl` and `mtlUrl` links may point to files either hosted on cloud storage, CDNS, or stored on MongoDB. For MERN VR Game, we will assume makers will add URLs to their own hosted OBJ, MTL, and equirectangular image files.

Translation values

The position of the VR object in the 3D space will be defined with the `translate` values in the following keys:

- **translateX**: Translation value of the object along the X-axis
- **translateY**: Translation value of the object along the Y-axis
- **translateZ**: Translation value of the object along the Z-axis

All translation values are numbers in meters.

Rotation values

The orientation of the 3D object will be defined with the `rotate` values in the following keys:

- **rotateX**: Rotation value of the object around the X-axis, in other words, turning the object up or down
- **rotateY**: Rotation value of the object around the Y-axis that would turn the object left or right
- **rotateZ**: Rotation value of the object around the Z-axis, making the object tilt forward or backward

All rotation values are in numbers or string representations of a number in degrees.

Scale value

The `scale` value will define the relative size appearance of the 3D object:

scale: A number value that defines uniform scale across all axes

Color

If the 3D object's material texture is not provided in an MTL file, the color value can define the default color of the object.

color: A string value representing color values allowed in CSS

With this game data structure capable of holding details of the game and its VR objects, we can implement the game in React 360 accordingly with sample data values.

Static data versus dynamic data

In the next chapter, we will update the React 360 code to fetch game data dynamically from the backend database. For now, we will start developing the game features here with dummy game data set to `state` with the defined game data structure.

Sample data

For initial development purposes, the following sample game data can be set to state to be rendered in the game view:

```
game: {
  name: 'Space Exploration',
  world: 'https://s3.amazonaws.com/mernbook/vrGame/milkyway.jpg',
  answerObjects: [
    {
      objUrl: 'https://s3.amazonaws.com/mernbook/vrGame/planet.obj',
      mtlUrl: 'https://s3.amazonaws.com/mernbook/vrGame/planet.mtl',
      translateX: -50,
      translateY: 0,
      translateZ: 30,
      rotateX: 0,
      rotateY: 0,
      rotateZ: 0,
      scale: 7,
      color: 'white'
    }
  ],
  wrongObjects: [
    {
      objUrl: 'https://s3.amazonaws.com/mernbook/vrGame/tardis.obj',
      mtlUrl: 'https://s3.amazonaws.com/mernbook/vrGame/tardis.mtl',
      translateX: 0,
      translateY: 0,
      translateZ: 90,
      rotateX: 0,
      rotateY: 20,
      rotateZ: 0,
      scale: 1,
      color: 'white'
    }
  ]
}
```

Building the game view in React 360

We will apply the React 360 concepts, and use the game data structure to implement the game features by updating the code in index.js and client.js. For a working version, we will start with the state initialized using the sample game data from the previous section.

/MERNVR/index.js:

```
export default class MERNVR extends React.Component {

    constructor() {
        super()
        this.state = {
                game: sampleGameData
                ...
            }
    }

...
}
```

Update client.js and mount to Location

The default code in `client.js` attaches the mount point declared in `index.js` to the Default Surface in the React 360 app, where the Surface is a cylindrical layer for placing 2D UI. In order to use the 3D meter-based coordinate system for a layout in 3D space, we need to mount to a `Location` instead of a Surface. So update `client.js` to replace the `renderToSurface` with a `renderToLocation`.

/MERNVR/client.js:

```
r360.renderToLocation(
  r360.createRoot('MERNVR', { /* initial props */ }),
  r360.getDefaultLocation()
)
```

 You can also customize the initial background scene by updating the code r360.compositor.setBackground(**r360.getAssetURL('360_w orld.jpg')**) in `client.js` to use your desired image.

Defining styles with StyleSheet

In `index.js`, we will update the default styles created using `StyleSheet.create` with our own CSS rules, to be used with the components in the game.

/MERNVR/index.js:

```
const styles = StyleSheet.create({
            completeMessage: {
                margin: 0.1,
                height: 1.5,
                backgroundColor: 'green',
                transform: [ {translate: [0, 0, -5] } ]
            },
            congratsText: {
                fontSize: 0.5,
                textAlign: 'center',
                marginTop: 0.2
            },
            collectedText: {
                fontSize: 0.2,
                textAlign: 'center'
            },
            button: {
                margin: 0.1,
                height: 0.5,
                backgroundColor: 'blue',
                transform: [ { translate: [0, 0, -5] } ]
            },
            buttonText: {
                fontSize: 0.3,
                textAlign: 'center'
            }
        })
```

World background

In order to set the the game's 360 degree world background, we will update the current background scene using the `setBackgroundImage` method from the `Environment` API inside `componentDidMount`.

/MERNVR/index.js:

```
componentDidMount = () => {
    Environment.setBackgroundImage(
        {uri: this.state.game.world}
    )
}
```

This will replace the default 360 background in the starter React 360 project with our sample game's world image fetched from cloud storage. If you are editing the default React 360 application and have it running, refreshing the `http://localhost:8081/index.html` link on the browser should show an outer space background, that can be panned around using the mouse:

To generate the preceding screenshot, the `View` and `Text` components in the default code were also updated with custom CSS rules to show this **hello** text on the screen.

Adding 3D VR objects

We will add 3D objects to the game world using `Entity` components and the sample object details in the `answerObjects` and `wrongObjects` arrays.

First, we will concatenate the `answerObjects` and `wrongObjects` arrays in `componentDidMount` to form a single array containing all the VR objects.

`/MERNVR/index.js`:

```
componentDidMount = () => {
  let vrObjects =
this.state.game.answerObjects.concat(this.state.game.wrongObjects)
  this.setState({vrObjects: vrObjects})
    ...
}
```

Then in the main view, we will iterate over the `vrObjects` array to add the `Entity` components with details of each object.

/MERNVR/index.js:

```
{this.state.vrObjects.map((vrObject, i) => {
    return (
                <Entity key={i} style={this.setModelStyles(vrObject, i)}
                  source={{
                    obj: {uri: vrObject.objUrl},
                    mtl: {uri: vrObject.mtlUrl}
                  }}
                />
        )
    })
}
```

The obj and mtl file links are added to source and the transform style details are applied in the Entity component's styles with setModelStyles(vrObject, index).

/MERNVR/index.js:

```
setModelStyles = (vrObject, index) => {
    return {
        display: this.state.collectedList[index] ? 'none' : 'flex',
        color: vrObject.color,
        transform: [
          {
            translateX: vrObject.translateX
          }, {
            translateY: vrObject.translateY
          }, {
            translateZ: vrObject.translateZ
          }, {
            scale: vrObject.scale
          }, {
            rotateY: vrObject.rotateY
          }, {
            rotateX: vrObject.rotateX
          }, {
            rotateZ: vrObject.rotateZ
          }
        ]
    }
}
```

The display property will allow us to show or hide an object based on whether it has been already collected by the player or not.

The `translate` and `rotate` values will render the 3D objects in the desired positions and orientations across the VR world.

Next, we will update the `Entity` code further to enable user interactions with the 3D objects.

Interacting with VR objects

In order to make the VR game objects interactive, we will use the React 360 event handlers, such as `onEnter` and `onExit` with `Entity`, and `onClick` with `VrButton`, to add rotation animation and gameplay behavior.

Rotation

We want to add a feature that starts rotating a 3D object around its Y-axis whenever a player focuses on the 3D object, that is, the platform cursor begins intersecting with the `Entity` rendering the specific 3D object.

We will update the `Entity` component from the previous section to add the `onEnter` and `onExit` handlers.

`/MERNVR/index.js`:

```
<Entity
    ...
    onEnter={this.rotate(i)}
    onExit={this.stopRotate}
/>
```

The object will start rotating on enter, and stop when the platform cursor exits the object and it is no longer in the player's focus.

Animation with requestAnimationFrame

In the `rotate(index)` and `stopRotate()` methods, we will implement rotation animation behavior using `requestAnimationFrame` for smooth animations on the browser.

The `window.requestAnimationFrame()` method asks the browser to call a specified callback function to update an animation before the next repaint. With `requestAnimationFrame`, the browser optimizes the animations to make them smoother and more resource-efficient.

Using the `rotate` method, we will update the `rotateY` transform value of the given object at a steady rate on a set time interval with `requestionAnimationFrame`.

`/MERNVR/index.js`:

```
this.lastUpdate = Date.now()
rotate = index => event => {
    const now = Date.now()
    const diff = now - this.lastUpdate
    const vrObjects = this.state.vrObjects
    vrObjects[index].rotateY = vrObjects[index].rotateY + diff / 200
    this.lastUpdate = now
    this.setState({vrObjects: vrObjects})
    this.requestID = requestAnimationFrame(this.rotate(index))
}
```

The `requestAnimationFrame` will take the `rotate` method as a recursive callback function, then execute it to redraw each frame of the rotation animation with the new values, and in turn update the animation on the screen.

The `requestAnimateFrame` method returns a `requestID`, which we will use in `stopRotate` to cancel the animation in the `stopRotate` method.

`/MERNVR/index.js`:

```
stopRotate = () => {
  if (this.requestID) {
    cancelAnimationFrame(this.requestID)
    this.requestID = null
  }
}
```

This will implement the functionality of animating the 3D object only when it is in the viewer's focus. As seen in the following image, the 3D Rubik's cube rotates clockwise around its Y-axis while it is in focus:

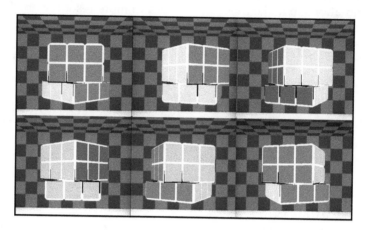

Though not covered here, it is also worth exploring the React 360 Animated library, which can be used to compose different types of animations. Core components can be animated natively with this library, and it is possible to make other components animatable using `createAnimatedComponent()`. This library was originally implemented from React Native, and to learn more you can refer to the React Native documentation.

Clicking the 3D objects

In order to register the click behavior on each 3D object added to the game, we need to wrap the `Entity` component with a `VrButton` component that can call the `onClick` handler.

We will update the `Entity` component added inside the `vrObjects` array iteration code, to wrap it with the `VrButton` component. The `VrButton` will call the `collectItem` method when clicked, and pass it the current object's details.

/MERNVR/index.js:

```
<VrButton onClick={this.collectItem(vrObject)} key={i}>
    <Entity ... />
</VrButton>
```

When a 3D object is clicked, the `collectItem` method needs to perform the following actions with respect to the game features:

- Check whether the clicked object is an `answerObject` or a `wrongObject`
- Based on the object type, play the associated sound
- If the object is an `answerObject`, it should be collected and disappear from view
  - Update collected objects list
- Check whether all instances of `answerObject` were successfully collected with this click
  - If yes, show the game completed message to the player and play the sound for game completed

Hence, the `collectItem` method will have the following structure and steps:

```
collectItem = vrObject => event => {
  if (vrObject is an answerObject) {
    ... update collected list ...
    ... play sound for correct object collected ...
    if (all answer objects collected) {
      ... show game completed message in front of user ...
      ... play sound for game completed ...
    }
  } else {
    ... play sound for wrong object clicked ...
  }
}
```

Next, we will look at the implementation for these steps.

Collecting the correct object on click

When a user clicks on a 3D object, we need to first check whether the clicked object is an answer object. If it is, this *collected* object will be hidden from view and a list of collected objects will be updated along with the total number to keep track of the user's progress in the game.

To check whether the clicked VR object is an `answerObject`, we will use the `indexOf` method to find a match in the `answerObjects` array:

```
let match = this.state.game.answerObjects.indexOf(vrObject)
```

If the `vrObject` is an `answerObject`, `indexOf` will return the array index of the matched object, otherwise it will return −1 if no match is found.

To keep track of collected objects in the game, we will also maintain an array of Boolean values in `collectedList`, and the total number of objects collected so far in `collectedNum`:

```
let updateCollectedList = this.state.collectedList
let updateCollectedNum = this.state.collectedNum + 1
updateCollectedList[match] = true
this.setState({collectedList: updateCollectedList,
               collectedNum: updateCollectedNum})
```

Using the `collectedList` array, we will also determine which `Entity` component should be hidden from the view because the associated object was collected. The `display` style property of the relevant `Entity` will be set based on the Boolean value of the corresponding index in the `collectedList` array, while setting the style for the `Entity` component using the `setModelStyles` method, as shown earlier in the *Adding 3D VR objects* section:

```
display: this.state.collectedList[index] ? 'none' : 'flex'
```

In the following image, the treasure chest can be clicked to be collected as it is an `answerObject`, whereas the flower pot cannot be collected because it is a `wrongObject`:

When the treasure chest is clicked, it disappears from the view as the `collectedList` is updated, and we also play the sound effect for collection using `AudioModule.playOneShot`:

```
AudioModule.playOneShot({
    source: asset('collect.mp3'),
})
```

But when the flower pot is clicked, and it is identified as a wrong object, we play another sound effect indicating it cannot be collected:

```
AudioModule.playOneShot({
    source: asset('clog-up.mp3'),
})
```

As the flower pot was identified to be a wrong object, the `collectedList` was not updated and it remains on the screen as seen in the following screenshot:

The complete code in the `collectItem` method that executes all these steps when an object is clicked will be as follows.

/MERNVR/index.js:

```
collectItem = vrObject => event => {
  let match = this.state.game.answerObjects.indexOf(vrObject)
  if (match != -1) {
    let updateCollectedList = this.state.collectedList
    let updateCollectedNum = this.state.collectedNum + 1
    updateCollectedList[match] = true
```

```
this.checkGameCompleteStatus(updateCollectedNum)
    AudioModule.playOneShot({
      source: asset('collect.mp3'),
    })
    this.setState({collectedList: updateCollectedList, collectedNum:
updateCollectedNum})
  } else {
    AudioModule.playOneShot({
      source: asset('clog-up.mp3'),
    })
  }
}
```

After a clicked object is collected, we will also check whether all the answerObjects have been collected, and the game is complete with the checkGameCompleteStatus method, as discussed in the next section.

Game completed state

Every time an answerObject is collected, we will check whether the total number of collected items is equal to the total number of objects in the answerObjects array to determine whether the game is complete by calling checkGameCompleteStatus.

/MERNVR/index.js:

```
if (collectedTotal == this.state.game.answerObjects.length) {
    AudioModule.playEnvironmental({
        source: asset('happy-bot.mp3'),
        loop: true
    })
    this.setState({hide: 'flex', hmMatrix: VrHeadModel.getHeadMatrix()})
}
```

If the game is indeed complete, we will perform the following actions:

- Play the audio for game completed, using AudioModule.playEnvironmental
- Fetch the current headMatrix value using VrHeadModel so it can be set as the transform matrix value for the View component containing the game completion message
- Set the display style property of the message View to flex, so the message renders to the viewer

The `View` component containing the message congratulating the player for completing the game will be added to the parent `View` component as follows.

/MERNVR/index.js:

```
<View style={this.setGameCompletedStyle}>
    <View style={this.styles.completeMessage}>
        <Text style={this.styles.congratsText}>Congratulations!</Text>
        <Text style={this.styles.collectedText}>
            You have collected all items in {this.state.game.name}
        </Text>
    </View>
    <VrButton onClick={this.exitGame}>
        <View style={this.styles.button}>
            <Text style={this.styles.buttonText}>Play another game</Text>
        </View>
    </VrButton>
</View>
```

The call to the `setGameCompletedStyle()` method will set the styles for the message `View` with the updated `display` value and `transform` matrix value.

/MERNVR/index.js:

```
setGameCompletedStyle = () => {
    return {
        position: 'absolute',
        display: this.state.hide,
        layoutOrigin: [0.5, 0.5],
        width: 6,
        transform: [{translate: [0, 0, 0]}, {matrix: this.state.hmMatrix}]
    }
}
```

This will render the `View` with the completion message at the center of the user's current view, regardless of whether they are looking up, down, behind, or forward in the 360 degree VR world:

The final text in the `View` message will act as a button, as we wrapped this `View` in a `VrButton` component that calls the `exitGame` method when clicked.

`/MERNVR/index.js`:

```
exitGame = () => {
    Location.replace('/')
}
```

The `exitGame` method will use the `Location.replace` method to redirect the user to an external URL that may contain a list of games.

The `replace` method can be passed any valid URL, and once this React 360 game code is integrated with the MERN VR Game application in Chapter 11, *Making the VR Game Dynamic Using MERN*, `replace('/')` will take the user to the home page of the application.

Bundling for production and integration with MERN

Now that we have features of the VR game implemented and functional with sample game data, we can prepare it for production and add it to our MERN base application to see how VR can be added to an existing web application.

React 360 tools provide a script to bundle all the React 360 application code into a few files that we can just place on the MERN web server and serve as content at a specified route.

Bundling React 360 files

To create the bundled files, we can run the following command from the React 360 project directory:

```
npm run bundle
```

This generates compiled versions of the React 360 application files in a folder called build. The compiled bundle files are client.bundle.js and index.bundle.js. These two files, in addition to index.html and the static-assets/ folder, make up the production version of the whole React 360 application that was developed:

    -- static_assets/

    -- index.html

    -- index.bundle.js

    -- client.bundle.js

Integrating with MERN application

We will need to add these three files and the static_assets folder to our MERN application, then make sure the bundle file references are accurate in index.html, and finally load the index.html at a specified route in the Express app.

Add the React 360 production files

With consideration to the folder structure in the MERN skeleton application, we will add the `static_assets` folder and the bundle files to the `dist/` folder to keep our MERN code organized and have all the bundles in the same location. The `index.html` file will be placed in a new folder, named `vr`, in the `server` folder:

```
-- ...
-- client/
-- dist/
    --- static_assets/
    --- ...
    --- client.bundle.js
    --- index.bundle.js
-- ...
-- server/
    --- ...
    --- vr/
        ---- index.html
-- ...
```

Updating references in index.html

The generated `index.html` file, as shown here, references the bundle files, expecting these files to be in the same folder:

```html
<html>
  <head>
    <title>MERNVR</title>
    <style>body { margin: 0 }</style>
    <meta name="viewport" content="width=device-width, initial-scale=1,
user-scalable=no">
  </head>
  <body>
    <!-- Attachment point for your app -->
    <div id="container"></div>
    <script src="./client.bundle.js"></script>
    <script>
      // Initialize the React 360 application
      React360.init(
        'index.bundle.js',
        document.getElementById('container'),
        {
          assetRoot: 'static_assets/',
        }
```

```
      )
    </script>
  </body>
</html>
```

We need to update `index.html` to refer to the correct location of the `client.bundle.js`, `index.bundle.js`, and `static_assets` folders.

First, update the reference to `client.bundle.js` as follows:

```
<script src="/dist/client.bundle.js" type="text/javascript"></script>
```

Then, update `React360.init` with the correct reference to `index.bundle.js`, and `assetRoot` set to the correct location of the `static_assets` folder:

```
React360.init(
        './../dist/index.bundle.js',
        document.getElementById('container'),
        { assetRoot: '/dist/static_assets/' }
    )
```

The `assetRoot` will tell React 360 where to look for asset files when we use `asset()` to set resources in the components.

Now, if we set up an Express route in the MERN application to return the `index.html` file in the response, then visiting the route in the browser will render the React 360 game.

Trying out the integration

To test out this integration, we can set up an example route, as follows:

```
router.route('/game/play')
    .get((req, res) => {
        res.sendFile(process.cwd()+'/server/vr/index.html')
})
```

Then run the MERN server, and open the route in the browser at `localhost:3000/game/play`. This should render the React 360 game implemented in this chapter from within our MERN application.

Summary

In this chapter, we used React 360 to develop a web-based VR game that can be easily integrated into MERN applications.

We began by defining simple VR features for the gameplay, then set up React 360 for development, and looked at key VR concepts such as equirectangular panoramic images, 3D positions, and coordinate systems in the 360-degree VR world. We explored the React 360 components and API required to implement the game features, including components such as `View`, `Text`, `Entity`, and `VrButton`, along with the `Environment`, `VrHeadModel` and `NativeModules` APIs.

Finally, we updated the code in the starter React 360 project to implement the game with sample game data, then bundled the code files and discussed how to add these compiled files to an existing MERN application.

In the next chapter, we will develop the MERN VR Game application, complete with a game database and APIs so we can make the game developed in this chapter dynamic by fetching data from the game collection in MongoDB.

Making the VR Game Dynamic Using MERN

11

In this chapter, we will extend the MERN skeleton application to build the MERN VR game application, and use it to make the static React 360 game developed in the previous chapter dynamic by replacing the sample game data with game details fetched directly from the MERN server.

To make MERN VR Game a complete and dynamic game application, we will implement the following:

- A game model schema to store game details in MongoDB
- APIs for game CRUD operations
- React views for game create, edit, list, and delete
- Updating the React 360 game to fetch data from API
- Loading the VR game with dynamic game data

Dynamic MERN VR Game

Registered users on MERN VR Game will be able to make and modify their own games by providing an equirectangular image for the game world, and the VR object resources, including transform property values for each object to be placed in the game world. Any visitor to the application will be able to browse through all the games added by the makers, and play any game to find and collect the 3D objects in the game world that are relevant to the clue or description of each game:

The code for the complete MERN VR Game application is available on GitHub at `github.com/shamahoque/mern-vrgame`. You can clone this code and run the application as you go through the code explanations in the rest of this chapter.

The views needed for the features related to creating, editing, and listing VR games will be developed by extending and modifying the existing React components in the MERN skeleton application. The component-tree pictured next shows all the custom React components that make up the MERN VR Game frontend developed in this chapter:

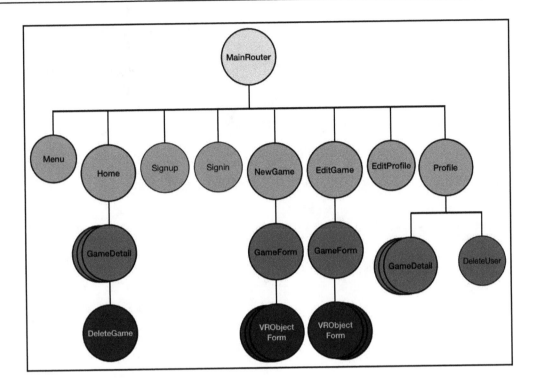

Game model

In Chapter 10, *Developing a Web-Based VR Game*, the *Game data structure* section laid out the details needed for each game in order to implement the scavenger hunt features defined for the gameplay. We will design the game schema based on these specific details about the game, its VR objects, and also a reference to the game maker.

Game schema

In the Mongoose schema for the game model defined in game.model.js, we will add fields for the

- Game's name
- World image URL
- Clue text

- An array containing details of the VR objects to be added as collectable answer objects
- An array containing details of the VR objects that are wrong objects and cannot be collected
- Timestamps indicating when a game is created and updated
- A reference to the user who made the game

The `GameSchema` will be defined as follows.

`mern-vrgame/server/models/game.model.js`:

```
const GameSchema = new mongoose.Schema({
  name: {
    type: String,
    trim: true,
    required: 'Name is required'
  },
  world: {
    type: String, trim: true,
    required: 'World image is required'
  },
  clue: {
    type: String,
    trim: true
  },
  answerObjects: [VRObjectSchema],
  wrongObjects: [VRObjectSchema],
  updated: Date,
  created: {
    type: Date,
    default: Date.now
  },
  maker: {type: mongoose.Schema.ObjectId, ref: 'User'}
})
```

VRObject schema

The `answerObjects` and `wrongObjects` fields in the game schema will both be arrays of VRObject documents, and the VRObject Mongoose schema will be defined separately with fields for storing the URLs of the OBJ file and MTL file, along with the React 360 `transform` values for each VR object, the `scale` value, and `color` value.

mern-vrgame/server/models/game.model.js:

```
const VRObjectSchema = new mongoose.Schema({
  objUrl: {
    type: String, trim: true,
    required: 'ObJ file is required'
  },
  mtlUrl: {
    type: String, trim: true,
    required: 'MTL file is required'
  },
  translateX: {type: Number, default: 0},
  translateY: {type: Number, default: 0},
  translateZ: {type: Number, default: 0},
  rotateX: {type: Number, default: 0},
  rotateY: {type: Number, default: 0},
  rotateZ: {type: Number, default: 0},
  scale: {type: Number, default: 1},
  color: {type: String, default: 'white'}
})
```

When a new game document is saved to the database, the answerObjects and wrongObjects arrays will be populated with VRObject documents that adhere to this schema definition.

Array length validation in the game schema

The answerObjects and wrongObjects arrays in a game document must contain at least one VRObject document in each array when being saved in the game collection. To add validation for a minimum array length to the game schema, we will add the following custom validation checks to the answerObjects and wrongObjects paths in GameSchema.

mern-vrgame/server/models/game.model.js:

```
GameSchema.path('answerObjects').validate(function(v) {
  if (v.length == 0) {
    this.invalidate('answerObjects',
    'Must add alteast one VR object to collect')
  }
}, null)
```

```
GameSchema.path('wrongObjects').validate(function(v) {
  if (v.length == 0) {
    this.invalidate('wrongObjects',
    'Must add alteast one other VR object')
  }
}, null)
```

These schema definitions will cater to all the requirements for developing a dynamic VR game according to the specifications of the MERN VR Game.

Game APIs

The backend in the MERN VR Game will expose a set of CRUD APIs for creating, editing, reading, listing, and deleting games from the database, which can be used in the frontend of the application, including in the React 360 game implementation, with fetch calls.

The create API

A user who is signed in to the application will be able to create new games in the database using the create API.

Route

In the backend, we will add a POST route in game.routes.js, that verifies that the current user is signed in and authorized, and then creates a new game with the game data passed in the request.

mern-vrgame/server/routes/game.routes.js:

```
router.route('/api/games/by/:userId')
    .post(authCtrl.requireSignin, authCtrl.hasAuthorization,
gameCtrl.create)
```

To process the :userId param and retrieve the associated user from the database, we will utilize the userByID method from the user controller. We will also add the following to the game routes, so the user is available in the request object as profile.

mern-vrgame/server/routes/game.routes.js:

```
router.param('userId', userCtrl.userByID)
```

The `game.routes.js` file will be very similar to the `user.routes` file, and to load these new routes in the Express app, we need to mount the game routes in `express.js`, just as we did for the auth and user routes.

`mern-vrgame/server/express.js`:

```
app.use('/', gameRoutes)
```

Controller

The `create` controller method is executed when a POST request is received at `'/api/games/by/:userId'` with the request body containing the new game data.

`mern-vrgame/server/controllers/game.controller.js`:

```
const create = (req, res, next) => {
  const game = new Game(req.body)
  game.maker= req.profile
  game.save((err, result) => {
    if(err) {
      return res.status(400).json({
        error: errorHandler.getErrorMessage(err)
      })
    }
    res.status(200).json(result)
  })
}
```

In this `create` method, a new game document is created using the game schema and the data passed in the request body from the client side. Then this document is saved in the `Game` collection after the user reference is set as the game maker.

Fetch

On the frontend, we will add a corresponding `fetch` method in `api-game.js` to make a POST request to the `create` API by passing the form data collected from the signed-in user.

`mern-vrgame/client/game/api-game.js:`

```
const create = (params, credentials, game) => {
  return fetch('/api/games/by/'+ params.userId, {
      method: 'POST',
      headers: {
        'Accept': 'application/json',
        'Content-Type': 'application/json',
        'Authorization': 'Bearer ' + credentials.t
      },
      body: JSON.stringify(game)
  })
  .then((response) => {
    return response.json();
  }).catch((err) => console.log(err))
}
```

List API

It will be possible to fetch a list of all the games in the Game collection from the backend using the list API.

Route

We will add a GET route to the game routes to retrieve all the games stored in the database.

`mern-vrgame/server/routes/game.routes.js:`

```
router.route('/api/games')
    .get(gameCtrl.list)
```

A GET request to /api/games will execute the list controller method.

Controller

The list controller method will query the Game collection in the database to return all the games in the response to the client.

`mern-vrgame/server/controllers/game.controller.js:`

```
const list = (req, res) => {
  Game.find({}).populate('maker', '_id name')
  .sort('-created').exec((err, games) => {
```

```
    if(err) {
      return res.status(400).json({
        error: errorHandler.getErrorMessage(err)
      })
    }
    res.json(games)

  })
}
```

Fetch

In the frontend, to fetch the games using this list API, we will set up a fetch method in api-game.js.

mern-vrgame/client/game/api-game.js:

```
const list = () => {
  return fetch('/api/games', {
    method: 'GET',
  }).then(response => {
    return response.json()
  }).catch((err) => console.log(err))
}
```

List by maker API

The application will also allow us to fetch the games made by a specific user with the list by maker API.

Route

In the game routes, we will add a GET route to retrieve the games made by a specific user.

mern-vrgame/server/routes/game.routes.js:

```
router.route('/api/games/by/:userId')
    .get(gameCtrl.listByMaker)
```

A GET request to this route will execute the listByMaker method in the game controller.

Controller

The `listByMaker` controller method will query the Game collection in the database to get the matching games.

`mern-vrgame/server/controllers/game.controller.js`:

```
const listByMaker = (req, res) => {
  Game.find({maker: req.profile._id}, (err, games) => {
    if(err) {
      return res.status(400).json({
        error: errorHandler.getErrorMessage(err)
      })
    }
    res.json(games)
  }).populate('maker', '_id name')
}
```

In the query to the Game collection, we find all the games where the `maker` field matches the user specified in `req.profile`.

Fetch

In the frontend, to fetch the games for a specific user with this list by the maker API, we will add a `fetch` method in `api-game.js`.

`mern-vrgame/client/game/api-game.js`:

```
const listByMaker = (params) => {
  return fetch('/api/games/by/'+params.userId, {
    method: 'GET',
    headers: {
      'Accept': 'application/json'
    }
  }).then((response) => {
    return response.json()
  }).catch((err) => {
    console.log(err)
  })
}
```

Read API

Individual game data will be retrieved from the database using the `read` API at
`'/api/game/:gameId'`.

Route

In the backend, we will add a `GET` route that queries the `Game` collection with an ID and
returns the game in the response.

`mern-vrgame/server/routes/game.routes.js`:

```
router.route('/api/game/:gameId')
    .get(gameCtrl.read)
```

The `:gameId` param in the route URL will be processed first to retrieve the individual game
from the database. So we will also add the following to the game routes:

```
router.param('gameId', gameCtrl.gameByID)
```

Controller

The `:gameId` param in the request to the read API will call the `gameByID` controller
method, which is similar to the `userByID` controller method. It will retrieve the game from
the database and attach it to the `request` object to be used in the `next` method.

`mern-vrgame/server/controllers/game.controller.js`:

```
const gameByID = (req, res, next, id) => {
  Game.findById(id).populate('maker', '_id name').exec((err, game) => {
    if (err || !game)
      return res.status('400').json({
        error: "Game not found"
      })
    req.game = game
    next()
  })
}
```

The `next` method, in this case the `read` controller method, simply returns this `game` object
in the response to the client.

mern-vrgame/server/controllers/game.controller.js:

```
const read = (req, res) => {
  return res.json(req.game)
}
```

Fetch

In the frontend code, we will add a `fetch` method to utilize this read API to retrieve the details of an individual game according to its ID.

mern-vrgame/client/game/api-game.js:

```
const read = (params, credentials) => {
  return fetch('/api/game/' + params.gameId, {
    method: 'GET'
  }).then((response) => {
    return response.json()
  }).catch((err) => console.log(err))
}
```

This `read` API will be used for the React views fetching a game detail and also the React 360 game view, which will render the game interface.

Edit API

Authorized users who are signed in and also the maker of a specific game will be able to edit the details of that game using the `edit` API.

Route

In the backend, we will add a `PUT` route that allows an authorized user to edit one of their games.

mern-vrgame/server/routes/game.routes.js:

```
router.route('/api/games/:gameId')
    .put(authCtrl.requireSignin, gameCtrl.isMaker, gameCtrl.update)
```

A PUT request to `'/api/games/:gameId'` will first execute the `gameByID` controller method to retrieve the specific game's details. The `requireSignin` auth controller method will also be called to ensure the current user is signed in. Then the `isMaker` controller method will determine whether the current user is the maker of this specific game before finally running the game `update` controller method to modify the game in the database.

Controller

The `isMaker` controller method ensures that the signed-in user is actually the maker of the game being edited.

mern-vrgame/server/controllers/game.controller.js:

```
const isMaker = (req, res, next) => {
  let isMaker = req.game && req.auth && req.game.maker._id == req.auth._id
  if(!isMaker){
    return res.status('403').json({
      error: "User is not authorized"
    })
  }
  next()
}
```

The `update` method in the game controller will take the existing game details and the form data received in the request body to merge the changes, and save the updated game to the Game collection in the database.

mern-vrgame/server/controllers/game.controller.js:

```
const update = (req, res) => {
  let game = req.game
  game = _.extend(game, req.body)
  game.updated = Date.now()
  game.save((err) => {
    if(err) {
      return res.status(400).send({
        error: errorHandler.getErrorMessage(err)
      })
    }
    res.json(game)
  })
}
```

Fetch

The `edit` API is called in the view using a `fetch` method that takes the form data and sends it with the request to the backend along with user credentials.

`mern-vrgame/client/game/api-game.js`:

```
const update = (params, credentials, game) => {
  return fetch('/api/games/' + params.gameId, {
    method: 'PUT',
    headers: {
      'Accept': 'application/json',
      'Content-Type': 'application/json',
      'Authorization': 'Bearer ' + credentials.t
    },
    body: JSON.stringify(game)
  }).then((response) => {
    return response.json()
  }).catch((err) => {
    console.log(err)
  })
}
```

Delete API

An authenticated and authorised user will be able to delete any of the games they made on the application using the `delete` game API.

Route

In the backend, we will add a `DELETE` route that allows an authorized maker to delete one of their own games.

`mern-vrgame/server/routes/game.routes.js`:

```
router.route('/api/games/:gameId')
    .delete(authCtrl.requireSignin, gameCtrl.isMaker, gameCtrl.remove)
```

The flow of the controller method execution on the server after receiving the DELETE request at `'api/games/:gameId'` will be similar to the edit API, with the final call made to the `remove` controller method instead of `update`.

Controller

The `remove` controller method deletes the specified game from the database, when a
DELETE request is received at `'/api/games/:gameId'` and it has been verified that the
current user is the original maker of the given game.

`mern-vrgame/server/controllers/game.controller.js`:

```
const remove = (req, res) => {
  let game = req.game
  game.remove((err, deletedGame) => {
    if(err) {
      return res.status(400).json({
        error: errorHandler.getErrorMessage(err)
      })
    }
    res.json(deletedGame)
  })
}
```

Fetch

We will add a corresponding `remove` method in `api-game.js` to make a `delete` fetch
request to the delete API.

`mern-vrgame/client/game/api-game.js`:

```
const remove = (params, credentials) => {
  return fetch('/api/games/' + params.gameId, {
    method: 'DELETE',
    headers: {
      'Accept': 'application/json',
      'Content-Type': 'application/json',
      'Authorization': 'Bearer ' + credentials.t
    }
  }).then((response) => {
    return response.json()
  }).catch((err) => {
    console.log(err)
  })
}
```

With these game APIs in place, we can build out the React views for the application and also update the React 360 game view code to fetch and render dynamic game details.

Creating and editing games

Users registered on MERN VR Game will be able to make new games and modify these games from within the application. We will add React components that allow users to modify game details and VR object details for each game.

Making a new game

When a user signs into the application, they will see a **MAKE GAME** link on the menu that will navigate them to the NewGame component containing a form to create a new game.

Updating the menu

We will update the navigation menu to add the **MAKE GAME** button, as shown in the following screenshot:

In the Menu component, we will add the Link to the route for the NewGame component, right before the **MY PROFILE** Link, in the section that renders only when the user is authenticated.

mern-vrgame/client/core/Menu.js:

```
<Link to="/game/new">
  <Button style={isActive(history, "/game/new")}>
    <AddBoxIcon color="secondary"/> Make Game
  </Button>
</Link>
```

NewGame component

The NewGame component uses the GameForm component to render the form elements the user will fill out to create a new game:

The GameForm contains all the form fields, and it takes the onSubmit method that should be executed when the user submits the form, as a prop from the NewGame component along with any server-returned error messages.

mern-vrgame/client/game/NewGame.js:

```
<GameForm onSubmit={this.clickSubmit} errorMsg={this.state.error}/>
```

The clickSubmit method uses the create fetch method from api-game.js to make a POST request to the create API with the game form data and user details.

`mern-vrgame/client/game/NewGame.js`:

```
clickSubmit = game => event => {
  const jwt = auth.isAuthenticated()
  create({
    userId: jwt.user._id
  }, {
    t: jwt.token
  }, game).then((data) => {
    if (data.error) {
      this.setState({error: data.error})
    } else {
      this.setState({error: '', redirect: true})
    }
  })
}
```

We will add a `PrivateRoute` in `MainRouter`, so the `NewGame` component loads in the browser at the `/game/new` path.

`mern-vrgame/client/MainRouter.js`:

```
<PrivateRoute path="/game/new" component={NewGame}/>
```

Editing the game

Users will be able to edit the games they made using the `EditGame` component, which will render the game form fields pre-populated with the existing game's details.

EditGame component

Just like in the `NewGame` component, the `EditGame` component will also use the `GameForm` component to render the form elements, but this time the fields will show the current values of the game fields, and users will be able to update these values:

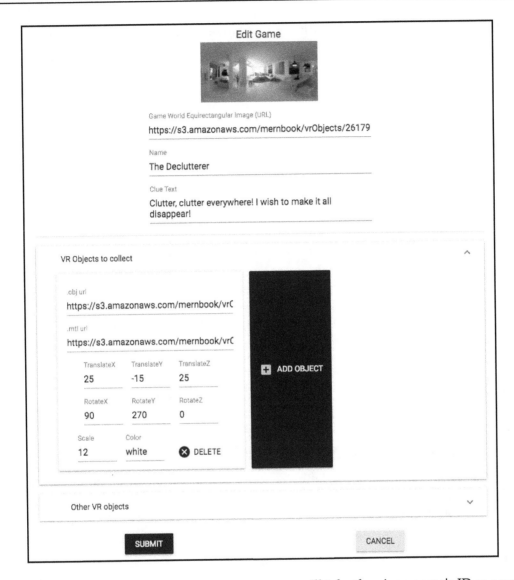

In the case of the EditGame component, GameForm will take the given game's ID as a prop so it can fetch the game details, in addition to the onSubmit method and server-generated error message, if any.

mern-vrgame/client/game/EditGame.js:

```
<GameForm gameId={this.match.params.gameId} onSubmit={this.clickSubmit}
errorMsg={this.state.error}/>
```

The `clickSubmit` method for the edit form will use the `update` fetch method in `api-game.js` to make a PUT request to the edit API with the form data and user details.

`mern-vrgame/client/game/EditGame.js`:

```
clickSubmit = game => event => {
    const jwt = auth.isAuthenticated()
    update({
      gameId: this.match.params.gameId
    }, {
      t: jwt.token
    }, game).then((data) => {
      if (data.error) {
        this.setState({error: data.error})
      } else {
        this.setState({error: '', redirect: true})
      }
    })
  }
```

The `EditGame` component will load in the browser at the `/game/edit/:gameId` path, declared in a `PrivateRoute` in `MainRouter`.

`mern-vrgame/client/MainRouter.js`:

```
<PrivateRoute path="/game/edit/:gameId" component={EditGame}/>
```

The GameForm component

The `GameForm` component used in both the `NewGame` and `EditGame` components contains the elements that allow users to enter game details and VR object details for a single game. It may start with a blank game object or load an existing game in `componentDidMount`.

`mern-vrgame/client/game/GameForm.js`:

```
state = {
    game: {name: '', clue:'', world:'', answerObjects:[], wrongObjects:[]},
    redirect: false,
    readError: ''
  }
```

If the `GameForm` component receives a `gameId` prop from the parent component, such as from the `EditGame` component, then it will use the read API to retrieve the game's details and set it to state to be rendered in the form view.

`mern-vrgame/client/game/GameForm.js`:

```
componentDidMount = () => {
    if(this.props.gameId){
        read({gameId: this.props.gameId}).then((data) => {
          if (data.error) {
            this.setState({readError: data.error})
          } else {
            this.setState({game: data})
          }
        })
    }
}
```

The form view in the `GameForm` component will essentially have two parts, one part that takes simple game details, such as name, world image link, and clue text as input, and a second part that allows users to add a variable number of VR objects to either the answer objects array or wrong objects array.

Inputing simple game details

The simple game details section will mostly be text input added using the Material-UI `TextField` component, with a change handling method passed to `onChange`.

Form title

The form title will either be `New Game` or `Edit Game`, depending on whether an existing game ID is passed as a prop to `GameForm`.

`mern-vrgame/client/game/GameForm.js`:

```
<Typography type="headline" component="h2">
    {this.props.gameId? 'Edit': 'New'} Game
</Typography>
```

Game world image

We will render the background image URL in an `img` element at the very top to show users the image they added as the game world image URL.

`mern-vrgame/client/game/GameForm.js`:

```
<img src={this.state.game.world}/>
<TextField id="world" label="Game World Equirectangular Image (URL)"
value={this.state.game.world} onChange={this.handleChange('world')}/>
```

Game name

The game name will be added in a single `TextField` of default type `text`.

`mern-vrgame/client/game/GameForm.js`:

```
<TextField id="name" label="Name" value={this.state.game.name}
onChange={this.handleChange('name')}/>
```

Clue text

The clue text will be added to a multiline `TextField` component.

`mern-vrgame/client/game/GameForm.js`:

```
<TextField id="multiline-flexible" label="Clue Text" multiline rows="2"
value={this.state.game.clue} onChange={this.handleChange('clue')}/>
```

Handle input

All the input changes will be handled by the `handleChange` method that will update the game values in state with the user input.

`mern-vrgame/client/game/GameForm.js`:

```
handleChange = name => event => {
    const newGame = this.state.game
    newGame[name] = event.target.value
    this.setState({game: newGame})
}
```

Modifying arrays of VR objects

In order to allow users to modify the arrays of `answerObjects` and `wrongObjects` that they wish to add to their VR game, `GameForm` will iterate through each array and render a `VRObjectForm` component for each object. With this, it will become possible to add, remove, and modify VR objects from the `GameForm` component:

Iterating and rendering the object details form

Using the Material-UI `ExpansionPanel` components, we will add the form interface seen previously to create a modifiable array of VR object details for each type of VR object array in the given game.

Inside the `ExpansionPanelDetails` component, we will iterate through the `answerObjects` array or the `wrongObjects` array to render a `VRObjectForm` component for each VR object.

`mern-vrgame/client/game/GameForm.js`:

```
<ExpansionPanel>
  <ExpansionPanelSummary expandIcon={<ExpandMoreIcon/>}>
    <Typography>VR Objects to collect</Typography>
  </ExpansionPanelSummary>
  <ExpansionPanelDetails>{
```

```
this.state.game.answerObjects.map((item, i) => {
  return <div key={i}>
            <VRObjectForm index={i} type={'answerObjects'}
              vrObject={item}
              handleUpdate={this.handleObjectChange}
              removeObject={this.removeObject}/>
      </div> })}
<Button color="primary" variant="raised"
onClick={this.addObject('answerObjects')}>
    <AddBoxIcon color="secondary"/> Add Object
</Button>
  </ExpansionPanelDetails>
</ExpansionPanel>
```

Each `VRObjectForm` will take as props the `vrObject` itself, the current `index` in the array, the type of object array, and two methods for updating the state in `GameForm` when the array details are modified by changing details or deleting an object from within the `VRObjectForm` component.

Adding a new object to the array

The button to add an object will allow users to add a new `VRObjectForm` component to take the details of a new VR object.

`mern-vrgame/client/game/GameForm.js`:

```
addObject = name => event => {
    const newGame = this.state.game
    newGame[name].push({})
    this.setState({game: newGame})
}
```

This will basically just add an empty object to the array being iterated with a call to the `addObject` method with the array type specified in the name value.

Removing an object from the array

Each VRObjectForm component can also be deleted to remove the object from the given array. GameForm will pass a removeObject method to the VRObjectForm component as a prop so the array can be updated in state when a user clicks delete on a specific VRObjectForm.

mern-vrgame/client/game/GameForm.js:

```
removeObject = (type, index) => event => {
    const newGame = this.state.game
    newGame[type].splice(index, 1)
    this.setState({game: newGame})
}
```

The object will be removed from the array by slicing at the given index from the array of the specified array type in name.

Handling the object detail change

The VR object details will update in the GameForm component state when the user changes input values in any of the VRObjectForm fields. To register this update, the GameForm passes the handleObjectChange method to the VRObjectForm component.

mern-vrgame/client/game/GameForm.js:

```
handleObjectChange = (index, type, name, val) => {
    var newGame = this.state.game
    newGame[type][index][name] = val
    this.setState({game: newGame})
}
```

The handleObjectChange method updates the field value of the specific object at the index in the array with the given type, so it is reflected in the game object stored in the state in GameForm.

VRObjectForm component

The VRObjectForm component will render the input fields to modify an individual VR object's details, which is added to the answerObjects and wrongObjects arrays of the game in the GameForm component:

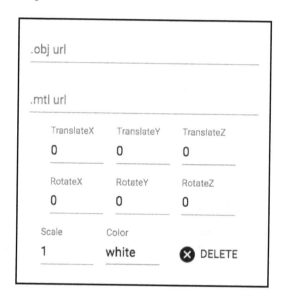

It may start with a blank VR object or load an existing VR object's details in componentDidMount.

mern-vrgame/client/game/VRObjectForm.js:

```
state = {
    objUrl: '', mtlUrl: '',
    translateX: 0, translateY: 0, translateZ: 0,
    rotateX: 0, rotateY: 0, rotateZ: 0,
    scale: 1, color:'white'
}
```

In componentDidMount, the state will be set with details of the vrObject passed as a prop from the GameForm component.

mern-vrgame/client/game/VRObjectForm.js:

```
componentDidMount = () => {
    if(this.props.vrObject &&
    Object.keys(this.props.vrObject).length != 0){
        const vrObject = this.props.vrObject
        this.setState({
            objUrl: vrObject.objUrl,
            mtlUrl: vrObject.mtlUrl,
            translateX: Number(vrObject.translateX),
            translateY: Number(vrObject.translateY),
            translateZ: Number(vrObject.translateZ),
            rotateX: Number(vrObject.rotateX),
            rotateY: Number(vrObject.rotateY),
            rotateZ: Number(vrObject.rotateZ),
            scale: Number(vrObject.scale),
            color:vrObject.color
        })
    }
}
```

The input fields to modify these values will be added using Material-UI TextField components.

3D object file input

The OBJ and MTL file links will be added for each VR object as text input using the TextField components.

mern-vrgame/client/game/VRObjectForm.js:

```
<TextField
    id="obj"
    label=".obj url"
    value={this.state.objUrl}
    onChange={this.handleChange('objUrl')}
/><br/>
<TextField
    id="mtl"
    label=".mtl url"
    value={this.state.mtlUrl}
    onChange={this.handleChange('mtlUrl')}
/>
```

Translate value input

The translate values of the VR object across the X, Y, and Z axes will be input in the `TextField` components of the `number` type.

`mern-vrgame/client/game/VRObjectForm.js`:

```
<TextField
    value={this.state.translateX}
    label="TranslateX"
    onChange={this.handleChange('translateX')}
    type="number"
/>
<TextField
    value={this.state.translateY}
    label="TranslateY"
    onChange={this.handleChange( 'translateY')}
    type="number"
/>
<TextField
    value={this.state.translateZ}
    label="TranslateZ"
    onChange={this.handleChange('translateZ')}
    type="number"
/>
```

Rotate value input

The `rotate` values of the VR object around the X, Y, and Z axes will be input in the `TextField` components of the `number` type.

`mern-vrgame/client/game/VRObjectForm.js`:

```
<TextField
    value={this.state.rotateX}
    label="RotateX"
    onChange={this.handleChange('rotateX')}
    type="number"
/>
<TextField
    value={this.state.rotateY}
    label="RotateY"
    onChange={this.handleChange('rotateY')}
    type="number"
/>
<TextField
```

```
        value={this.state.rotateZ}
        label="RotateZ"
        onChange={this.handleChange('rotateZ')}
        type="number"
/>
```

Scale value input

The `scale` value for the VR object will be input in a `TextField` component of
the `number` type.

`mern-vrgame/client/game/VRObjectForm.js`:

```
<TextField
    value={this.state.scale}
    label="Scale"
    onChange={this.handleChange('scale')}
    type="number"
/>
```

Object color input

The color value for the VR object will be input in a `TextField` component of the `text` type:

`mern-vrgame/client/game/VRObjectForm.js`:

```
<TextField
    value={this.state.color}
    label="Color"
    onChange={this.handleChange('color')}
/>
```

Delete object button

The `VRObjectForm` will contain a `Delete` button that will execute the `removeObject`
method received in the `GameForm` props form:

`mern-vrgame/client/game/VRObjectForm.js`:

```
<Button onClick={this.props.removeObject(this.props.type,
this.props.index)}>
      <Icon>cancel</Icon> Delete
</Button>
```

The `removeObject` method will take the value of the object array type and the array index position to remove the given object from the relevant VR objects array in the `GameForm` state.

Handling the input change

When any of the VR object details are changed in the input fields, the `handleChange` method will update the state of the `VRObjectForm` component, and use the `handleUpdate` method passed as a prop from `GameForm` to update the VR object in the `GameForm` state with the changed value for the object detail.

`mern-vrgame/client/game/VRObjectForm.js`:

```
handleChange = name => event => {
    this.setState({[name]: event.target.value})
    this.props.handleUpdate(this.props.index,
                            this.props.type,
                            name,
                            event.target.value)
}
```

With this implementation, the create and edit game forms are in place, complete with VR object input forms for arrays of varying sizes. Any registered user can use these forms to add and edit games on the MERN VR Game application.

Game list views

Visitors to MERN VR Game will access the games on the application from lists rendered on the home page and individual user profiles. The home page will list all the games on the application, and the games by a specific maker will be listed on their user profile page. The list views will iterate through game data fetched using the `list` APIs and render details of each game in the `GameDetail` component.

All games

The `Home` component will fetch the list of all the games in the game collection using the list API when the component mounts.

`mern-vrgame/client/core/Home.js`:

```
componentDidMount = () => {
    list().then((data) => {
      if (data.error) {
        console.log(data.error)
      } else {
        this.setState({games: data})
      }
    })
}
```

The list of games retrieved from the server will be set to state and iterated over to render a `GameDetail` component with each game in the list.

`mern-vrgame/client/core/Home.js`:

```
{this.state.games.map((game, i) => {
      return <GameDetail key={i} game={game}
updateGames={this.updateGames}/>
})}
```

The `GameDetail` component will be passed the game details and an `updateGames` method.

`mern-vrgame/client/core/Home.js`:

```
updateGames = (game) => {
    const updatedGames = this.state.games
    const index = updatedGames.indexOf(game)
    updatedGames.splice(index, 1)
    this.setState({games: updatedGames})
}
```

The `updateGames` method will update the list in the `Home` component when a user deletes their game from the `GameDetail` component that renders with an `edit` and `delete` option for the maker of the game:

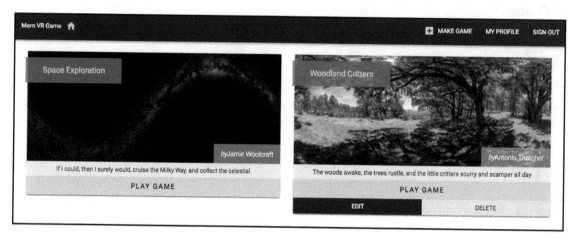

Games by a maker

The user `Profile` component will fetch the list of just the games made by the given user with the list by the maker API. We will update the `init` method in the `Profile` component to call the `listByMaker` fetch method after the user details are retrieved.

`mern-vrgame/client/user/Profile.js`:

```
init = (userId) => {
  const jwt = auth.isAuthenticated()
  read({
    userId: userId
  }, {t: jwt.token}).then((data) => {
    if (data.error) {
      this.setState({redirectToSignin: true})
    } else {
      this.setState({user: data})
      listByMaker({userId: data._id}).then((data) => {
        if (data.error) {
          console.log(data.error)
        } else {
          this.setState({games: data})
        }
      })
```

```
        }
    })
  }
```

Similar to how the game list is rendered in the Home component, we will set the list of games retrieved from the server to state in the Profile component, and iterate over it in the view to render the GameDetail components, which will be passed the individual game details and an updateGames method.

mern-vrgame/client/user/Profile.js:

```
{this.state.games.map((game, i) => {
    return <GameDetail key={i} game={game} updateGames={this.updateGames}/>
})}
```

This will render a GameDetail component for each game made by the specific user:

GameDetail component

The `GameDetail` component takes a game object as a prop, and renders the details of the game, along with a **PLAY GAME** button that links to the VR game view. It also shows `edit` and `delete` buttons if the current user is the maker of the game:

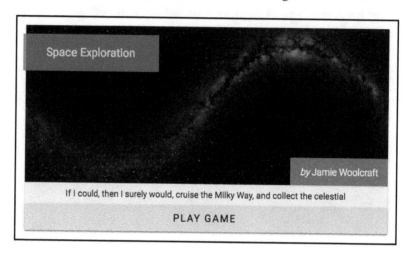

Game details

The game details, such as the name, world image, clue text, and maker name, are rendered to give the user an overview of the game.

`mern-vrgame/client/game/GameDetail.js`:

```
<Typography type="headline" component="h2">
    {this.props.game.name}
</Typography>
<CardMedia image={this.props.game.world}
        title={this.props.game.name}/>
<Typography type="subheading" component="h4">
    <em>by</em>
    {this.props.game.maker.name}
</Typography>
<CardContent>
    <Typography type="body1" component="p">
        {this.props.game.clue}
    </Typography>
</CardContent>
```

Play Game button

The `Play Game` button in the `GameDetail` component will simply be a `Link` component that points to the route that opens the React 360-generated `index.html` (implementation for this route on the server is discussed in the *Playing the VR game* section).

mern-vrgame/client/game/GameDetail.js:

```
<Link to={"/game/play?id=" + this.props.game._id} target='_self'>
    <Button variant="raised" color="secondary">
        Play Game
    </Button>
</Link>
```

The route to the game view takes the game ID as a `query` parameter. We set `target='_self'` on the `Link` so React Router skips transitioning to the next state and lets the browser handle this link. What this will do is allow the browser to directly make the request at this route, and render the `index.html` file sent by the server in response to this request.

Edit and delete buttons

The `GameDetail` component will show the `edit` and `delete` options only if the currently signed-in user is also the maker of the game being rendered.

mern-vrgame/client/game/GameDetail.js:

```
{auth.isAuthenticated().user
    && auth.isAuthenticated().user._id == this.props.game.maker._id &&
    (<div>
        <Link to={"/game/edit/" + this.props.game._id}>
            <Button variant="raised" color="primary"
          className={classes.editbutton}>
                Edit
            </Button>
        </Link>
        <DeleteGame game={this.props.game}
        removeGame={this.props.updateGames}/>
    </div>)}
```

If the user ID of the signed-in user matches the maker ID in the game, the `edit` button linking to the edit form view and the `DeleteGame` component are shown in the view.

Deleting a game

A signed-in user will be able to delete a specific game they made by clicking on the `delete` button visible to makers in the `GameDetail` component. The `GameDetail` component adds this `delete` option using a `DeleteGame` component.

DeleteGame component

The `DeleteGame` component added to the `GameDetail` component for each game takes the game details, and a `removeGame` method, as props from `GameDetail` that updates the parent component that `GameDetail` is a part of.

`mern-vrgame/client/game/GameDetail.js`:

```
<DeleteGame game={this.props.game} removeGame={this.props.updateGames}/>
```

This `DeleteGame` component is basically a button that, when clicked, opens a confirm dialog to ask the user whether they are sure they want to delete their game:

Delete The Declutterer

Confirm to delete your game The Declutterer.

CANCEL   CONFIRM

The dialog is implemented using the `Dialog` component from Material-UI.

`mern-vrgame/client/game/DeleteGame.js`:

```
<Button variant="raised" onClick={this.clickButton}>
   Delete
</Button>
<Dialog open={this.state.open} onClose={this.handleRequestClose}>
   <DialogTitle>{"Delete "+this.props.game.name}</DialogTitle>
   <DialogContent>
      <DialogContentText>
         Confirm to delete your game {this.props.game.name}.
      </DialogContentText>
   </DialogContent>
   <DialogActions>
```

```
            <Button onClick={this.handleRequestClose} color="primary">
                Cancel
            </Button>
            <Button onClick={this.deleteGame} color="secondary"
            autoFocus="autoFocus">
                Confirm
            </Button>
        </DialogActions>
    </Dialog>
```

Upon successful deletion, the dialog is closed and the parent component containing the `GameDetail` component is updated by calling the `removeGame` method passed in as a prop.

`mern-vrgame/client/game/DeleteGame.js`:

```
deleteGame = () => {
    const jwt = auth.isAuthenticated()
    remove({
      gameId: this.props.game._id
    }, {t: jwt.token}).then((data) => {
      if (data.error) {
        console.log(data.error)
      } else {
        this.props.removeGame(this.props.game)
        this.setState({open: false})
      }
    })
}
```

The `removeGame` method called in this `deleteGame` handler method updates the state of the parent, which could be the `Home` component or the user `Profile` component, so the deleted game is no longer shown in the view.

Playing the VR game

Users on MERN VR Game will be able to open and play any of the games from within the application. To enable this, we will set up a route on the server that renders `index.html`, which was generated with React 360, in the response to a GET request at the following path:

```
/game/play?id=<game ID>
```

The path takes a game ID value as a `query` parameter, which is used in the React 360 code to fetch the game details with the read API.

API to render the VR game view

The GET request to open the React 360 `index.html` page will be declared in `game.routes.js`, as follows.

`mern-vrgame/server/routes/game.routes.js`:

```
router.route('/game/play')
  .get(gameCtrl.playGame)
```

This will execute the `playGame` controller method to return the `index.html` page in response to the incoming request.

`mern-vrgame/server/controllers/game.controller.js`:

```
const playGame = (req, res) => {
  res.sendFile(process.cwd()+'/server/vr/index.html')
}
```

The `playGame` controller method will send the `index.html` placed in the `/server/vr/` folder to the requesting client.

In the browser, this will render the React 360 game code, which will fetch the game details from the database using the read API, and render the game world along with the VR objects that the user can interact with.

Updating the game code in React 360

With the game backend all set up in the MERN application, we can update the React 360 project code we developed in Chapter 10, *Developing a Web-Based VR Game*, to make it render games directly from the game collection in the database.

We will use the game ID in the link that opens the React 360 application to fetch game details with the read API from within the React 360 code, and then set the data to state so the game loads details retrieved from the database instead of the static sample data we used in Chapter 10, *Developing a Web-Based VR Game*.

Once the code is updated, we can bundle it again and place the compiled files in the MERN application.

Getting the game ID from a link

In the `index.js` file of the React 360 project folder, update the `componentDidMount` method to retrieve the game ID from the incoming URL and make a fetch call to the read game API.

/MERNVR/`index.js`:

```
componentDidMount = () => {
    let gameId = Location.search.split('?id=')[1]
    read({
        gameId: gameId
    }).then((data) => {
      if (data.error) {
        this.setState({error: data.error});
      } else {
        this.setState({
          vrObjects: data.answerObjects.concat(data.wrongObjects),
          game: data
        });
        Environment.setBackgroundImage(
          {uri: data.world}
        )
      }
    })
}
```

`Location.search` gives us access to the query string in the incoming URL that loads `index.html`. The retrieved query string is `split` to get the game ID value from the `id` query parameter attached in the URL. We need this game ID value to fetch the game details with the read API from the server, and set it to state for the game and `vrObjects` values.

Fetching the game data with the read API

In the React 360 project folder, we will add an `api-game.js` file that will contain a read `fetch` method that makes a call to the read game API on the server using the provided game ID.

/MERNVR/api-game.js:

```
const read = (params) => {
  return fetch('/api/game/' + params.gameId, {
    method: 'GET'
  }).then((response) => {
    return response.json()
  }).catch((err) => console.log(err))
}
export {
  read
}
```

This fetch method is used in `componentDidMount` of the React 360 entry component to retrieve the game details.

This updated React 360 code is available in the branch named 'dynamic-game' on the GitHub repository at: `github.com/shamahoque/MERNVR`.

Bundling and integrating the updated code

With the React 360 code updated to fetch and render game details dynamically from the server, we can bundle this code using the provided bundle script and place the newly compiled files in the `dist` folder of the MERN VR Game project directory.

To bundle the React 360 code from the command line, go to the React 360 MERNVR project folder and run:

npm run bundle

This will generate the `client.bundle.js` and `index.bundle.js` bundle files in the `build/` folder with the updated React 360 code. These files, along with the `index.html` and `static_assets` folders, need to be added to the MERN VR Game application code as discussed in Chapter 10, *Developing a Web-Based VR Game*, to integrate the latest VR game code.

With this integration completed, if we run the MERN VR Game application, and click the **Play Game** link on any of the games, it should open up the game view with the details of the specific game rendered in the VR scene, and allow interaction with the VR objects as specified in the gameplay.

Summary

In this chapter, we integrated the capabilities of the MERN stack technologies with React 360 to develop a dynamic VR game application for the web.

We extended the MERN skeleton application to build a working backend that stores VR game details. And allows us to make API calls to manipulate these details. We added React views that let users modify games and browse through the games with the option to launch and play the VR game at a specified route rendered directly by the server.

Finally, we updated the React 360 project code to pass data between the MERN application and the VR game view, by retrieving query parameters from the incoming URL, and using fetch to retrieve data with the game API.

This integration of the React 360 code with the MERN stack application produced a fully functioning and dynamic web-based VR game application, demonstrating how MERN stack technologies can be used and extended to create unique user experiences.

In the next chapter, we will reflect on the MERN applications built in this book, discussing not just the best practices the were followed, but also the scope for improvements and further development.

12
Following Best Practices and Developing MERN Further

In this chapter, we elaborate on some of the best practices applied while building the four MERN applications in this book, along with other practices not applied in this book, but that should be considered for real-world applications to ensure reliability and scalability as complexity grows. Finally, we wrap up with suggestions on enhancing, and steps for extending the applications built.

The topics covered in this chapter include the following:

- Separation of concerns with modularity in the app structure
- Considering the options for CSS styling solutions
- Server-side rendering with data for selected views
- Using ES6 class for stateful vs purely functional components
- Deciding on using Redux or Flux
- Security enhancements for storing user credentials
- Writing test code
- Optimizing bundle size
- How to add new features to existing applications

Separation of concerns with modularity

While building out the MERN stack applications, we followed a common folder structure across each application, which divided and grouped the code based on relevance and common functionality. The idea behind creating these smaller and distinct sections in the code is to make sure each section addresses a separate concern, so individual sections can be reused, as well as developed and updated independently.

Revisiting the application folder structure

More specifically, in the application folder structure, we kept the client-side and server-side code separate with further subdivisions within these two sections. This gave us some freedom to design and build the frontend and backend of the application independently:

```
| mern_application/
  | -- client/
  | -- server/
```

In the `client` and `server` sections, we divided the code further into subfolders that mapped to unique functionalities, such as models, controllers, and routes in the server to a specific feature, such as grouping all components related to a user on the client side.

Server-side code

On the server side, we divided the code according to functionality by separating code that defines business models from code implementing routing logic and code that responds to client requests at these routes:

```
| -- server/
  | --- controllers/
  | --- models/
  | --- routes/
```

In this structure, each folder contains code with a specific purpose:

- **models**: This folder is meant to contain all the Mongoose schema model definitions in separate files, each file representing a single model.
- **routes**: This folder contains all routes that allow the client to interact with the server - placed in separate files where each file may be associated with a model in the models folder.
- **controllers**: This contains all the controller functions that define logic to respond to incoming requests at the defined routes, divided into separate files corresponding to relevant model and route files.

As demonstrated throughout the book, these specific separations of concerns for the code on the server side allowed us to extend the server developed for the skeleton application by just adding the required model, route, and controller files.

Client-side code

The client-side code for the MERN applications consist primarily of React components. In order to organize the component code and related helper code in a reasonable and understandable manner, we separated the code into folders related to a feature entity or unique functionality:

```
| -- client/
   | --- auth/
   | --- core/
   | --- post/
   | --- user/
   | --- componentFolderN/
```

In the preceding structure, we placed all the auth-related components and helper code in the `auth` folder, common and basic components, such as the `Home` and `Menu` components, in the `core` folder, then we made `post` and `user` folders for all post-related or user-related components in the respective folders.

This separation and grouping of components based on features allowed us to extend the frontend views in the skeleton application for each application that followed, by adding a new feature-related component code folder, as required, to the client folder.

In the final section of this chapter, we demonstrate further the advantages of this modularized approach of separating the application code, as we outline the general workflow that can be adopted to add a new feature to any of the existing applications developed in this book.

Adding CSS styles

When discussing user interface implementations for the applications in this book, we chose not to focus on the details of the CSS styling code applied and relied mostly on the default Material-UI stylings. But given that implementing any user interface requires considering styling solutions, we will briefly look at some of the options available.

When it comes to adding CSS styles to the frontend, there are a number of options, each with pros and cons. In this section, we will discuss the two most common options, which are external style sheets and inline styles, along with a newer approach of writing CSS in JavaScript, or more specifically JSS, which is used in Material-UI components and hence also for the applications in this book.

External style sheets

External style sheets allow us to define CSS rules in separate files that can be injected into the necessary view. Placing CSS styles this way in external style sheets was once considered the better practice because it enforced the separation of style and content, allowing reusability and also maintaining modularity if a separate CSS file is created for each component.

However, as web development technologies continue evolving, the demands of better CSS organization and performance are no longer met by this approach. For example, using external style sheets while developing frontend views with React components limits control over updating styles based on the component state. Moreover, loading external CSS for React applications requires additional Webpack configurations with `css-loader` and `style-loader`.

When applications grow and share multiple style sheets, it also becomes impossible to avoid selector conflicts because CSS has a single global namespace. Hence, though external style sheets may be enough for simple and trivial applications, as an application grows, other options for using CSS become more relevant.

Inline styles

Inline CSS is a style defined and applied directly to individual elements in the view. Though this takes care of some of the problems faced with external style sheets, such as eliminating the issue of selector conflicts and allowing state-dependent styles, it takes away reusability and introduces a few problems of its own, such as limiting the CSS features that can be applied.

Using only inline CSS for a React-based frontend has important limitations for growing applications, such as poor performance because all the inline styles are recomputed at each render, and inline styles are slower than class names to begin with.

Inline CSS may seem like an easy fix in some cases, but does not serve as a good option for overall usage.

JSS

JSS allows us to write CSS styles using JavaScript in a declarative way. This also means all the features of JavaScript are now available for writing CSS, making it possible to write reusable and maintainable styling code.

JSS works as a JS to CSS compiler that takes JS objects, where keys represent class names, with values representing corresponding CSS rules, and then generates the CSS along with scoped class names.

In this way, JSS generates unique class names by default when it compiles JSON representations to CSS, eliminating the chances of selector conflicts faced with external style sheets. Moreover, unlike inline styles, CSS rules defined with JSS can be shared across multiple elements and all CSS features can be used in the definitions.

Material-UI uses JSS to style its components, and as a result we used JSS to apply Material-UI themes and also custom CSS to the components developed for the frontend views in all the applications.

Selective server-side rendering with data

When we developed the frontend of the base skeleton application in Chapter 4, *Adding a React Frontend to Complete MERN*, we integrated basic server-side rendering to be able to load client-side routes directly from the browser address bar when the request goes to the server. In this SSR implementation, while rendering the React components server-side, we did not consider loading the data from the database for the components that displayed data. The data only loads in these components when the client-side JavaScript takes over after the initial load of the server-side rendered markup.

We did update this implementation to add server-side rendering with data for the individual media detail pages in the MERN Mediastream application discussed in Chapter 9, *Customizing Media Player and Improve SEO*. In this case, we decided to render this specific view with data by injecting data into the server-side generated markup of the React frontend. The reasoning behind this selective server-side rendering with data only for specific views can be based on certain desired behaviors for the view in question.

When is SSR with data relevant?

Implementing server-side rendering with data for all the React views in an application can become complicated and additional work when it is necessary to consider views with client-side authentication or consisting of multiple data sources. In many cases, it may be unnecessary to tackle these complexities if the view does not require server-side rendering with data. In order to judge whether a view needs to be server-rendered with data, answer the following questions for the specific view to make your decision:

- Is it important for the data to be displayed in the initial load of the view when JavaScript may not be available in the browser?
- Do the view and its data need to be SEO-friendly?

Loading data in the initial load of the page may be relevant from a usability persepective, so it really depends on the use case for the specific view. For SEO, server-side rendering with data will give search engines easier access to the data content in the view, so if this is crucial for the view in question, then adding server-side rendering with data is a good idea.

Using ES6 class for stateful vs pure functional components

While building UI with React components, composing the views with more stateless functional components can make the frontend code manageable, clean, and easier to test. But some components will need the state or lifecycle hooks to be more than pure presentational components. In this section, we look at what it takes to build stateful and stateless functional React components, when to use one or the other and how often.

React components with ES6 class

React components defined using ES6 class have access to lifecycle methods, the `this` keyword, and can manage state with `setState` when building stateful components. Stateful components allow us to build interactive components that can manage changing data in state, and propagate any business logic that needs to be applied across the UI. Generally, for complex UI, stateful components should be higher-level container components that manage the state of the smaller stateless functional components they are composed of.

React components as pure functions

React components can be defined as stateless functional components using the ES6 class syntax or as pure functions. The main idea is a stateless component does not modify state and receives props.

The following code defines a stateless component using the ES6 class syntax:

```
class Greeting extends React.Component {
  render() {
    return <h1>Hello, {this.props.name}</h1>
  }
}
```

The same can also be defined using JavaScript pure functions, as follows:

```
function Greeting(props) {
  return <h1>Hello, {props.name}</h1>
}
```

A pure function always gives the same output when given the same input without any side effects. Modeling React components as pure functions enforces creation of smaller, more defined, and self-contained components that emphasize UI over business logic as there is no state manipulation in these components. These kinds of components are composable, reusable, and easy to debug and test.

Designing the UI with stateful components and stateless functional components

While thinking about the component composition for a UI, design the root or a parent component as a stateful component that will contain child components or the composable components that only receive props and cannot manipulate state. All the state-changing actions using setState and life-cycle issues will be handled by the root or parent component.

In the applications developed for this book, there is a mixture of stateful higher-level components and smaller stateless components. For example, in the MERN Social application, the Profile component modifies the state for stateless child components, such as the FollowProfileButton and FollowGrid components. There is scope for refactoring some of the larger components that were developed in this book into smaller, more self-contained components, and this should be considered before extending the applications to incorporate more features.

The main takeaway that can be applied to new component design or refactoring existing components, is that as the React application grows and gets more complex, it is better to have more stateless functional components added to higher-level stateful components that are in charge of managing state for its inner components.

Using Redux or Flux

When React applications begin to grow and get more complex, managing communication between components can become problematic. When using regular React, the way to communicate is to pass down values and callback functions as props to the child components. But this can be tedious if there are a lot of intermediary components that the callback must pass through. To address these state communication and management-related issues as the React application grows, people turn to using React with libraries and architecture patterns such as Redux and Flux.

It is outside the scope of this book to delve into the details of integrating React with the Redux library or the Flux architecture, but the reader may consider these options for their growing MERN applications while keeping the following in mind:

- Redux and Flux utilize patterns that enforce changing states in a React application from a central location. A trick to avoid using Redux or Flux in React applications of manageable sizes, is moving all state changes up the component tree to parent components.
- Smaller applications work just as well without Flux or Redux.

 You can learn more about using React with Redux at `https://redux.js.org/`, and Flux at `facebook.github.io/flux/`.

Enhancing security

In the MERN applications developed for this book, we kept the auth-related security implementations simple by using JSON Web Tokens as an authentication mechanism and by storing hashed passwords in the User collection. In this section, we will go over these choices and point to possible enhancements.

JSON web tokens – client-side or server-side storage

With the JWT authentication mechanism, the client side becomes responsible for maintaining user state. Once the user signs in, the token sent by the server is stored and maintained by the client-side code on browser storage, such as `sessionStorage`. Hence, it is also up to the client-side code to invalidate the token by removing it when a user signs out or needs to be signed out. This mechanism works out well for most applications that need minimal authentication to protect access to resources. However, for instances where it may be necessary to track user sign-ins, sign-outs, and to let the server know that a specific token is no longer valid for sign-in, just the client-side handling of the tokens is not enough.

For these cases, the implementation discussed for handling JWT tokens on the client side can be extended to storage on the server side as well. In the specific case of keeping track of invalidated tokens, a MongoDB collection can be maintained by the server to store these invalidated tokens as reference, somewhat similar to how it is done for storing session data on the server side.

The thing to be cautious about and to keep in mind is that storing and maintaining auth-related information on both the client and server side may be overkill in most cases. Hence it is entirely up to the specific use case and the related trade-offs to be considered.

Securing password storage

While storing user credentials for authentication in the User collection, we made sure that the original password string provided by the user is never stored directly in the database. Instead we generated a hash of the password along with a salt value using the `crypto` module in Node.

In `user.model.js` from our applications, we defined the following functions to generate the hashed `password` and `salt` value:

```
encryptPassword: function(password) {
    if (!password) return ''
    try {
      return crypto
        .createHmac('sha1', this.salt)
        .update(password)
        .digest('hex')
    } catch (err) {
      return ''
```

```
    }
  },
  makeSalt: function() {
    return Math.round((new Date().valueOf() * Math.random())) + ''
  }
```

With this implementation, every time a user enters a password to sign in, a hash is generated with the salt. If the generated hash matches the stored hash, then the password is correct, otherwise the password is wrong. So in order to check whether a password is correct, the salt is required, and hence it is stored with the user details in the database along with the hash.

This is standard practice for securing passwords stored for user authentication, but there are other advanced approaches that may be explored if a specific application's security requirements demand it. Some options that can be considered include multi-iteration hashing approaches, other secure hashing algorithms, limiting login attempts per user account, and multi-level authentication with additional steps such as answering security questions or entering security codes.

Writing test code

Though discussing and writing test code is outside the scope of this book, it is crucial for developing reliable software. In this section, first we will look at the testing tools available to test the different parts of a MERN application. Then, to help get started with writing test code for the MERN applications developed in this book, we will also discuss a real example of adding a client-side test to the MERN Social application from Chapter 5, *Starting with a Simple Social Media Application*.

Testing with Jest

Jest is a comprehensive testing framework for JavaScript. Though it is more commonly known for testing React components, it can be used for general-purpose testing with any JavaScript library or framework. Among the many JavaScript testing solutions in Jest, it provides support for mocking and snapshot testing, comes with an assertion library, and tests in Jest are written in the **behavior driven development** (**BDD**) style. Besides testing the React components, Jest can be also be adapted to write test code for the Node-Express-Mongoose-based backend as required. Hence, it is a solid testing option to add test code for the MERN applications.

To learn more about Jest, read the docs at `https://facebook.github.io/jest/docs/en/getting-started.html`.

Adding a test to the MERN Social application

Using Jest, we will add a client-side test to the MERN Social application and demonstrate how to get started with adding tests to MERN applications.

Before writing the test code, first we will set up for testing by installing the necessary packages, defining the test run script, and creating a `tests` folder for the test code.

Installing the packages

The following npm packages will be required in order to write test code and run the tests:

- **jest**: To include the Jest testing framework
- **babel-jest**: To compile JS code for Jest
- **react-test-renderer**: To make a snapshot of the DOM tree rendered by a React DOM without using a browser

To install these packages as `devDependencies`, run the following `npm install` command from the command line:

```
npm install --save-dev jest babel-jest react-test-renderer
```

Defining the script to run tests

In order to run the test code, we will update the run scripts defined in `package.json`, to add a script for running tests with `jest`:

```
"scripts": {
  "test": "jest"
}
```

In the command line, if we run `npm run test`, it will prompt Jest to find the test code in the application folders and run the tests.

Adding a tests folder

To add the client-side test in the MERN Social application, we will create a folder called tests in the client folder, which will contain test files relevant to testing the React components. When the test command is run, Jest will look for the test code in these files.

The test case for this example will be a test on the Post component, and tests for the Post component will be added in a file called post.test.js in the tests folder.

Test case

We will write a test to check whether the delete button on a post is only visible when the signed-in user is also the creator of the post. This means that the delete button will only be a part of the Post view, if the user._id of the authenticated user is the same as the postedby value of the post data being rendered.

Adding the test

In order to implement this test case, we will add code which takes care of the following:

- Defines dummy data for a post and an auth object
- Mocks auth-helper.js
- Defines the test and within the test definition
    - Declares the post and auth variables
    - Sets the return value of the mocked isAuthenticated method to the dummy auth object
    - Uses renderer.create to create the Post component with the required dummy props passed and wrapped in MemoryRouter to provide the props related to react-router
    - Generates and matches snapshots

The code in post.test.js to incorporate the steps described for this specific test will be as follows:

```
import auth from './../auth/auth-helper.js'
import Post from './../post/Post.js'
import React from 'react'
import renderer from 'react-test-renderer'
import { MemoryRouter } from 'react-router-dom'
```

```
jest.mock('./../auth/auth-helper.js')

const dummyPostObject = {"_id":"5a3cb2399bcc621874d7e42f",
                         "postedBy":{"_id":"5a3cb1779bcc621874d7e428",
                         "name":"Joe"}, "text":"hey!",
                         "created":"2017-12-22T07:20:25.611Z",
                         "comments":[], "likes":[]}
const dummyAuthObject = {user: {"_id":"5a3cb1779bcc621874d7e428",
                               "name":"Joe",
                               "email":"abc@def.com"}}

test('delete option visible only to authorized user', () => {
  const post = dummyPostObject
  const auth = dummyAuthObject

  auth.isAuthenticated.mockReturnValue(auth)

  const component = renderer.create(
     <MemoryRouter>
         <Post post={post} key={post._id} ></Post>
     </MemoryRouter>
  )

  let tree = component.toJSON()
  expect(tree).toMatchSnapshot()
})
```

Generating a snapshot of the correct Post view

The first time this test is run, we will provide it with the values required to generate the correct snapshot of the Post view. The correct snapshot for this test case will contain the delete button when the `user._id` of the auth object is equal to the `postedBy` value of the post object. This snapshot generated when the test is first run will be used for comparison for future test executions.

 Snapshot testing in Jest basically records snapshots of rendered component structures to compare them to future renderings. When the recorded snapshot and the current rendering don't match, the test fails, indicating that something has changed.

Running and checking the test

In the code that we just added to the `post.test.js`, the dummy `auth` object and `post` object refer to the same user, thus running this test in the command line will prompt Jest to generate a snapshot that will contain the delete option and also pass the test.

To run the test, go into the project folder from the command line:

```
npm run test
```

The test output will show that the test passed:

```
> mern-social@1.0.0 test /Users/shoque/packtBook/mern-social
> jest

 PASS  client/tests/post.test.js
  ✓ Test for Post (112ms)

Test Suites: 1 passed, 1 total
Tests:       1 passed, 1 total
Snapshots:   1 passed, 1 total
Time:        1.436s, estimated 2s
Ran all test suites.
```

The recorded snapshot that is generated, when this test runs successfully for the first time, is added automatically to a `_snapshots_` folder in the `tests` folder. This snapshot represents the state where the delete button is rendered in the view since the authenticated user is also the creator of the post.

We can now check whether the test actually fails when the component is rendered with an authenticated user that is not the creator of the post. To perform this check, we will update the dummy data objects by changing `user._id` to not match the `postedBy` value, then run the test again. This will give us a failed test, as the current rendering will no longer have a delete button that is present in the recorded snapshot.

As seen in the test log pictured next, the test fails and indicates that the rendered tree does not match the recorded snapshot since the elements representing the delete button are missing in the received value:

```
> mern-social@1.0.0 test /Users/shoque/packtBook/mern-social
> jest

FAIL  client/tests/post.test.js
 X Test for Post (175ms)

 ● Test for Post

   expect(value).toMatchSnapshot()

   Received value does not match stored snapshot 1.

   - Snapshot
   + Received

   @@ -37,51 +37,10 @@
                className="MuiTypography-root-45 MuiTypography-body2-53 M
   lorSecondary-66 MuiCardHeader-subheader-40"
                >
                  Fri Dec 22 2017
                </span>
              </div>
   -          <div
   -            className="MuiCardHeader-action-37"
   -          >
   -            <button
   -              aria-label="delete"
   -              className="MuiButtonBase-root-78 MuiIconButton-root-69"
   -              disabled={false}
   -              onBlur={[Function]}
```

With this screenshot, we have a client-side test for checking whether a signed-in user can view the delete button on their posts. Using this setup, more tests can be added for the MERN application utilizing the capabilities of Jest.

Writing test code will make the application you develop reliable and also help ensure code quality. Another good practice for improving and maintaining code quality is using a linting tool with your project. Linting tools perform static analysis on the code to find problematic patterns or behaviors that violate specified rules and guidelines. Linting code in a JavaScript project can improve overall code readability and also help find syntax errors before the code is executed. For linting in MERN-based projects, you can explore ESLint, which is a JavaScript linting utility that allows developers to create their own linting rules.

Optimizing the bundle size

As you develop and grow a MERN application, chances are the size of the bundles produced with Webpack will also grow, especially if large third-party libraries are used. Larger bundle sizes will effect performance and increase the initial load time of the application. We can make changes in the code to ensure we don't end up with large bundles and also utilize features packed in Webpack 4 to help optimize bundling. In this section, we will highlight some key concepts that can give us control in producing smaller bundles and decreasing load time.

 Before going into the code to update it for bundle size optimization, you can also get familiar with the default optimization options that are now part of Webpack 4. In the MERN applications, we used the `mode` config to utilize the default settings for both development and production mode. To get an overview of the options available, check out this article at `https://medium.com/webpack/webpack-4-mode-and-optimization-5423a6bc597a`.

Code splitting

Instead of loading all the code at once in one bundle, we can use the code-splitting feature supported by Webpack to lazy-load parts of the application code as currently needed by the user. After we modify the application code to introduce code splitting, Webpack can create multiple bundles rather than one large bundle. These bundles can be loaded dynamically at runtime, allowing us to improve the performance of the application.

 To learn more about code splitting support in Webpack and how to make necessary changes to the setup and configuration, check out the guides in the documentation at `https://webpack.js.org/guides/code-splitting/`.

There are several ways to introduce code splitting for the application code, but the most important syntax you will come across for this purpose is the dynamic `import()`. In the next section, we will look at how to use `import()` with our MERN applications.

Dynamic import()

Dynamic `import()` is a new function-like version of the regular import and it enables the dynamic loading of JS modules. Using `import(moduleSpecifier)` will return a promise for the module namespace object of the requested module. When using regular static imports, we import a module at the top of the code and then use it in the code:

```
import {  convert } from './metric'
...
console.log(convert('km', 'miles', 202))
```

If we were to use dynamic `import()` instead of adding the static import at the beginning, the code would look like this:

```
import('./metric').then({ convert } => {
    console.log( convert('km', 'miles', 202) )
})
```

This allows importing and loading the module when the code requires it. While bundling the application code, Webpack will treat calls to `import()` as split points and automatically start code splitting by placing the requested module and its children into a separate chunk from the main bundle.

In order to optimize the bundling of the frontend React code by applying code splitting at a given component, we need to pair dynamic `import()` with React Loadable—a higher-order component for loading components with promises. As an example, we will look at the shopping cart developed in `Chapter 7`, *Extending the Marketplace for Orders and Payments*. While building the interface of the cart, we composed the `Cart` component by importing and adding the `Checkout` component to the view as follows:

```
import Checkout from './Checkout'
class Cart extends Component {
    ...
    render(){
        ...
        <Checkout/>
    }
    ...
}
```

To introduce code splitting here and import the `Checkout` component dynamically, we can replace the static import at the beginning with a `Loadable` Checkout, as shown in the following code:

```
import Loadable from 'react-loadable'
const Checkout = Loadable({
  loader: () => import('./Checkout'),
  loading: () => <div>Loading...</div>,
})
```

Making this change and using Webpack to build the code again will produce a `bundle.js` file of reduced size, and generate another smaller bundle file representing the split code, which will now only load when the `Cart` component is rendered.

Using this mechanism, we can apply code splitting across our application code as required. The thing to keep in mind is that effective code splitting will depend on using it correctly and applying it at the right places in the code—places that will benefit in optimization from resource-load prioritization.

 Route-based code splitting can be an effective approach for introducing code splitting in React apps that use routes to load components in the view. To learn more about implementing code splitting, specifically with React Router, check out the article at `https://tylermcginnis.com/react-router-code-splitting/`.

Extending the applications

Throughout the chapters in this book, as we developed each application, we added features by extending the existing code in a common and repeatable number of steps. In this final section, we will review these steps and set a guideline for adding more features to the current versions of the applications.

Extending the server code

For a specific feature, that will require data persistence and APIs to allow the views to manipulate the data, we can start by extending the server code and adding the necessary models, routes, and controller functions.

Adding a model

For the data persistence aspect of the feature, design the data model considering the fields and values that need to be stored. Then, define and export a Mongoose schema for this data model in a separate file in the `server/models` folder.

Implementing the APIs

Next, design the APIs relevant for the desired feature, in order to manipulate and access the data that will be stored in the database based on the model.

Adding controllers

With the APIs decided, add the corresponding controller functions that will respond to the requests to these APIs in a separate file in the `server/controllers` folder. The controller functions in this file should access and manipulate the data for the model defined for this feature.

Adding routes

To complete the implementation of the server-side APIs, corresponding routes need to be declared and mounted on the Express app. In a separate file in the `server/routes` folder, first declare and export the routes for these APIs, assigning the relevant controller functions that should be executed when a specific route is requested. Then, load these new routes on the Express app in the `server/express.js` file, like the other existing routes in the application.

This will produce a working version of the new backend APIs that can be run and checked from a REST API client application, before going on to build and integrate frontend views for the feature being developed.

Extending the client code

On the client side, first design the views required for the feature, and determine how these views will incorporate user interaction with the data relevant to the feature. Then add the fetch API code to integrate with the new backend APIs, define the new components that represent these new views, and update the existing code to include these new components in the frontend of the application.

Adding the API fetch methods

In the client folder, create a new folder to house the components and helper code relevant to the feature module being developed. Then to integrate the new backend APIs, add and export the corresponding fetch methods in a separate file in this new components folder.

Adding components

Create and export new React components that represent views for the desired feature, in separate files in the new folder. Integrate auth into these new components using the existing auth-helper methods.

Loading new components

In order to incorporate these new components into the frontend, the components either need to be added into existing components or rendered at their own client-side routes.

Updating frontend routes

If these new components need to be rendered at individual routes, update the `MainRouter.js` code to add new routes that load these components at given URL paths.

Integrating with existing components

If the new components will become part of existing views, import the component into the existing component to add it to the view as desired. The new components can also be integrated with existing components, such as in the `Menu` component, by linking to new components that were added with individual routes.

With the components integrated and connected with the backend, the new feature implementation is complete. These steps can be repeated to add on new features to the applications.

Summary

In this final chapter, we reviewed and elaborated on some of the best practices used while building the MERN applications in this book, highlighted areas of improvement, gave pointers to address issues that may crop up when applications grow, and finally set down the guidelines to continue developing more features into the existing applications.

We saw that modularizing the application's code structure helped extend the application easily, choosing to use JSS over inline CSS and external style sheets kept the styling code contained and easy to work with, and only implementing server-side rendering for specific views as required kept unnecessary complications out of the code.

We discussed the benefits of creating fewer stateful components that are composed of smaller and more defined stateless functional components, and how this can be applied while refactoring existing components or designing new components to extend the applications. For growing applications that may run into issues of managing and communicating state across hundreds of components, we pointed to options such as Redux or Flux that may be considered to address these issues.

For applications that may have higher demands for stricter security enforcement, we looked back at our existing implementation of user auth with JWT and password encryption, and discussed possible extensions for improved security.

We used Jest to demonstrate how test code can be added to the MERN applications, and discussed how good practices, such as writing test code and using a linting tool, can improve code quality besides ensuring reliability in an application.

We also looked at bundle optimization features, such as code splitting, that can help to improve performance by reducing the initial bundle size, and by lazy-loading parts of the application as required.

Finally, we reviewed and set down the repeatabe steps that were used throughout the book, and can be used as a guideline moving forward to extend the MERN applications by adding more features.

Other Books You May Enjoy

If you enjoyed this book, you may be interested in these other books by Packt:

React Design Patterns and Best Practices
Michele Bertoli

ISBN: 978-1-78646-453-8

- Write clean and maintainable code
- Create reusable components applying consolidated techniques
- Use React effectively in the browser and node
- Choose the right styling approach according to the needs of the applications
- Use server-side rendering to make applications load faster
- Build high-performing applications by optimizing components

Full-Stack Vue.js 2 and Laravel 5
Anthony Gore

ISBN: 978-1-78829-958-9

- Core features of Vue.js to create sophisticated user interfaces
- Build a secure backend API with Laravel
- Learn a state-of-the-art web development workflow with Webpack
- Full-stack app design principles and best practices
- Learn to deploy a full-stack app to a cloud server and CDN
- Managing complex application state with Vuex
- Securing a web service with Laravel Passport

Leave a review - let other readers know what you think

Please share your thoughts on this book with others by leaving a review on the site that you bought it from. If you purchased the book from Amazon, please leave us an honest review on this book's Amazon page. This is vital so that other potential readers can see and use your unbiased opinion to make purchasing decisions, we can understand what our customers think about our products, and our authors can see your feedback on the title that they have worked with Packt to create. It will only take a few minutes of your time, but is valuable to other potential customers, our authors, and Packt. Thank you!

Index